John Stewart

Highways and Hedges

Fifty Years of Western Methodism

John Stewart

Highways and Hedges
Fifty Years of Western Methodism

ISBN/EAN: 9783744775212

Printed in Europe, USA, Canada, Australia, Japan

Cover: Foto ©ninafisch / pixelio.de

More available books at **www.hansebooks.com**

HIGHWAYS AND HEDGES;

OR,

FIFTY YEARS OF WESTERN METHODISM.

BY

REV. JOHN STEWART,

OF THE OHIO CONFERENCE.

CINCINNATI:
HITCHCOCK AND WALDEN.
NEW YORK:
CARLTON AND LANAHAN.
1870.

Entered, according to Act of Congress, in the year 1870,

BY JOHN STEWART,

In the Office of the Librarian of Congress, Washington.

PREFACE.

THE time was when the publication of a book was a notable event, and only men of great ability were expected to become authors. Now, however, the facilities for book-making are so multiplied, and the popular taste for reading so developed, that the annual crop of books is looked for with as much regularity as the crop of corn. But as in agriculture, so in book-making, the fondest hopes are sometimes cut short by an "untimely frost." It has been said by some one that "an author, like a fat man in a crowd, must elbow others out of the way to make room for himself." Not being a fat man, and now within four years of four-score, I can not jostle much with others in the crowd. A half century spent mostly upon horseback, traversing large circuits and districts in the States of Ohio, Virginia, Kentucky, Pennsylvania, Indiana, and Illinois, has brought me in contact with most of the men and measures that have molded the institutions, and gathered the membership of the Methodist Episcopal Church on this continent, and which have sent its streams of influence to Europe, Asia, and Africa. From the store-house of my memory I have endeavored to record some things which I thought would be of interest to the present generation, and of value to the future historian. I have also ventured some opinions in regard to men and measures, and some counsels to ministers and laymen. I am conscious of the decay of memory, and, doubtless, other powers of mind, less observed by myself than others, are failing also; hence it becomes me to ask forbearance for whatever errors may be found in my book, consequent upon the infirmities of age. I have never kept an extensive journal, and only the brief notes of my circuit "diaries" to prompt my memory. The book, such as it is, has been called out by the partiality of my friends, and I doubt not they will treat it with the same courtesy that they have so long extended to its author.

At the close of my *fiftieth year* in the regular work, in obedience to a request of my Conference, I delivered a semi-centennial sermon before that body. My brethren had the kindness to spread the following upon their journal:

"*Resolved*, That having heard with much pleasure, and, we trust, with profit, the very interesting and instructive semi-centennial sermon, delivered this day before the Conference, by our venerable and beloved brother, John Stewart, we do hereby very respectfully request him to have it published, in such form as he may think best, for our benefit, as well as for the interest of those who were not present at its delivery. B. N. SPAHR."

This was followed up by solicitations from my friends that I would prepare and publish an autobiography. After a good deal of hesitation I have yielded to that solicitation, and here is the result of my effort.

I have given the names of those admitted on trial into the Ohio Conference from the year 1816 to the year 1866, a period of fifty years. I have also given the names and brief biographical notices of those of her members that have fallen in death during that period. This arrangement gives somewhat of a monotonous beginning to the several chapters, but will be convenient for reference. Though I have expressed my views fully of the characteristics of my colleagues and presiding elders, and the many preachers who have been associated with me during the years of my pastorate and presiding eldership, yet I have been so fortunate in these associations, that there have been very few of them of whom I found it necessary to say aught but good.

If my book shall meet the reasonable expectations of my friends, and above all if it shall be made a blessing to others after I shall have gone to join my comrades in the Church above, I shall not have labored or prayed in vain.

THE AUTHOR.

MONROE, WIS., *June* 10, 1870.

CONTENTS.

CHAPTER I.

Birth and ancestry—Father heads a small colony and emigrates to the Hockhocking Valley, in Ohio—Incidents of the journey—George Barris—Builds a cabin—Establishes Sabbath services in his cabin—Travels twenty-five miles to class-meetings—Induces Revs. Jacob Young and George C. Light to visit the Hockhocking Valley—They establish the first permanent societies in the region—Names of members of first class at Daniel Stewart's—Class at South Town—Family religion—The subject of this narrative converted—Eliphalet Case—Hunting and praying—Philadelphia Case—Rev. Marcus Lindsey—Rev. Joseph Pownell—Revival—Singular mode of appointing new leader—E. T. Webster attends class and is awakened—The subject of this narrative is licensed to exhort—Appointments: Smith's, M'Keever's, Pilcher's, and Lotridge's—Doings of mother Ruter—Rev. T. A. Morris—Glorious time at Milton Buckingham's—The young exhorter becomes tempted—He eludes his companion and starts for home—Meets Lindsey at Athens, and counsels with him—Teaches school and holds prayer and class-meetings—Licensed to preach—Visits a camp-meeting near Circleville...................PAGE 15

CHAPTER II.

Ohio Conference at Louisville, Kentucky, October 3, 1816—Appearance of the preachers—List of those received on trial—Vast boundaries of the Conference—Appointments of the preachers—The writer employed as assistant on Letart Falls circuit—Struggle and decision—Reception by colleague and people—Opens his work at King's, at mouth of Mill Creek—Large circuit: partly in Ohio and partly in Virginia—Twenty-eight appointments every four weeks—Sketch of first sermon—Revivals—Received for year's labor $25 in depreciated money—Question as to life-work—The farm and plenty, or the circuit and poverty—Decides for God—Recommendation carried up to the Ohio Conference... ....PAGE 27

CHAPTER III.

Conference at Zanesville, Ohio, October 3, 1817—Bishop Roberts—List of persons received on trial—The writer the only survivor of the class—Bishop Roberts's sermon on Sabbath—Samuel Parker sent as missionary to Natchez—His feeble health, and affectionate parting with his brethren—The writer appointed to Little Kanawha circuit—Plan of circuit—Writer's views of preaching and other duties—He and his colleague blaze their pioneer path through the forest—Rude but cheerful hospitality—Amusing experiences—Bear meat and bear skins—"Not all gold that glitters"—Preacher deceived by outward appearances—Revs. David Smithers, Samuel Briggs, and Reese Wolf: their peculiarities and worth as local preachers—Transferred to Fairfield circuit—Jacob Young's notice of the change in his autobiography—Mistakes corrected—Rev. Michael Ellis—His fatherly welcome—Reminiscences of appointments and fellow-workers—Charges that have grown out of this circuit—Some of the local preachers were men of great ability and worth—Biographical sketch of Rev. Michael Ellis—The quarterly-meeting of those days—Writer's first sermon in presence of his colleague—Rev. J. M'Mahon's criticism—Rev. James Quinn's amusing experience—Conference year two months shorter than usual—Round exchanged with Rev. Job Baker..PAGE 33

CHAPTER IV.

Conference at Steubenville, Ohio, August 7, 1818—Persons received on probation—Conference business—William Burke—Mahoning circuit—First call—Rev. Shadrach Bostwick—Revival—Horatio Day—Conversions—Eric Circuit—Dr. Samuel Adams—Dr. D. D. Davisson—Rev. Alfred Brunson—Dr. Menarey—Revs. Smith, Leach, and Miller useful local preachers—Great revival and ingathering—Exchange one round with Rev. Isaac C. Hunter, the supply on Lake circuit, New York—Accompany Rev. J. B. Finley to Chautauqua camp-meeting—Large circuit—Erie—Waterford—M'Connelsville—Meadville—Mercer—Rev. Samuel Gregg's mistakes corrected—Horseback journey to Cincinnati—Proposition to found an institution of learning agitated—Indian missionary work—Delegates elected to General Conference—Persons admitted on probation—Ordained deacon—Postpone matrimonial engagement in view of missionary work—Sketches of J. Young and J. B. Finley..PAGE 44

CHAPTER V.

Volunteers for frontier work—Blue River circuit, Indiana—Marriage and retirement of my colleague—Bishop Roberts moves into the bounds of the circuit—Character and popularity among the people—Experience with a young Calvinistic missionary—Lewis Roberts and family—Wedding scenes—Muskatatack camp-meeting—

CONTENTS.

The jerks—List of appointments—General Conference, and exciting scenes ....PAGE 61

CHAPTER VI.

Mt. Carmel circuit, Ill.—Conference at Shiloh, Ill., September, 1820—Bishop Roberts presiding in bed—Camp-meeting—Received on trial—Plan of Mt. Carmel circuit—Leading Methodist families of 1821 in that circuit—Camp-meetings—Remarkable conversions—Ohio Conference, and list of persons received on trial...................PAGE 72

CHAPTER VII.

A horse-thief pursued, captured, and punished—Societies organized for protection—Return to Ohio...PAGE 85

CHAPTER VIII.

Vincennes circuit, Indiana—Marriage—Conference at Lebanon, Ohio, September, 1821—Persons admitted on trial—Camp-meeting on Mt. Carmel circuit—Conference at Cape Girardeau, Missouri—Camp-meeting—Persons admitted on trial—Ordination to elder's orders—Sickness—Vincennes—General Harrison—Representative Methodists of the circuit—Birth of a son—Plan of circuit.....PAGE 97

CHAPTER IX.

Sketch of the early life and Christian experience of Mrs. Stewart..PAGE 106

CHAPTER X.

Ohio Conference at Marietta, September, 1822—Transfer to Ohio Conference—Madison circuit, Indiana—Delegates to General Conference—Preacher's family to "board around"—Local preachers—Route of travel—Controversy with Baptists—Camp-meeting—Valuable families from Ohio—Camp-meeting—Bishop Roberts's great sermon..PAGE 120

CHAPTER XI.

Muskingum circuit, Ohio—Conference at Urbana, September, 1823—Death of Rev. Charles Trescott—Rev. Thomas Beacham—Plan of circuit—Membership—Salary—Wife teaches school—Local preachers—Rev. C. Springer—Visit from Bishop Roberts and Rev. Martin Ruter—Delegates to General Conference—Presiding elder question—Lay delegation discussed ....PAGE 126

CHAPTER XII.

Marietta circuit, Ohio—Conference at Zanesville, Ohio, 1824—Deceased preachers—Incident of travel—Revival—Waterford—Parks—

Itinerant feature of Church polity—Whitney—Crawford—Daniels—
Birth of second son—Plan of circuit...PAGE 133

CHAPTER XIII.

Guyandotte circuit, Virginia—Conference at Columbus, Ohio, October, 1825—Nathan Walker deceased—Rugged mountain ride—Search for a house—Sheep turned out and shepherd turned in—Outline of the circuit—Local preachers—Spurlock—M'Comas—Barboursville—Ladeley Public whipping-post and characteristic scenes...PAGE 140

CHAPTER XIV.

Deer Creek circuit, Ohio Conference at Hillsboro, October 4, 1826 — John Walker deceased Rev. John Ferree—Rev. Russel Bigelow--Conversion of a young skeptic—Parsonage at Dry Run—Kind neighbors Domestic incidents—Serious illness of wife and prayer answered in her recovery—Dr. Deming Third son born—Radical excitement—Anecdote of father Timmons Camp-meeting—Conference at Cincinnati, September 19, 1827—Delegates to General Conference—John Sale deceased—Returned to Deer Creek circuit—Move to Greenfield—General Conference and its exciting questions—Nicholas Snethen and Thomas Bond..PAGE 146

CHAPTER XV.

Miami circuit, Ohio—Conference at Chillicothe, September 18, 1828—Camp-meeting—William R. Anderson—J. M. Trimble's first Conference exhortation—The great Freemason excitement—List of appointments—Prosperous year—closed with camp-meeting—Conference at Urbana, September 3, 1829— Returned to Miami circuit with James Laws for colleague—Camp-meeting—Incidents of the meeting—First daughter born...PAGE 159

CHAPTER XVI.

Oxford circuit, Ohio—Conference at Lancaster, Ohio, September 8, 1830—Pleasant year—Build parsonage in Oxford—Conference at Mansfield, Ohio, September 8, 1831—Michael Ellis deceased—Delegates elected to the General Conference Returned to Oxford circuit—Miami State University--Second daughter born—Rev. Moses Crume—Local preachers—Aaron Powers and the Mormons—Names of precious memory—Camp-meeting—Collision with Kidwell of the "Star of the West"..PAGE 167

CHAPTER XVII.

Bellefontaine circuit, Ohio Conference at Dayton, Ohio, September 19, 1832—Bishop Emory—Rev. J. G. Bruce and Peter Sharp—Camp-meeting—Local preachers and model private members—Kindness of brother Messick—Deputation from the Flat-Head Indians this year resulted in founding a mission among them..........PAGE 173

CHAPTER XVIII.

Troy circuit—Conference at Cincinnati, August 21, 1833—Rev. John Ulin deceased—Arza Brown—Richard Brandriff—Local preachers and lay members..........PAGE 177

CHAPTER XIX.

Adelphi circuit, Ohio—Conference at Circleville, Ohio, August 20, 1834—Sargent and Callahan deceased—Plan of the circuit—Haunted house—New parsonage—Great camp-meeting—Incident—Camp-meeting near the falls of the Hockhocking—Conference at Springfield, Ohio, August 19, 1835—Philip Gatch, William Page, and Russel Bigelow deceased—Delegates to General Conference..........PAGE 181

CHAPTER XX.

Athens circuit, Ohio—Conference at Chillicothe, Ohio, 1836—William Phillips deceased—Return home - Conference at Xenia, Ohio, September 27, 1837—John A. Waterman and Erastus Felton deceased—Ohio State University..........PAGE 190

CHAPTER XXI.

Felicity circuit, Ohio—Conference at Columbus, Ohio, September 26, 1838—Rev. J. B. Finley deceased—Augusta College, its professors, successes, and downfall—Hon. David Fisher—Holly Raper—John Patterson—James Armstrong—Erection of church in Augusta—Church in Higginsport..........PAGE 198

CHAPTER XXII.

Georgetown circuit, Ohio—Conference in Cincinnati, Ohio, September 18, 1839—Preachers deceased—Delegates to General Conference—Protracted meetings—Camp-meeting—Conference at Zanesville, Ohio, September 30, 1840—Persons admitted on trial—Charles R. Baldwin and Jeremiah Hill deceased—Controversy on baptism—Protracted meetings—Camp-meeting—Decease of venerable mother—Sickness of daughters Incidents and triumphant death of the girls—Local preachers—Prominent laymen..........PAGE 204

CHAPTER XXIII.

Bainbridge circuit—Conference at Urbana, Ohio, August 25, 1841—R. W. Finley deceased—Pleasant year—Closing camp-meeting near Bainbridge—Conference at Hamilton and Rossville, Ohio, September 28, 1842—William B. Christie and Isaac C. Hunter deceased—Protracted meetings—Wonderful outpourings of the Spirit—Building a church—Revival incidents Writer's second son licensed, and recommended to the traveling connection..................................PAGE 219

CHAPTER XXIV.

Kanawha district, Virginia Conference at Chillicothe, Ohio, September 23, 1843—Rev. A. Hance deceased—Appointed presiding elder—Delegates to General Conference—Territory and population of the district—Preachers—Charges Great Variety Amusing anecdote—General Conference at New York, May, 1844—Plan of separation—Intense excitement—Ohio Conference at Marietta, Ohio, September 4, 1844 Bishop Soule—J. W. Kanaga deceased—Bishop's cabinet—Inside view—Stormy times—"Abolitionism"—Conference at Cincinnati, Ohio, September 3, 1845—Exciting times—Bishops Soule and Hamline—Brothers Collins, Jones, and Farnandis deceased Doctrines of the Church on slavery—Position of the writer—Outrage at Parkersburg—Correspondence with Bishop Soule—State of the district...PAGE 233

CHAPTER XXV.

Portsmouth district—Conference at Piqua, Ohio, September 2, 1846—Deaths—Preachers on district—Residence—Conference at Columbus, Ohio, September 1, 1847—Delegates to General Conference—Journey to Pittsburg—Session of General Conference—Dr. Dixon—Conference at Newark, Ohio, September 27, 1848 James Quinn and William Parish—Preachers on Portsmouth district—Kentucky work included—Cholera—Kentucky hospitality—Conference at Dayton, Ohio, September 26, 1849—Deaths reported—Pew question—Visit to Iowa—Reminiscences...PAGE 261

CHAPTER XXVI.

Deer Creek circuit, Ohio—Conference at Chillicothe, Ohio, September 18, 1850—Pleasant charge—Conference met at Springfield, Ohio, September 17, 1851—Deaths—Returned to Deer Creek circuit—Colleague, Samuel Middleton—Sickness of wife—Reminiscences and reflections—Delegation to General Conference................PAGE 279

CHAPTER XXVII.

London circuit, Ohio—Conference met at Zanesville, September 1, 1852—Deaths—Colleague, Rev. James Brown—Appointments—"A mere garden spot"—Gracious revivals, and a happy year—Conference met at Lancaster, Ohio, September 7, 1853—Deaths—Returned to London circuit—Colleague, Rev. J. Crum—Revival fires spread over the circuit—Incidents—Washington Withrow's conversion—Buys a horse for the preacher—Names of noble-hearted laymen—Critical illness of wife—Prayer prevails—Journey to Wisconsin..........PAGE 284

CHAPTER XXVIII.

Pickerington circuit and Lancaster district—Conference met at Portsmouth, Ohio, September 6, 1854—No deaths reported—Journey to Wisconsin—Settlement at Pickerington—List of eight appointments—Pleasant home and surroundings—Names of some of those excellent families—Conference met at Athens, Ohio, September 5, 1855—Death—Pleasant Conference—Delegates to General Conference—Returned to Pickerington circuit—Rev. J. L. Grover resigns the district—The writer appointed to fill the vacancy—The work and the preachers—Pleasant and profitable year..................PAGE 291

CHAPTER XXIX.

Jackson district—Conference met at Newark, Ohio, September 3, 1856—Deaths—The field and the workmen on Jackson district—Live at Jackson—Conference met at Chillicothe, August 26, 1857—List of those received on trial—Death—Preachers for Jackson District—Sickness and death of venerable father—Conference met at Marietta, Ohio, August 25, 1858—List of preachers for Jackson district—Conference met at Columbus, Ohio, August 31, 1859—List of those received on trial—Bishop Morris's Sabbath sermon—Preachers on Jackson district—Pleasant years—Stewart Chapel..............PAGE 297

CHAPTER XXX.

Minister at large—Western tour—Conference at Gallipolis, Ohio, September 19, 1860—Deceased, Jacob Young and Samuel Harvey—Semi-centennial celebration resolved on—Permission to travel at large during the year—Visit Chicago, Monroe, Madison, Freeport, Rockford, Burlington, Mt. Pleasant, Fort Madison, West Point, Chambersburg, St. Louis, Springfield, Indianapolis, Cincinnati, Covington, Columbus, etc. Preached about one hundred sermons and visited a multitude of friends—Impressions of persons and places visited—Programme for memorial services......................PAGE 305

CHAPTER XXXI.

Frankfort circuit—Conference held its fiftieth session at Circleville, Ohio, September 11, 1861—Semi-centennial celebration—Colleague, W. W. Cherington—Old friends—Nine appointments—Attended many funerals—War excitement—Cherished names....................PAGE 319

CHAPTER XXXII.

Deer Creek circuit and Chillicothe district—Conference at Zanesville, Ohio, September 3, 1862—J. W. Clark, Uriah Heath, and John P. Calvert deceased—Historical succession of preachers on Deer Creek circuit from A. D. 1800 to 1863—Colleague, Rev. T. J. N. Simmons; Z. Connell, presiding elder—Conference at Lancaster, Ohio,

September 3, 1863 Neither probationers nor deaths Returned to Deer Creek circuit. Death of presiding elder—Writer appointed to the district—The work and workmen on the district—Continued military excitement...PAGE 322

CHAPTER XXXIII.

West Rushville circuit—Conference at Chillicothe, Ohio, October 8, 1864—Edward Estell and Zachariah Connell deceased Reunion of the members of Cincinnati and Ohio Conferences. Grand patriotic address of Bishop Simpson—Circuit plan of four appointments—Mode of pastoral work—Rebel sympathizers—Neighbors and choice spirits...PAGE 329

CHAPTER XXXIV.

Royalton circuit, Ohio—Conference at Columbus, Ohio, September 21, 1865—John C. Havens, Henry Wharton, and Leonidas L. Hamline deceased—Kind attention from brethren and Conference—Request of Conference that the writer should deliver semi-centennial sermon at its next session—Colleague, Rev. John W. White—Nine appointments—Meditations...PAGE 333

CHAPTER XXXV.

Superannuated life—Conference at Columbus, Ohio, September 26, 1866—Semi-centennial sermon made the order of the day for Monday, 10 o'clock—Conference request publication—Superannuated—Resolution of respect—Journey to the North-west—Settled at Monroe, Wisconsin—Welcomed—Letter of welcome from Dr. Brunson—Rev. Aspinwall—Called on to preach—Letter to Ohio Conference—Assist son on Joliet district, Rock River Conference—Concluding adieu to Methodists..PAGE 337

APPENDIX.

I. COMMEMORATION SERMON—Delivered by request of the Ohio Conference on the occasion of its fiftieth anniversary, at Circleville, Ohio, September 16, 1864 ....PAGE 345

II. SEMI-CENTENNIAL SERMON—Delivered by request of the Ohio Conference on the completion of half a century in the regular work, at Columbus, Ohio, October 1, 1866..................................PAGE 377

HIGHWAYS AND HEDGES:

OR,

FIFTY YEARS OF WESTERN METHODISM.

CHAPTER I.

BIRTH AND EARLY LIFE.

I WAS born in Sussex county, New Jersey, June 8, 1795. My ancestors, on my father's side, were of Scotch origin. My great-grandfather, Daniel Stewart, emigrated to America at an early day, and settled in Litchfield, Connecticut. My father, Daniel Stewart, was born November, 1762, in Litchfield, Connecticut. Before he had reached his majority the Revolutionary War broke out. He warmly espoused the cause of the struggling colonies, and offered himself for the service. He was accepted, but being too young for the ranks was put in charge of a wagon. His position was one of hardship and danger, but he endured cheerfully, and had the pleasure of living to see the country that he had assisted in wresting from British domination taking a front rank in the great brotherhood of nations. He married Miss Ruth Fulford, and settled in Sussex county, New Jersey. About the beginning of the present century he formed the acquaintance of a man who owned a large tract of land in the valley of the Hockhocking, in the then wilds of the Ohio Territory. The man was very anxious to dispose of the property, and my father purchased it, and determined to emigrate to that place and open a farm. One of his brothers, Archelaus Stewart, determined to accompany him. The two families commenced making their arrangements. My father sold off his personal property at public auction, and as he was compelled to give a credit to the purchasers, he removed his family to New York city and engaged in temporary business. When the sale notes were due we returned to Sussex, closed up the business, made a short visit among old friends, and then set out upon the long journey. Kind neighbors bid us good-by with many tears, and shuddered in view of the hardships we were to encounter on the journey and after we should reach our destination. We had two wagons and five horses. In view of difficult roads and the amount of our load, it was necessary that some of the company should walk most of the time. Though only seven years old, I walked almost the entire journey. At the difficult mountain ascents we doubled teams, and thus, though our progress was slow it was sure. After more than a month of weary marching we caught our first view of the beautiful Ohio River at Wheeling. We purchased of Mr. Palmer, who kept the ferry at Wheeling, an old ferry-boat. One of the party took the horses through by land. We packed the goods on the boat and floated down the river. The scenery was wild, but beautiful and exciting. As we were floating quietly along one day, one of our company saw an object reclining on the limb of a tree which overhung the water. A closer inspection revealed the fact that it was a huge bear lazily enjoying the sunshine. With a trusty rifle in hand, one of the party landed and soon brought old bruin down with a deadly shot. When we reached the mouth of the Hockhocking we landed, and after providing ourselves with suitable barge-poles, commenced the laborious work of poling our boat and cargo up that stream to the place of our destination. The knowledge of the fact that we were so near to our new home inspired us all with fresh courage, and we worked with a will. The first day of January, 1803, we tied up our boat at the mouth of Federal Creek, and were made welcome to the hospitalities of the log cabin of George Barris. The land which my father owned was in this immediate vicinity, and with his usual promptness and enterprise, he gathered a sufficient force to put up with great dispatch quite a pretentious cabin for those days. I shall not indulge in many reminiscences of those pioneer days at present, as I shall have occasion to refer to them frequently as I progress with my narrative. Though we were in the dense forest, where the wild whoop of the Indian was a more familiar sound than that of the church-going bell, yet we were at home, and we addressed ourselves to the task of making that home as attractive as possible. My uncle built his cabin a few miles further up the river. The settlers were few and far between, and school and Church privileges far away. My father and his brother and their wives were the only Methodists within the bounds of what now constitutes Athens county. They acknowledged God, and erected the family altar in their houses. They also met regularly at my father's house on the Sabbath-day, at twelve o'clock, to worship God publicly. The service consisted of singing, prayer, and the reading of one of Mr. Wesley's sermons. In view of seniority and superior education, my father usually read the sermons. Though they enjoyed times of refreshing at these family gatherings, and realized the faithfulness of God's promises to two or three gathered together, yet they longed for the ministration of the Word from God's living ministers. In the course of time my father learned that there was Methodist circuit preaching at or near Rev. Reece Wolf's, three miles above Parkersburg, Va., a distance of twenty-three miles from our house. My father went, found that preaching-place, handed in his letter, and attended the service, making the journey of forty-six miles each time with more of fidelity than many professors attend religious duty who live within a stone's throw of the house of God. It was impracticable, however, for the families to attend, and at length, by earnest solicitation, the preachers consented to make a tour of observation up the valley of Hockhocking. Jacob Young, then a single man, in the vigor and ambition of early life, led the way. The scattering pioneers received him so gladly, that he determined to expand the already enormous boundaries of the Little Kanawha circuit to embrace these Ohio neighborhoods. Rev. Geo. C. Light, the junior preacher followed in his turn, and the result was the establishment of several classes. The first was organized at my father's house, and comprised six members, namely: Daniel Stewart, Ruth Stewart, Archelaus Stewart, Lydia Stewart, William Pilcher, and Letta Pilcher. Not long afterward Harrison Long and Lydia Long, Job Ruter and wife, parents of the Ruter family, brother and sister Case, Rev. John and Palace Green, and others, were added to the class. Another class was organized in what was then called Southtown—now called Alexander—about six miles south of where Athens now stands. Those pioneer societies still live, and they who planted them and they who were the original members of them live also, but not on earth—the pioneer preachers and the pioneer members are now safe at home.

My father had a large family—nine sons and five daughters. He opened up a large farm on heavily-timbered land, and educating his family to habits of industry and economy, accumulated a large property. During more than sixty years of membership in the Methodist Church, I never knew him to omit family prayers, morning or evening. He usually had a good many hands about him, but it mattered not what was the press of business or who were present, he neither omitted or abridged the service. He read a chapter—usually in course—sang a hymn, and offered prayer. For many years the regular preaching was on week days. He gave all his hired help privilege to attend, without any deduction from their day's wages. My mother died in 1839. She was a strong-minded, kind-hearted, noble, Christian woman, having been a faithful member of the Methodist Church about fifty years. My father married again in his eightieth year. The woman that he selected, Mrs. Lovica Willard, was an excellent Christian woman, and they lived together some sixteen years, being a great help and comfort to each other. During the last years of my father's life he was nearly blind and unable to kneel, but his wife would read the chapter and then read a hymn, after which she would kneel down, and father would lead in prayer, sitting in his chair, or call on his companion, or the hired girl, if a Christian, or any praying visitor who might chance to be present. This punctuality in the maintenance of the exercises of religion in the family had a salutary influence on the whole household. All of my brothers and sisters embraced religion in early life, and the most of them made a permanent home in the visible Church. In his ninety-seventh year my father fell asleep in Jesus, and about one year afterward my step-mother was called to her rest, in the eightieth year of her age.

As my father's house was a home for the traveling preachers and the preaching-place, I was early brought under the influence of their public and private teaching. The Holy Spirit strove with me, and deeply convicted me of the necessity of a change of heart. I often commenced seeking it, and often gave up seeking it, as I passed up from childhood to manhood. The restraints thrown around me were so numerous and strong that I was kept from running into open wickedness. I was kept within the bounds of what the superficial of this world call morality; but in my most careless state I never thought that morality would save me. When I was about twenty years of age the Spirit called me again with great earnestness, and I determined, not without a severe struggle of mind, to give up the amusements which so engrossed the young, and enter upon the work of seeking my soul's salvation with full purpose of heart. I sought the Lord by day and by night, read the Scriptures much, spent much time in secret prayer, and realized that though I was doing the work of repentance and faith, the work was delightful to me in some respects though painful in others. I was distressed with the remembrance of my long procrastination, but comforted with the assurance that I was now honestly and earnestly seeking God. After several months of seeking, it occurred to me that I might find helps in the Church that would be of value to me. On one occasion I remained for the class-meeting after preaching. Before the preacher commenced to lead it, he asked the leader if any person had remained who was not a member. His attention was directed to me, and he gave me such counsel as suited my case. The preacher was Rev. Marcus Lindsey, a man of precious memory, who turned many to righteousness. I did not join that day, but began at once to persuade others to come to the Savior that I so much desired to serve. On one occasion Eliphalet Case came to our house, intending to go out with my brother Charles hunting that night. Charles not being at home, Eliphalet remained and lodged with me. After we had retired I told him that I was seeking religion, and that I intended to be a Christian if none of my young companions would go with me. I talked on until I supposed he had gone to sleep, but as soon as I ceased talking he expressed his pleasure that I had introduced the subject, and promised that he would join me in the enterprise. Soon after this we went one night together to the woods as though we were going hunting; we had a precious time in prayer. I now think that had I been more thoroughly instructed I would have made a profession of the love of God that night. A few days after this, Philadelphia Case was on a visit to our house. As I walked home with her in the evening, while I was exhorting her to become a Christian, she burst into tears and promised that she would from that time commence seeking the Lord. When brother Pownell, the junior preacher, came round I joined the Church, and two weeks from that time, when brother Lindsey came, these two young friends joined. My withdrawal from the dancing circle and joining the Church produced a profound impression through the whole circle of our acquaintance. Many of them came to class to see and hear, and within a few months the society had so enlarged that the preacher thought it best to divide it and appoint another leader. Brother Lindsey told the society that he was going to appoint another leader, and that if they wished to advise him of their wishes, each person might come up and whisper the name of their choice in his ear. In that way I was nominated for leader. He objected at first to appointing me, as I was a probationer, but when it appeared to be the wish of the young converts so generally, he acquiesced and appointed me. It was a great undertaking for me, but I went forward in the fear of God, and he greatly blessed me. Ebenezer T. Webster, then a wild young man, heard that I was to lead the class at Wm. Pilcher's, and though he had spent the previous night at the card-table, he resolved to attend the class-meeting. He did so, and before it closed he determined to give his heart to God. He afterward entered the ministry, and proclaimed the Gospel with a tongue of fire for many years. One day, as the congregation was assembling for preaching, brother Lindsey took me out one side and sat down on a log; and after talking with me a little while, he handed me a license to exhort, and said, "You must go and do the best you can." I tried to excuse myself, but he insisted, and that day announced four appointments for me, each of which I was to fill every four weeks. The appointments were as follows: 1. Smith's, at Wesley; 2. M'Keever's, on Federal Creek; 3. Wm. Pilcher's, on Hocking; and, 4. Lotridge's, in Carthage. I afterward learned that Mother Ruter, the mother of Calvin and Martin Ruter, had been moving in the matter, urging the pastor to thrust me out into the work. We all had unbounded confidence in him. Indeed, Marcus Lindsey was one of our denominational giants. Standing full six feet in his boots, and weighing two hundred pounds, his commanding presence instantly arrested the attention of a congregation. He had keen, black eyes, and a strong voice, full of melody. He was a master in song, exhortation, prayer, and preaching. He excelled, too, as pastor, administrator of discipline, and in looking after the general interests of the Church. Taking him in all the relations and responsibilities of a Methodist preacher, he had few, if any, superiors. In the Spring he went to Baltimore to attend the General Conference, and left the circuit in the care of Rev. T. A. Morris, now well known to the Church, but then a supply under the presiding elder. At his request my father consented that I should accompany him around the circuit. The first appointment was at Carthage. We stopped at Milton Buckingham's, and while I was leading in family prayer the power of God came down and we had a wonderful blessing. Brother and sister Buckingham shouted all over the house. We went on to

Lotridge's; then to Stubb's school-house; then to Smith's, on Tupper's Plains; then to Jacob Humphrey's, where we were to spend the Sabbath. Brother Morris had preached at each place, and I had attempted to exhort, but at each appointment I had less and less liberty, until now I seemed to be completely shut up. I went out into the woods Sabbath morning, and threw myself on the earth and pleaded with God to help me if he had work for me to do; still I was enveloped in darkness, and had no liberty. I begged brother Morris to let me go home, but he insisted that I should go on. At Newberry and at Daniel Goss's it was the same way. On our way to Marietta we were overtaken with a terrible thunder-storm. I was seized with the impression that God was displeased with me, but brother Morris calmly and delightfully discoursed upon the grandeur of the lightning's flash and the thunder's roar. That night we lodged at brother Whitney's. I still pleaded to go home but he would not consent. At the mouth of Duck Creek we separated, with instructions that I should meet him next day, but as soon as he was out of sight I mounted my horse and fled for home. On my way home I learned that brother Lindsey had returned from General Conference and was at Athens. I turned my horse toward Athens, and finding brother Lindsey told him the whole story. He gave me a narrative of his experience—he had started too soon—his way closed up—he waited until it opened, and then went forward. He said, "John, you are called to the work of the ministry, but the time has not come. Keep yourself unencumbered and in due time the way will be clear." I returned home, and after a little time took charge of a school, taught two terms, seeking all the time to improve myself, and do all the good I could holding prayer and class meetings. The members of the Church were still urging their convictions that I should enter the work of the ministry, and notwithstanding my natural timidity and a profound sense of my unworthiness, such were the movings of the Spirit upon my heart that I did not dare to commit myself permanently to any other vocation in life.

When the preachers started to Conference they instructed me to attend to the appointments during their absence. I consented to do so, and started to fulfill the promise. Finding, however, that the appointments had not been announced, and hearing of a camp-meeting near Circleville, O., I turned my course toward that; and, indeed, my steps seemed to be directed by a kind Providence. I was desirous there to obtain instructions and help such as I needed. An immense concourse of people had gathered, and many preachers of a high order were present to labor, such as Wm. Swazey, Moses Trader, and Michael Ellis. Swazey was a great revivalist, and was here in his element. He had charge of the meeting, and managed it with much wisdom and energy. But the pulpit giant of the meeting was the venerable Ellis. Physically of almost giant proportions, his head whitened by the frosts of more than seventy Winters, many years of close communion with God and successful labors in his vineyard had made such an impress upon his commanding countenance as attracted the attention and awed the hearer at first sight. When I first saw him standing before the great audience, on Saturday, at 11 o'clock, A. M., he seemed to my mind to answer Daniel's description of the ancient of days—I was spell-bound from the beginning. As he read his hymn he spake as a man of authority, and the people catching the inspiration of the occasion, lifted up their voices and made the grand old forest reverberate with their singing. He kneeled to lead the devotions of the people, and it was apparent that he was addressing one with whom he was intimately acquainted and on terms of closest friendship. The windows of heaven were opened in answer to his prayer, and heavenly influences were poured out upon the people. When he rose to announce his text all eyes were fixed upon him, and large expectations were evidently awakened. He read 1 Cor. i, 30: "But of him are ye in Christ Jesus, who of God is made unto us wisdom, and righteousness, and sanctification, and redemption." It was soon evident that he was a workman that needeth not to be ashamed, and that the highest expectation would be fully met. His words were well chosen and fitly spoken, like apples of gold in pictures of silver; they were uttered in tones of thunder, and seemed to emit flashes of living light. With the theme of holiness he was evidently thoroughly familiar, theoretically, practically, and experimentally, and as he unfolded it a Divine power attended his utterances. It far excelled any thing I had heard before. It seemed to me that in that discourse he had exhausted that great theme. The work of awakening, and conversion, and sanctification went on with great power. That night was one never to be forgotten. The hour of midnight found the worshipers at their places with unabated interest. But admonished that it was needful that they must take some bodily rest preparatory to the duties of the Sabbath, they formed in line and marched around the encampment, singing the triumphant songs of Zion. The procession more than circled the whole encampment, and then with happy hearts we returned to the tents for repose.

At the break of day the trumpet sounded to call the people up; then it sounded again to call them to family prayers in the tents, and then, after an unostentatious breakfast was dispatched, the trumpet called the congregation, at eight o'clock, to hear the preaching of the Word. The people came with promptness to their places in the congregation, evidently hungry for the Word. The sermon was attended with power. The hour of eleven came around, and the great

Sabbath congregation, surging and excited, crowded the forest temple. At the sounding of the trumpet the venerable Ellis appeared again on the stand. His text on this occasion was John xv, 1: "I am the true vine, and my Father is the husbandman." In the midst of the excitement of this great hour of the meeting, he stood before the vast audience more grand and impressive than on Saturday. He appeared indeed a fit embassador from the court of heaven. His theme was again holiness, and though it had appeared to me on Saturday that he had exhausted the theme, it now seemed clothed in fresh beauty and grandeur. I was lost in wonder, admiration, and delight. The sermon and the influence produced by it beggars all description. No doubt its fruits will be seen in eternity. The Sabbath night was spent as Saturday night, only with increased power. I had never witnessed or enjoyed such a meeting before, and although I have since witnessed vaster audiences and larger numbers of conversions at camp-meetings, I have never heard the theme of holiness so ably expounded and earnestly advocated by one who seemed such an embodiment and exposition of the doctrine as the venerable Ellis. I returned to my home a better man, better understanding the doctrines and the privileges of Christianity, and more than ever feeling the importance of the mission of the Christian minister. Hitherto my mind had been in conflict in regard to my future. Possibly it will appear in eternity that this meeting was the pivot on which my life turned. A few months after this Rev. Cornelius Springer carried up from the society to which I belonged a recommendation to the quarterly conference, and I was licensed to preach.

CHAPTER II.

MY FIRST CIRCUIT—LETART FALLS.

1816-17.

OCTOBER 3, 1816, the Ohio Conference met in Louisville, Kentucky. There being no railroads in those days, the great majority of the preachers came on horseback, many of them giving evidence, by their homespun and threadbare garments, that they had had hard work and poor pay. Their happy countenances, however, gave evidence of devotion to their work, and satisfaction in the prosecution of it. Since the last session of the Conference, the venerable Asbury had gone home to his reward, and the General Conference, which had held its session in Baltimore during the month of May, had elected Enoch George and Robert R. Roberts to strengthen the Episcopacy. These were men of rare talents and piety, and with M'Kendree, who the Western preachers almost worshiped, made an able and efficient Board of Bishops. The Ohio Conference, on this occasion, was favored with the presence of all of the board. The session was a pleasant and profitable one. The principal matter of the Conference was the distribution of the laborers over the vast fields to be cultivated. This great wheel of the itinerancy which is central to our ecclesiastical system, has always imposed the gravest responsibility on the superintendents, and tried most thoroughly the self-sacrificing spirit of both the preachers and the people; yet it seems to me that in those days, when the greatest sacrifices were made, the wheel moved with as little friction as now. There was but little disposition to interfere in regard to the appointments either on the part of the preachers or the people, but both looked to God in earnest prayer and strong faith, and regarded the appointments as coming from him.

From this Conference J. B. Finley, then a young man, full of courage and fire, led forth into the Ohio district, as his helpers, Hatton, Goddard, Baker, Booth, Davidson, Dixon, Westlake, M'Elroy, Knox, and Kent.

David Young, then physically, as well as intellectually and morally, a noble specimen of a man, led forth into the Scioto district, as his helpers, Ellis, Hooper, W. Westlake, R. A. Finley, Swayze, Peter, Truitt, Tivis, Waddle, Glaze, Samuel Brown, and T. Sewell.

Moses Crume, a man of large physical proportions and great moral worth, led into the Miami Valley Cummins, Goddard, W. P. Finley, Bigelow, Lawrence, Hunt, Sale, Brooke, Griffith, Williams, Strange, Pavery, and Sharpe.

Jacob Young led forth as his helpers to the Muskingum district, Somerville, Solomon, James Quinn, John M'Mahon, Watterman, Carr, Ruark, Springer, Thomas A. Morris, Graham, Hamilton, and Lane.

Samuel Parker led forth into the Kentucky district James Simmons, Hunt, Chenowith, Lakin, Baker, Linville, Dumint, West, Cunningham, Holdman, and S. Spurlock.

Under the leadership of these presiding elders these men were soon scattered over the large Conference then comprising all of the State of Ohio, and large portions of Kentucky, Pennsylvania, and Virginia, and soon forest and village was vocal with the earnest appeals and invitations of these men, determined to win the people to Christ.

The following preachers were received on trial at this session of the Conference: Ezra Booth, Thomas A. Morris,

MY FIRST CIRCUIT—LETART FALLS.

William Westlake, Thomas Carr, Stephen Spurlock, Samuel Glaze, Samuel Baker, Daniel D. Davisson, John C. Brooks, William Williams, William Holdman, Samuel Demint, John Lindville, Simon Peter. Of these Thomas A. Morris, now senior Bishop of the Methodist Episcopal Church, and Daniel D. Davisson are still living.

Having been licensed to preach, as previously stated, I started the first day of March, 1817, under instructions from the presiding elder, Rev. J. Young, to assist Rev. John Summerville on the Letart Falls circuit. I dared not refuse, though I felt that of myself I was utterly inadequate to the greatness of the work. I knew He who commissioned the first band of Christian missionaries had said to them, "Go," and "lo, I am with you." Taking fast hold on this promise, I mounted my horse and turned my face toward my life-work. Little did I then think that half a century of itinerating was before me, or that I would be still upon the walls of Zion when the hosts of Methodism should celebrate the close of the first hundred years of the history of this wonderful spiritual movement on this continent. The Rev. John Summerville received me with kindness, and gave me the plan of appointments, commencing at King's, at the mouth of Mill Creek, near Buffington's Island, on the Ohio River. We took a line of appointments along both sides of the river down to Burlington, making twenty-eight appointments in the round, allowing less than one rest day per week during the whole year. The scope of territory occupied was about equal to a presiding elder's district at this time in that portion of the Ohio Conference. I preached my first sermon at brother King's, at the mouth of Mill Creek. Brother Summerville preached at noon and announced for me at night. The people as well as the preacher in charge came together at night, with more or less of curiosity to hear what kind of a young man the presiding elder had sent to assist in the work. Under a painful sense of responsibility, I announced for my text, "Mary has chosen that good part."

After pressing upon the congregation the fact that each probationer has life and death placed before him, and is left to make a deliberate and intelligent choice of the "good part" which secures the favor of God, or of the part which hypocrites and unbelievers have in the lake that burneth with fire and brimstone, I dwelt upon the impotency of any power on earth or in hell to rob the faithful Christian of the good part. But I apprehend that my outline was not very clearly brought out, and that, to my more experienced colleague, there was not in the sermon much promise of excellence in pulpit performance. I inferred this from a *gentle hint* he gave me after we had retired to bed at night. "Brother John," said he, "if I had not known what your text was I should not have gathered it from any thing that you said in your sermon." This remark was certainly not much calculated to flatter my vanity.

The circuit being so large, and our time so fully occupied, the preachers had but little opportunity of being together. Yet we occasionally crossed each other's paths, and I received counsel and instruction from my superior. During the six months that I labored on the Letart circuit I had the privilege of seeing some good revivals of religion, the evidences that we had not labored in vain. After an absence of forty years I returned to travel over much of the same territory as presiding elder, and found great satisfaction in calling up the memories of the scenes and associations of those days of my itinerant life. If I should record here the names of the officers of the Church, or the kind people who welcomed me to their homes and gave me the best fare which their pioneer cabins afforded, there are few now living who would be found upon the roll. I fancy, however, that a host of them who have passed over the river are waiting to welcome me to the mansion-house above, when the time for my departure shall come. To the few who still linger in the Church below I would extend my hand, and bid them be faithful until we hail the sainted above.

At the close of the year I returned to my father's house to report the labors of the year, and to enjoy a brief reunion with my former classmates and the friends of my boyhood.

The session of the Conference, to be held at Zanesville, Ohio, was near at hand, and I had been recommended to be received on trial as a traveling preacher. My pecuniary prospects were not particularly bright in the direction of an itinerant life. Six months of hard labor had brought me only twenty-five dollars, or about four dollars per month, and that in depreciated currency. On the other hand, my father was a large land-owner and very prosperous farmer, and, with my strong hands and willingness to labor, there could be but little doubt of success in making money, should I give up the ministry and devote myself to secular pursuits. I had not, however, any serious struggle of mind in regard to this. I think I chose as honestly and fairly as did Moses, having "respect to the recompense of reward." And now, after more than five decades of sacrifice and toil in the rougher departments of Methodist preacher life, I am prepared fully to indorse the faithfulness of the Savior's promise to Peter when he inquired, "What shall we have therefor?" He assured them that they should have manifold more in this life, besides the priceless rewards of the life to come. I doubt whether any young man who gives himself up to the work of preaching the Gospel ever loses any thing, even in a pecuniary sense, by so doing. "There is that giveth and yet increaseth" applies not only to those who give money, but who give up the opportunity of making money, for the sake of Christ and his kingdom. To refuse to preach the Gospel because it does not promise to pay pecuniarily, or to turn aside from the work of the ministry for the purpose of making money, is usually to array ourselves against the plans of the Great Head of the Church, who is the God of providence; if then we make money, is it not after he has said, "Let him alone, he is joined to his idols?" I stood there on the threshold of decision. The spirit of this world seemed to say, "On one side is the farm, a settled home, future wealth, and ease and comfort; on the other side a wandering life, poverty, and continual privations." But my heart said, "The Savior says go, the Church says go, and if I can be successful in rescuing one soul from the jaws of death and hell, it will be a life spent more grandly, it will bring a happier termination and a more glorious hereafter, than could I have all that heart could wish of this world's goods, but spend life out of the path of duty. My decision was taken, and I offered myself to the Ohio Conference to become a traveling preacher, so long as God and the Church should have need of my services.

CHAPTER III.

LITTLE KANAWHA CIRCUIT, VIRGINIA AND OHIO, AND FAIRFIELD CIRCUIT, OHIO.

1817-18.

THE Conference met in Zanesville, Ohio, October 3, 1817. Bishop Roberts presided with great dignity and acceptability. On Sabbath he preached a powerful sermon from "Behold the Lamb of God," etc. At this Conference Rev. Samuel Parker, who was a man of superior ability and much popularity, was appointed to go as missionary to the Natchez country. In view of his feeble health, and the unhealthy character of the region to which he was going, the parting scene was a very tender one. Alas! it turned out as many feared—we saw his face no more. He fell far away from home, but he fell at his post, with his harness on, and his history will be precious as long as the history of the Church endures.

The following preachers were received on trial at this Conference: Bennet Dowler, Ira Eddy, Allen Wiley, Peter Stephens, Calvin Ruter, Philip Greene, John Stewart, Job M. Baker, John P. Taylor, Thomas Lowry, and Richard Corwine. None of this class survives except myself. The venerable Greene has fallen asleep in Jesus since I commenced this narrative. Why the Master spares me beyond the rest of my class I know not. May I watch, and wait, and be ready!

I was appointed as junior preacher to LITTLE KANAWHA

circuit in Virginia. Rev. John Graham was appointed to the charge of the circuit. He was an Irishman, of respectable preaching talent, affable in his manners, and being one of the sweet singers of Israel, he made a fine impression among the people. The circuit embraced an immense field, being about five hundred miles in circumference. It was the nucleus of what grew up into the Kanawha district, and was afterward widely known and as widely dreaded by the young men of the Ohio Conference as "Brush College." It embraced a very considerable portion of what is now the West Virginia Conference.

Our route commenced at Bellville, about ten miles below Parkersburg, on the Ohio River, and extended up the river to the mouth of Grave Creek, a little below Wheeling; thence down the river again to the mouth of Middle Island River; thence up the latter stream to near its head; thence over to Hews River, to brother Thomas Cunningham's; thence across over on to the head-waters of Little Kanawha River; thence down it to the mouth of Reeder Creek and to Elizabeth; thence over on to the waters of Elk River, and thence across to the Ohio River at Bellville, the place of starting. The mind now sweeps around that vast field almost without an effort; but to climb its mountains, and ford or ferry its streams, and penetrate its pathless forests more than fifty years ago, required much of courage and endurance. It was a five weeks' circuit, and we had about thirty-five appointments, or an average of one for each day. In modern times protracted meetings have come much into use, and the preachers generally regard them as making a heavy draft on the strength of the pastors; but so far as the preachers were concerned, in the days of which I am now writing, it was a protracted meeting from the first day spent on the circuit until we started for Conference. Indeed, the preachers generally—bishops, presiding elders, and circuit preachers—expected to preach every day if there was opportunity. This daily vocal exercise, accompanied with daily horseback exercise and coarse diet, was, doubtless, far more favorable to health than the habits of the present day. Now the majority of the pastors are shut in in their studios, at hard mental labor during the week, and take but little vocal or bodily exercise, and then on Sabbath preach twice or three times. No wonder that so many constitutions are prematurely broken down. I am not sure but a return to the circuit system, notwithstanding the embarrassments that are in the way of it, would prove a blessing to both preachers and people. If, however, this may not be, let the pastors, for the security of their own health, as well as the spiritual interests of the Church, spend at least one-half of each day in *pastoral visiting*, and a large measure of the time devoted to these visits in *vocal prayer* in the families visited. If this is done, ministerial life will be prolonged and ministerial efficiency greatly increased.

Some of our rides between appointments were forty miles and more, and much of the way no roads. We would carry the tomahawk with us, and blaze our path on the trees through the forest, or follow the blazed tracks that had been made by our predecessors. Notwithstanding the utmost care, we would frequently lose our path. Being a pretty good woodsman I seldom lost much in distance, and would come out near the place aimed for. I would often reach the neighborhood of my appointment after a hard day's travel, weary and hungry, and well prepared to appreciate the rude but cheerful hospitality extended to me in the cabins of the pioneers.

I remember one cabin to which I was welcomed, in which there was neither chair, nor bedstead, nor table, nor floor. To do me special honor, they set out the iron bake-oven, and putting the lid on it, gave it to me for a seat, while they gathered about me with wonder and kindness, to hear the news or receive such instructions as I had to impart. They spread for me, in due time, a sumptuous repast of bear-meat and corn-bread. When the evening was far spent, we gathered about the family altar and spent a time in devotion. Then one of the family climbed up to the loft and threw down a quantity of robes, taken from the wild animals that the hunter had gathered. These were spread on the ground-floor before and on each side of the spacious fire-place, and soon parents, and children, and preacher were hid beneath the robes, and wandering in the mysteries of dream-land. There was, however, considerable difference in the style of living among our people in those days. There were many, and some in almost every neighborhood, who had emerged from the rudeness of the scene above described, and whose houses presented many of the conveniences and embellishments of the older settlements. The external appearance of the people at meeting was not always, however, an infallible index to the state of things at their homes. I learned this the next day, after enjoying the rude hospitality above described. There was a lady in my congregation very neatly dressed, and her general appearance suggested the idea that if she should invite me to go home with her, I should be glad to accept the invitation. At the close of the services I threw myself in her way, and secured the invitation. I accompanied her, and was treated with marked kindness, but I had no sooner entered the house than I found that I had made a grand mistake. I would have changed back again for the ground beds and bear-meat, But I will not particularize. The people gave us as good as they used themselves, and seasoned their hospitality with the heartiest welcome and good wishes.

At the end of six months I was changed from this to

what in some respects was regarded a much more desirable field of labor. As the Little Kanawha was a five weeks' circuit, six months only took me three times around this vast circuit. During that time, however, I had formed a great many acquaintances and friendships, which are still green in memory.

Among the local preachers was the Rev. David Smithers, an able minister, and a man of genuine devotion to the cause of God; also, Rev. Samuel Briggs, a man of marked eccentricities of character, and the Rev. Reese Wolf, a man of marked peculiarities, but truly a man for the times. He was a thorough Methodist, well acquainted with our doctrine and Church polity. He was fearless and efficient, widely known, and deservedly popular. In after years he moved to Ohio, where we shall meet with him again in the course of our narrative.

FAIRFIELD CIRCUIT.

At midwinter the mail brought me an order from my superior—Rev. Jacob Young, presiding elder of the district—to leave Little Kanawha and go to Fairfield circuit, Ohio. In his autobiography he makes this brief allusion to the change: "Brother McMehan wished to retire from the work for reasons best known to himself. I deem it the worst step he ever took; so it turned out, and he regretted it for many years. I let him go, and put the well-known John Stewart in his place, then a lovely boy, full of zeal and good works. He and brother Quinn worked together in great harmony." The venerable author makes a mistake in regard to my colleague. The preacher in charge was not James Quinn, but Rev. Michael Ellis, one of the grandest men that ever occupied an American pulpit. The reader has already been informed, in a preceding chapter, of my journey of a hundred miles to the

Pickaway camp-meeting to hear this man of God expound the way of salvation, and how my young soul was blessed under his ministry. My heart bounded with joy that I should now be associated with him, and have him for my teacher and friend. The venerable man had passed his three-score years and ten, and had been the people's mouth to God and God's mouth to the people already for between thirty and forty years.

On Christmas day I closed my labors on Little Kanawha circuit, and on New-Year's day—January 1, 1818—I opened my mission on Fairfield circuit. The venerable Ellis received me as a son in the Gospel, and gave me his godly counsel and benediction. We had from twenty-five to thirty appointments, the names of some of which have passed from my memory. Among those now remembered are Lancaster, Nimrod Bright's, James Collins's, on Raccoon; David Dutcher's, below the falls of Hockhocking; Zeller's, Rushville, Peter Black's, Somerset, Jesse Cartliche's, Rehobeth, Chilcoat's, Springer's, Asbury's, Dillen's Furnace, Flint Ridge, Clay Lick, Pitser's Hog Run, David Swazy's, Baker's, and Thornville. This was one of the old, and one of the best, circuits in those days. Out of it have grown the following charges: Lancaster, Logan, Baltimore, Rehobeth, Somerset, Maxville, Asbury, Lexington, and East and West Rushville. The following were among the local preachers on that circuit: Alexander M'Cracken, Jesse Cartlich, Jesse Stoneman, Noah Fidler, David Dutcher, Aaron Young, George Gardner, Nimrod Bright. Some of these were men of mark, and had done and were still doing good service for Christ and his Church. Stoneman and Fidler had been efficient traveling preachers.

In the bounds of this circuit there was much of wealth and refinement, and the Methodist Episcopal Church had taken a strong hold upon the people, her membership on the circuit already numbering eight hundred and eighty-four. I applied myself diligently to my studies as my circumstances would allow, and stimulated by the influences of my colleague, was inspired with a lofty and increasing ambition to accomplish successfully my mission. We did not witness the extensive ingathering that we desired, but had times of refreshing from the presence of the Lord.

My heart prompts me to spread on these pages a still further record of my appreciation of my excellent colleague. Rev. Michael Ellis was stationed in Baltimore as early as 1784, and was that year ordained deacon at the same Conference that Asbury was ordained to the Episcopacy. After traveling a few years in Virginia, he found it necessary, in view of the support of his family, to retire from the regular work for a time, and give a portion of his attention to secular affairs. About the year 1810 his name appears on the Conference roll again. His children had now grown to that age that they could support the family, while he gave himself to the work again. Finley, in his Sketches of Western Methodism, thus speaks of him after his readmission: "He was appointed to the West Wheeling circuit, in the bounds of which he had labored for many years as a local preacher with great acceptability and usefulness. The next year he was returned to the same circuit, and such was his increasing popularity, even in the vicinity of home, that he would have been gladly received another year but for disciplinary restrictions. He was a Bible student, deeply versed in the science of salvation, and one of the soundest, clearest doctrinal preachers we have ever heard. He studied divinity in the school of Christ, and was trained under the professorship of Wesley and Fletcher. His heart was deeply imbued with the grace of God, and having obtained the fullness of the blessing of the Gospel of Christ, the perfect love that swelled his heart rolled out to bless mankind. We doubt whether he ever preached a sermon in which he did not introduce the doctrine of Christian perfection, as taught in the Bible and preached by Wesley and Fletcher. It was the plain, old-fashioned, unvarnished doctrine of entire sanctification, without any reference whatever to the philosophy of the intellect, the emotions, and volitions—a simple faith that brought into the soul the life and love of God. One of his favorite texts in the latter days of his ministry was, 'Jesus Christ, who is made unto us wisdom, and righteousness, and sanctification, and redemption.' These doctrines he compared to a ladder, the foot of which rested on earth and the top reached into heaven. Justification, sanctification, and redemption were the successive rounds of the ladder over which the soul passes in its course to heaven. He would clearly describe the doctrine of justification by showing the nature and condition thereof, and its attestation by the Holy Spirit. Then he would describe the nature and condition of sanctification, and, finally, what the Bible teaches in regard to redemption and glorification in heaven. He seemed to be the living impersonation of his theme, passing through all the successive stages of his theme to its close, when he would give a shouting peroration that would make every heart feel that the preacher knew and felt what he preached."

The doctrine of entire sanctification was recognized in those days as a distinctive feature of Wesleyan theology, and multitudes of professors of religion in other branches of the Church regarded the doctrine as unscriptural and dangerous. But now, thank God! the evangelical Churches have come to recognize the doctrine as Scriptural, and very many of their preachers and members preach and profess it. Let us, as Methodists and the successors of Wesley and Fletcher, hold fast to the doctrine, and urge entire purity of heart upon ourselves and all with whom we have to do. Holiness to the Lord is the grand secret of success and power.

The few months spent on Fairfield were months of enjoyment and profit to me, and I found on return that I had been correcting some pulpit habits which threatened to be of disadvantage to me. The circumstance that first called my attention to these habits was somewhat amusing, and a good deal annoying to me at the time. It was the first Sabbath that I spent on Fairfield circuit, and was a quarterly meeting. A quarterly meeting in those days was so different from what they are in these days, that many of my readers, I presume, have but little idea of the interest that gathered around such a meeting half a century ago. Fancy a circuit spreading over half a dozen large counties, and local preachers and exhorters, stewards and private members coming on horseback on Friday to stay over Saturday and Sunday, on purpose to worship God and advance his cause.

The meeting here referred to was held at Rushville, and embraced the first Sabbath of the new year. Rev. Jacob Young, the presiding elder, Rev. James Quinn, Rev. Michael Ellis, the preacher in charge, and Rev. J. M'Mahon, the eloquent preacher, who was about retiring from the work, and whose place I was to supply, were all there. With such an array of talent and experience about me, the announcement that I was to preach Sabbath night almost overwhelmed me with embarrassment. I announced for my text Isaiah iii, 10: "Say ye to the righteous that it shall be well with him," etc. I was badly frightened, labored hard, and sweat profusely. In the morning Rev. J. M'Mahon came to my bed and said, "Well, brother John, how often do you suppose that you said 'it appears' last night while you were preaching?" I was mortified above measure, and poured out my complaint to brother Quinn. He saw that I needed encouragement, and he gave me a bit of his own experience. "Do you see," said he, "that I have no pocket flaps?" "Yes, sir." "Well, I had unconsciously fallen into a habit of putting my hands into my pockets and taking them out again until it attracted attention. Some one took occasion to count the number of times that I put my hands into my pockets while preaching a sermon. Afterward he told me of it, and to break myself of the habit I had the pockets removed. It cured me, and brother M'Mahon's criticism will do you good." It did do me good, not only in that particular habit, but in causing me to give closer attention to my pulpit habits. Whenever a minister falls into any peculiarity of style in the pulpit, whether of language, tone, or gesture, which diverts the attention of the hearers from the message to the messenger there is a loss of efficiency. The most enviable efficiency is secured when the people forget the preacher in his theme, and go from the sanctuary revolving the thoughts that have been brought out in the sermon. In those days we had few of the advantages of ministerial association that are enjoyed by the preachers of the present day, and if we, who formed our habits on vast circuits and among comparatively uncultivated people, contracted some mannerisms it is hardly to be marveled at. The young men of this day have no apology.

The Conference was to meet at Steubenville, Ohio, August 7th. This arrangement made the Conference year two months shorter than usual. My library, wardrobe, and effects generally being packed into my saddle-bags, I made my way to Athens county, to visit my parents and friends during the session of the Conference. In those days the Conference probationers were not expected to attend the Conference, but were expected to keep up the appointments during the absence of the preacher in charge. On this occasion I exchanged one round with brother Baker, his parents living in the bounds of my circuit and my parents living in the bounds of his circuit.

CHAPTER IV.

MAHONING CIRCUIT AND ERIE CIRCUIT.

1818-19.

THE Conference at Steubenville, which met August 7, 1818, was one of power and glory. Bishops M'Kendree and George were present in the spirit of the Master. The preachers seemed to have a peculiar unction in the pulpit labors, and a gracious revival of religion broke out among the people. That was not an unusual state of things at our Annual Conferences in those days. Happy would it be for us if we had more of the revival power at our Conferences in these days. On the Sabbath-day Rev. John Collins thrilled the audience by singing a popular melody called the "Market Song," and he and Asa Shinn preached with wonderful power and effect. Joshua Soule, at that time Book Agent, was with us, to represent our publishing interest. That interest was then in its infancy, and was rather a system of colportage among ourselves than the mammoth publishing establishment having to do with the book market of the world, as now. The case of Rev. Wm. Burke — one of our greatest men, but unfortunate in some of his movements — caused some lively discussion, but the business of the Conference was conducted with a good degree of harmony and dispatch. At this session of the Conference the following preachers were admitted on trial: Samuel Adams, Samuel Brockunier, Ed. Taylor, James Smith, Dennis Goddard, Charles Elliott, Thos. M'Clary, Green-berry R. Jones, J. Whittaker, H. Holland, Henry Matthews, Z. Connell, L. Swormstedt, J. T. Wells, Arthur Elliott, A. S. M'Clain, B. Spurlock, J. Harber, J. Farrow. When, at the close of the session, the Bishop stood up before the Conference with the list of appointments in his hands, but few, besides God, the Bishop, and the presiding elders, knew any thing of the contents of the paper; but preachers and people lifted up their hearts to God, asking that he would give them a new baptism of the itinerant spirit, and send them to their work full of heavenly fire. I was appointed to "MAHONING CIRCUIT" with Calvin Ruter. I was well pleased with the appointment and my colleague. Within the past ten months I had swept over much of the southeastern and central part of the State, and now my field spread out over the Western Reserve. I should have more of the Yankee element in my congregations, but expected to find Methodism substantially the same as among the more emotional people farther south. Calvin Ruter and myself were linked together by peculiar ties. We had been brought up together in the same neighborhood, belonged to the same society, commenced our ministerial life as supplies under the same elder the same year, were received on trial in the traveling connection at the same Conference. We were now happy to be associated as colleagues. Soon after Conference we set out together to our new field of labor. We went in the spirit of our commission, and all things were propitious. Our first call was ordered of Providence. Doubtless the misfortunes of a Conference year have often resulted from unfavorable impressions made by the first contact of the preacher with the people of his new charge. A cold, formal, or repulsive reception has thrown its dark shadow over the whole year, while a hearty and smiling welcome has thrown sunshine and blessing through all the months of the year. Our first call was upon the Rev.

Shadrach Bostwick, a man of God, whose name is written in sunbeams on thousands of hearts. He entered the traveling connection in 1791. In the year 1803 he came West as a missionary, and after planting Methodism in the Western Reserve, he married and located—located so far as Conference relation was concerned, but in no other sense. Skillful and popular as a practicing physician, he was industrious and successful as a preacher of the Gospel. He was not jealous of the popularity of the circuit preachers, or inclined to complain and embarrass. He welcomed us to the circuit and his home, gave us advice and co-operation, and inspired us with assurance of success. We sent out our appointments, and as we went along the line the Spirit of God assisted us, and a mighty work of salvation visited the people. The revival fire spread over the circuit, and sinners were awakened daily. Upward of two hundred were added to the Church during the year.

I shall never forget how the God of grace revealed himself at Deerfield. I was to preach in a school-house. At the appointed time a large congregation crowded the place. While I was preaching the power of God came down, and the people, young and old, fell like men slain in battle until the floor was almost literally covered with the slain of the Lord. Among them Horatio Day was stretched upon the floor at full length. I heard his cry above that of others, saying, "God be merciful to me a sinner!" Approaching, I found him in deep distress. Turning his eyes toward me he exclaimed, "Do you think the Lord will have mercy on me? I am an old sinner and a great sinner." I replied, "Christ is a great Savior; he has a 'balm for every wound and a cordial for every fear.'

'His blood can make the foulest clean,
His blood availed for me.'"

The broken-hearted man had reached an extremity of

extremities. He was evidently in a region lying between hope and despair—bordering on hope, also bordering on despair. I endeavored to keep the promises before his eyes; now urging him to claim them and now dictating prayer. Suddenly his change came, and he exclaimed in rapture, "O how light it is!" He sprang to his feet, then mounted the bench, then leaped on to the table. Heaven seemed to beam in his countenance as he exclaimed, "I do not think that the people in heaven can look more beautiful than the people in this congregation." True, the change that had passed on the congregation was great, but it was chiefly the change that had been wrought in his own soul that made all around wear an aspect so lovely. Old things had passed away, and all things had become new.

At the next door from where the above scene occurred lived a young lady of fashion and fortune, who moved in what are called the "higher circles" of society—higher, indeed, in the sense of self-exaltation, but obnoxious to that teaching of the Book, "He that exalteth himself shall be abased." This young lady had opportunities to test the ability of the world to satisfy the longings of the immortal mind beyond what falls to the common lot. She had eagerly passed along the avenues that promise happiness, but had found nothing substantial and satisfying. She listened to the testimony of those who declared that they had found real and permanent enjoyment in the religion of Jesus Christ. As she mused with herself she said, "These are persons in whose truth and sincerity I can rely." She retired to her bed full of anxiety about her soul. Sleep passed from her eyes and slumber from her eyelids. The night passed slowly away, and the morning found her among the most unhappy of probationers. At the break of day, however, she deliberately resolved that she would seek Christ. Taking the Bible in her hand, she repaired to a neighboring forest with this desperate resolve, that she would not return to the house, eat, drink, or sleep until she had made her peace with God. Having penetrated the shadows of the forest, she selected the spot where she intended to die if she failed to obtain the mercy of God. The day passed wearily and painfully. Now she was searching the Scriptures as for hidden treasures, and now upon her knees in broken-hearted supplication. All seemed to be blackness overhead and all around. She felt that she was stumbling upon the dark mountains, and feared that she would go down to the pit. But she was not so far from the kingdom of Christ as she feared. Already the angels were rejoicing in heaven as her sighs, and tears, and prayers, and confessions evidenced her repentance. After the turn of the day, the family, having missed her since morning, became uneasy. An alarm was made, and the neighborhood turned out to search for her. To do the work effectually, they organized into companies and districted the territory to be searched over. Just as the sun was going down, the time hallowed by the incarnate Savior by wonderful deeds of mercy, He appeared to her the chiefest among ten thousand and the one altogether lovely. He spake her sins forgiven, her sky serene; he turned her night to day, her hell to heaven, and set the captive free. About this time one of the searching parties thought they heard the distant sound of a female voice. They paused and listened; it was surely the voice of singing; it was one of the songs of Zion, and it was the voice of the lady for whom they had been so anxiously seeking. They hastened to her, and she talked to them in the language of Canaan. The joy that had commenced in heaven had come down to earth, and the glad acclaim, "The dead's alive, the lost is found!" kindled rapture on earth. This incident gave a new interest to the work in the neighborhood, so that there and elsewhere the work of God went on grandly, and much people were added to the Lord.

The relations between the ministers, traveling and local, and between the preachers and people were most happy, and we looked forward almost with regret that one short year in all probability must sunder these ties of association. For in those days very rarely did unmarried men remain more than one year on the same circuit. In the midst of these musings, however, a letter from the presiding elder, J. B. Finley, fell like a bomb-shell among us. The letter announced that he had directed Dr. Samuel Adams, of the Erie circuit to take my place on Mahoning circuit, and he now directed me to take Dr. Adams's place on Erie circuit. The reason of the change was that Dr. D. D. Davisson, Adams's colleague had married, which made the burden on Erie circuit too great as to support, and as Ruter and myself were both single men, this arrangement would equalize the burden on the two circuits. I could not murmur, yet I parted from my colleague, and the the young converts, and the fathers and mothers in Israel who had lavished so much kindness on me, with a sad heart.

Among the ministers resident in this circuit, and whose acquaintance I had formed, and from whom I had received welcome and help, were Dr. Bostwick, of whom I have already spoken; Rev. Alfred Brunson, who still—1868—stands on the walls of Zion, a young man then, diligently plying his trade as a shoemaker, and, as he had opportunity, proclaiming the acceptable year of the Lord. He was a young man of vigorous intellect, inclined to take large views of his subject, and to treat it with a decided and earnest logic. Afterward he gave himself fully to the work, and upon the broad prairies of the North-west did much of pioneer work, and connected himself with almost every active movement in Church and State. His literary and theological attainments were recognized in the conferring of the degree of Doctor of Divinity upon him; and now, while I write these lines, the venerable Doctor is presiding over the metropolitan district of the West Wisconsin Conference. Dr. Menary, and brothers Smith, Leach, and Miller were all local preachers—good, true, and useful. Promising to visit the charge again on my way to Conference at the end of the year, I responded to the command of my superior in office, and turned my face eastward to Erie circuit.

ERIE CIRCUIT.

Rev. D. D. Davisson, the preacher in charge of ERIE CIRCUIT, received me with great kindness, and I found him to be not only an able theologian and faithful pastor, but a kind and profitable colleague. The Christian friendship thus formed strengthened with years, and shall be renewed and perpetuated in heaven. The circuit had not the revival spirit equal to the one that I had left, but I entered upon my work feeling that I was in the path of duty, and that God was with me.

The first quarterly meeting held on the circuit after I came to it was a camp-meeting. An immense concourse of people attended. Rev. J. B. Finley, the presiding elder, preached with great power, and all the preachers seemed to be anointed for the work, and entered into it with heart and soul. The fires of reformation burned brightly, and before the meeting closed the hallowed influences pervaded the congregation, and many were gathered to Christ. Those who were blessed at the meeting carried the good influence to their home communities, and so spread it, in a measure, all around.

Rev. Isaac C. Hunter, the supply on Lake circuit, in the State of New York, attended this camp-meeting. His friends lived in the bounds of this circuit, and as he desired to remain and spend a little more time with them, he proposed to exchange one round with me. After consultation with the presiding elder in regard to the matter, it was so arranged, and I spent a month pleasantly and profitably, I hope, in preaching the Gospel to the people of his charge. The engagement ended, each of us returned to our appointed field and work.

During this year brother Finley invited me to accompany him to the Chatauque camp-meeting. The invitation was the more cheerfully accepted by me as the Rev. John Summerville, my first colleague, was the preacher in charge on that circuit, and I should thereby have the pleasure of visiting with him again. My former colleague received me with great kindness, and after hearing me preach, flattered me greatly as to my proficiency since we traveled together on the Letart Falls circuit. I preached a sermon from 1 Timothy iv, 10: "Therefore we labor and suffer reproach, because we trust in the living God, who is the Savior of all men, specially of those that believe." It was greatly blessed to the congregation. The following is substantially the outline of the sermon:

I. We shall speak of the living God as a Savior.

1. The living God. There is one Being, self-existent and self-dependent—who exists, and can not but exist. If there ever was a time when that Being did not exist, that time would be now, for no being can be the author of his own existence. God lives. He has life in himself. He imparts life to all his creatures, both celestial and terrestrial, whether vegetable, animal, or rational. He exists under three adorable distinctions, as Father, Son, and Holy Spirit. The fact we believe because it is clearly revealed, but the mode of the fact transcends our reason, and is enveloped in mystery.

2. This God is a Savior—the only Savior—an all-sufficient Savior—able to save to the uttermost!

The log-cabin Episcopal parsonage occupied by Bishop Roberts was within the bounds of this circuit, and the influence of the good man was all-pervading. It was a large circuit, and swept over a considerable portion of Western Pennsylvania. Among the prominent appointments were Erie, Waterford, M'Connellsville, Meadville, and Mercer. As I was only a few months on this circuit, and that time broken by the visits above referred to, I shall refrain from entering into much detail of names and circumstances, lest I should make mistakes.

Rev. Samuel Gregg has written an interesting history of the growth of Methodism in the bounds of the Erie Conference. In his notice of myself, however, he has fallen into several mistakes. He states that I was received into the Ohio Conference on trial at Zanesville, Ohio, September 3, 1817, ordained deacon in 1819, ordained elder in 1821, and then transferred to the Missouri Conference. In this he makes a mistake, for I was transferred at the same time that I was ordained deacon. I was transferred back to Ohio after three years of missionary work. He further states that I itinerated effectively forty-three years and superannuated; he should have said fifty years. He falls into error, also, in regard to the time that I have served in the presiding eldership; he should have said thirteen years. They are not matters of any great importance, and yet such inaccuracies in a work professing to be history tend to weaken confidence in the reliability of the work.

Closing up my work on this circuit, I visited Mahoning circuit, according to promise, on my way to Conference, and we had a joyful time together. How sweet and strong are the bands that unite the hearts that have been touched with the loadstone of Divine love before the mercy seat!

Blessed memories come crowding upon my heart, and I anticipate a glad reunion with those cherished friends in the mansion-house on high. Its glittering dome rises before the eyes of my faith, and the light streams from its windows, and I fancy that the hands of its inmates are stretched out to beckon and welcome me there!

About the 1st of August brother Ruter and myself started in company toward Cincinnati, where the Conference was to meet on the 7th. We had time to review our past history, and lay plans for the future. To us both it was a time of peculiar interest, in view of the fact that we were both expecting to be received into the Conference, and ordained to the office of deacons in the Church of God. Bishops George and Roberts assisted, and business of varied character and vast importance came before the Conference, and was dispatched much more rapidly than business is dispatched in other than ecclesiastical bodies—the matter of founding an institution of learning of a high grade to meet the growing want of our people, the support of the wonderful work among our Indian tribes which had so strangely commenced under the self-appointed missionary labors of a colored man from Marietta, and the vexed question of slavery. Besides this, we had to elect delegates to the General Conference, which was to meet the following May. The delegates chosen were John Collins, Jacob Young, J. B. Finley, William Dixon, Alexander Cummins, Jonathan Stamper, James Quinn, and Walter Griffith. To me the events of greatest importance at this Conference were my ordination to the order of deacon and response to the call for volunteers for frontier work. The vows of ordination were solemn and searching, and the service was peculiarly impressive. The Macedonian cry came from Missouri and Illinois, and the Bishops pleaded earnestly and pathetically for volunteers. My mind was intensely exercised in regard to the matter. A matrimonial contract of four years' standing I had expected to consummate after taking the order of deacon and coming into full connection in the Conference. To place myself in a position that would almost necessitate the further postponement of that engagement, without having the opportunity of consulting with the other party to the contract, was a matter of no small embarrassment. On the other hand, I knew her devotion to the cause of Christ so well that I was persuaded that she would desire that I should go wherever my labors could conduce most to the upbuilding of the cause of Christ. With this conviction, I placed my name on the roll of volunteers, and was transferred to the Missouri Conference, with the promise of a transfer back to the Ohio Conference after two years of missionary labor. During the two years and a half that I had itinerated I had experienced much of toil and much of triumph, and felt to be fully committed to the itineracy as my life-work; but, could I have consulted my own preference, I should not have severed myself, even for a year, from the companionship of that noble band of men belonging to the Ohio Conference. My presiding elders and colleagues were specially dear to me, and it was like leaving home, and father, and brothers to be separated from them.

Rev. JACOB YOUNG, my first presiding elder, was a man of marked and strong points of character. He was born in Pennsylvania in 1776, a few months before the Declaration of Independence, but emigrated in early life, with his parents, to the wilds of Kentucky. He had become profane and wicked, but soon after their settlement in their new home, he was powerfullly awakened, and, after a desperate struggle, soundly converted to God. To his surprise his father, who had been brought up an Episcopalian, was highly displeased when he learned what had transpired, and complained bitterly that his son should have so disgraced the family in a strange land. The only defense that Jacob made was to take up the Bible, and after reading a lesson, kneeled down in the midst of the family and lifted up his voice in prayer. That voice they had often heard in outbursts of anger and profanity, but never before had it thrilled them as now. Before he rose from his knees the whole family was moved, and melted, and reconciled. Very soon afterward, through his instrumentality, his parents and nearly all the family were converted, and joined the Methodist Episcopal Church. Samuel Parker, who afterward became a prince in Israel, was at that time the leader of the class with which Jacob was connected, and he and others soon became convinced that God designed the young man for the ministry, and urged him into the work. In 1802 he commenced his itinerant career on Wayne circuit. He rose rapidly in the estimation of the Church, and soon occupied a commanding position. In 1816, when I became one of his assistants, he being presiding elder of the Muskingum district, he was looked up to as one of the master minds of the denomination. Without either the advantages of a classical education or the graces of rhetoric, such were the clearness of his theological views, the strength of his logic, and the earnestness of his ministrations, that multitudes listened to him with pleasure and profit. He was a progressive man, identifying himself with every movement in the Church promising to promote the education and salvation of the people. His name was frequently placed upon the list of delegates to General Conference, and the Indiana Asbury University conferred upon him the degree of D. D. In 1855 having so far failed in health as to preclude his further labors in the regular pastoral work, he took a superannuated relation. In a note to one of his friends, he thus expressed his feelings in view of his surroundings at that time: "After having gone in and out before the Church for fifty-four years, I am now compelled to retire. I am now in the neighborhood of total blindness. My strength is ebbing out with great rapidity. I shall soon be done with life and its cares. While you are actively and successfully doing the work of your great Master, I shall be sitting in my lonely cottage, repenting of all my former wrongs, believing in Jesus Christ, and trying to love God with all my heart. How gloomy is the end of human life unconnected with that which is to come! My highest enjoyment in time, next to religion, will be in going to the house of God. I have spent a long life in trying to do good, and am anxious to do good to the very last hour of my life. My trust is in my Redeemer." When the time for his departure came he was ready, and he graduated full of honors and went up to wear his crown.

Rev. JAMES B. FINLEY, my second presiding elder, was born in the State of North Carolina, in the year 1780, in the month of July. His life from early childhood was full of romantic interest; and throughout all the wide field of his travels as a Methodist preacher, multitudes of hearts have been thrilled with his weeping narratives of his youthful wickedness, his remarkable conversion, and the labors and triumphs of his itinerant life. He had been educated by his Calvinistic parents in the sternest doctrines of their confession of faith, his father being a minister in the Presbyterian Church.. His mind, however, early revolted against the doctrine of unconditional election and reprobation. One Sabbath, at the close of the usual family catechetical instruction, his father said to him, "James, do you pray?" He replied, "No, father, I do not." "Why do you not pray, my son?" "Because I do not see any use in it. If I am one of the elect, I will be saved in God's good time; if I am one of the non-elect, praying will do me no good, as Christ did not die for them." The exercises of his mind on this subject had well-nigh landed him in permanent infidelity. During this period of mental perplexity, he came in contact with a treatise on the final redemption of all from hell. This doctrine he grasped with avidity, and at once became a defiant advocate of the doctrine. One of the elders of the Church of which his father was pastor undertook to reason him out of this heresy, when the following conversation occurred:

"Did Christ die for all men?"

"No, he did not die for any but the elect."

"Will the reprobate be damned?"

"Yes, God for the praise of his glorious justice has decreed his damnation."

"For what is the reprobate damned?"

"Because it is so decreed, even so according to the good pleasure of God's will."

"But the Scriptures say that the reprobate is damned for unbelief. 'He that believeth not shall be damned.' Now, if Christ did not die for him, according to your system he is to be damned for not believing what is in itself not true. In other words he is to be damned for not believing a lie."

In this unhappy state of mind—a source of great grief to his parents and Christian friends—he gave way to the depravity of his nature, and excelled in wickedness. When his parents had emigrated to the West, they had settled for awhile in Kentucky, and his father had been pastor of a Church at Cane Ridge. Now, hearing that a camp-meeting was to be held within the bounds of his father's old parish, he determined to attend it. He was now married, and lived at New Market, in Highland county, Ohio. Having invited a friend to accompany him, they went to the meeting. The immense multitude assembled—estimated by some to number twenty-five thousand—was in a state of the greatest excitement. The noise was like the roar of Niagara. He counted seven preachers addressing different portions of the multitude at the same time, having for their pulpit either a stump, wagon, or fallen tree. The wonderful phenomenon of sinners falling as dead—rising as from death in transports of joy—produced a profound impression on his mind. He remained until he could endure it no longer, and then, in company with his friend, started for home again. Both deeply absorbed in their own thoughts, they rode mostly in silence until they came to the Blue Lick Knobs. His feelings now overmastered him, and he exclaimed, "Captain, if you and I do n't stop our wickedness the devil will get us both!" His deep emotion found response in the heart of his companion, and they both wept bitterly. They stopped that night at Mayslick, and spent the night in weeping and prayer. At daybreak he retired to the woods to pray, and soon fell to the ground, and cried to God in such agony that the neighbors heard him, and gathered about him. Among them was a converted German, who enjoyed religion. He took Finley to his house, and prayed and sang with him in German and in broken English until about nine o'clock, when God revealed his pardoning love. He laughed and shouted, to the amazement of all but the Dutch brother. Now, with a happy heart, he pressed his way on toward home, and told his young wife what great things God had done for him. He soon became perplexed in regard to a Church home. He could not subscribe to a Calvanistic creed, and, after turning toward the Newlights and Shaking Quakers, he could find no people who held the truth as he now believed it, and thus failing of the Christian fellowship that he needed, he, after a time, relapsed into carelessness, and then into sin, and at length plunged deeper into rebellion than ever before. After several miserable years, he was persuaded by his wife to accompany her to a Methodist meeting. His prejudices against that people were very strong, and he went reluctantly. But during the class meeting his prejudices gave way, and the Spirit of God again came to him in mighty awakening power. To the questions of the leader he only answered by sobs and tears. The next Thursday he set apart as a day of fasting and prayer, and spent it mostly alone in the forest, with his Bible and God. About midnight, kneeling by a poplar-tree, he was enabled to take hold of Christ with a heart that believeth unto "righteousness," and then he went home filled with peace. The next morning he obtained the witness of his acceptance in such demonstration that he fell his full length in the snow, and then, springing to his feet, went shouting the high praises of God, and declared to his wife what God had done for him. He now felt that he had a work to do for God, and commenced to hold prayer and class meetings in his own house. A Methodist preacher came and organized a class, and recognized Finley as a worker, and encouraged him to extend his missionary endeavors, and even to try to preach. In 1809, at the urgent request of Rev. John Sale, presiding elder, he consented to go around the Scioto circuit. He opened his more public labors at the house of brother Lucas. He was licensed to preach at the camp-meeting at Benjamin Turner's, in Paint Creek Valley, the next August. He was recommended by the same quarterly conference to the traveling connection, received at the approaching Conference, and sent to Wells Creek circuit.

Having extended my account of the early experience of brother Finley far beyond what I had intended, I shall only add a few general remarks in regard to his ministerial career, in this part of my narrative, and will have more to say of him when I come to the time of his death. In consequence of his native ability and remarkable adaptation to the work to which he was called, he took at once rank among his brethren. He was fearless, and indefatigable, and eloquent. With the hunter, or legislator, or the wild Indian he could make himself at home, and generally before the interview ended he became the center of attraction and interest. Whether as junior preacher, preacher in charge, presiding elder, delegate to General Conference, missionary among the Indians, or chaplain to the State-prison, from fiery youth to venerable and honored age, he was a man of mark. He was not equal to some of his brethren in critical exposition or consecutive argument, but he had few superiors in the impressive application of Gospel truth, and in the effectiveness of his flashes of logic. He seldom perhaps carried the fortifications of the enemy by a regular siege, but he usually took them by storm. At the time that I first became associated with him he was approaching the zenith of his popularity, and his mighty voic, whether in its plaintive and pathetic wail or in its thunder tones of exhortation, seldom failed to penetrate to the very citadel of the soul. Doubtless while I, now an old man, write this brief memorial of James, he "shines as a star in the kingdom of God forever."

CHAPTER V.

BLUE RIVER CIRCUIT, MISSOURI CONFERENCE.

1819-20.

CONFERENCE met at Cincinnati, August 7, 1819, and the following persons were admitted on trial: John Manary, Isaac C. Hunter, Abner Goff, James Gilruth, Thomas R. Ruckle, Josiah Foster, Peter Warner, James Murray, John Kinney, Henry S. Farnandis, Andrew Kinear, Adbel Coleman, Benjamin T. Crouch, Moses Henkle, Thos. Hitt, Wm. H. Raper, Robert Delap, Isaac Collard, Horace Brown, David Dyke, John P. Keach, John P. Durbin, Francis Wilson, Nathaniel Harris. This class has furnished the Church some of its ablest administrators and advocates, and one of them, Dr. Durbin, still holds a position of responsibility and honor second to none in the gift of the Church. The following were elected delegates to General Conference: John Collins, Jacob Young, James B. Finley, Wm. Dixon, A. Cummings, I. Stamper, Jas. Quinn, and W. Griffith.

In response to the Macedonian cry from the lips of the eloquent Bishops George and Roberts, Calvin W. Ruter, Job M. Baker, John Everhart, Samuel Hamilton, and myself volunteered for pioneer missionary work without any missionary appropriations, and were transferred to the Missouri Conference, which then spread over the States of Indiana, Illinois, Missouri, and Arkansas.

I was appointed to BLUE RIVER CIRCUIT, in the State of Indiana, as preacher in charge, the Rev. Joseph Pownell being the junior preacher. My home was across the State of Ohio eastward, while my circuit lay across the State of Indiana westward. Were you to fancy the young itinerant, with carpet bag in hand, hurrying down to the depot to fly across the State and say good-by to the loved ones at home, and then across two States to report for service the next Sabbath, the scene would indeed be a *fancy* one. The scream of a railroad whistle had not then been heard in the valley of the Mississippi. The locomotion practiced by the itinerants of that day was on horseback. To have visited home before going to my distant field of labor would have consumed weeks of precious time. With my vows of ordination fresh upon me, and my heart full of zeal, I mounted my horse and turned my face toward the field of future labors. I anticipated enjoyment and profit in my association with brother Pownell. He had received me into the Church, as stated in a previous chapter, and we had a warm attachment for each other. I learned, however, before reaching the circuit, that he was about to be married, and that he had expected to take a location. As he was not present at the Conference, however, and the presiding elder not being fully informed in regard to his wishes, and knowing that the people of Blue River circuit desired his return the appointment was made. Upon my arrival on the circuit he welcomed me, and invited me to perform the marriage service for him. Having been ordained to the office of deacon at the recent Conference, this was the first time that I had officiated in this way, but, after preparing myself thoroughly, the parties gave me the credit of acquitting myself very satisfactorily. The woman to whom he was married, Miss Arnold, was a lady of intelligence and piety, and made him an excellent companion and helpmate. He gave me a liberal fee, which I presented to his wife. During the year they gave me valuable assistance and encouragement in my work. Afterward they settled near Columbus, Indiana, where they maintained an excellent Christian character. Though they have long since crossed the river, the recollections of them are precious to me.

Bishop Roberts, who had been living in the bounds of Erie circuit, Penn., my last field of labor, moved to Bono, on White River, in the bounds of Blue River circuit, at the beginning of this year. This was peculiarly gratifying to me. He was gentlemanly, affable, and exceedingly condescending and communicative. I can never cease to remember and appreciate him as a citizen, a minister, and a Bishop. He gave us invaluable help during the year, both in the pulpit and otherwise. His praise was in the mouths of all, and through his instrumentality Methodism took a higher position and received a mighty impulse.

At one of our quarterly meetings, held at Paoli, he gave us very efficient help. Rev. Samuel Hamilton, the presiding elder, then in the full tide of popularity, was with us, and we had a time of interest and power Saturday and Saturday night. The love-feast on Sabbath morning was a time of refreshing. At the close of the love-feast it was reported to the presiding elder that a Presbyterian missionary, just from the East, was tarrying over the Sabbath in the place and wished to preach to our congregation. Brother Hamilton, with great meekness, not knowing that Bishop Roberts would be present, gave the stranger the eleven o'clock hour. The missionary took for his text, "What think ye of Christ?" His discourse was a cold, dry, theorizing disquisition. He manifested none of the unction essential to success, and the disappointed congregation endured it as patiently as could have been expected. Soon after he commenced, Bishop Roberts entered the house and seated himself near the fire. The meeting was in the court-house, and the preacher occupied the judge's desk. As soon as he had finished his discourse, the presiding elder arose and informed the congregation that one of the superintendents of the Methodist Episcopal Church was present, and that he would in a few minutes address the congregation. Soon he was erect, and slowly moving toward the stand he was to occupy. As very few of the congregation had ever seen a Methodist Bishop they were all eye and all ear. His appearance was venerable and commanding. As he announced his hymn the worshipers began to partake of his own devout spirit, and sang with the spirit and the understanding. They kneeled in prayer, and as he spake to God in their behalf the whole congregation felt shocks of Divine power, and realized that they were in the presence of God. Prayer ended, he announced for his text, "Wherefore seeing we also are compassed about with so great a cloud of witnesses," etc. He commenced by saying, "You have just had a theoretical discourse, and I now propose giving you a practical one." Immediately every eye and every ear was under his control, and the audience was spell-bound for an hour and a half. The court-house was crowded, and such overwhelming power attended the Word that the audience rose *en masse* and stood with open mouths each to receive his portion. The effect was wonderful and never to be forgotten. I thought the visiting clergyman departed a wiser man, possibly entertaining corrected views of the mission and power of the pulpit.

The home-life and arrangements of Bishop Roberts were as simple as his ministry was mighty. The following representation of his episcopal palace will give the reader a good idea of the magnificence of his new episcopal residence: When he moved into it it consisted of rough log walls, clapboard roof and sleepers, and had neither chimney, door, windows, floor, or loft, or furniture. His brother Lewis had erected it, but it remained in this unfinished condition when the Bishop moved his family into it. The first meal consisted of potatoes, roasted in the ashes, and served to the family on one of the sleepers instead of a table and dishes. With his family gathered about the simple meal, he devoutly asked the blessing of God at the beginning and returned thanks at the close of the repast. At night the wolves gave them such an equivocal serenade, that a large fire was kindled in front of the opening of the cabin to deter them from entering. Having made their beds on some puncheons, and having committed himself and family to the watchcare of the Almighty, they laid them down and slept sweetly. He commissioned me to purchase some furniture for him, which I did, and in due time the cabin was supplied with what was deemed sufficient for pioneer life and comfort. Perhaps the moving cause of his establishing his home here was the fact that his brother, Lewis Roberts, had settled here some years before. Lewis was a man of large natural endowments, a good historian, and an excellent Christian gentleman, universally respected. Though gifted in conversation and able to command the attention of any company, yet so timid was he that he could never be prevailed upon to pray vocally even in his own family circle. He was accustomed, however, to read the Scriptures, and then the family would kneel and spend a time in silent family prayer.

The traveling preachers were always welcomed and always benefited by their sojourn at the houses and in the families of these noble brothers. A day spent at the episcopal parsonage always did me great good, for, while Bishop Roberts never compromised the dignity and purity of the Christian Bishop, and gave needful advice and instruction to his junior brethren, he could adapt himself to the wants of the company he entertained, and so completely disembarrass them that they would feel at home and happy. He was often cheerful even to pleasantry. I shall never forget the mirth-provoking manner in which he narrated to me his first experience in the business of solemnizing marriages. One of Lewis Roberts's sons was about to be married, and had invited his uncle, the Bishop, to officiate. Knowing, however, that the Bishop might be called away on more important business, I was invited to be present also, so as to supply any lack of service. At the time appointed, as I was on my way to the place, I fell in company with the Bishop, also on his way to the wedding. He said to me, "I suppose that you are to marry them."

"Only in case you failed to be present."

"I would prefer," said the Bishop, "that you do it."

"In no case could I consent, as you are to be present."

"Are you not authorized to perform the marriage service?"

I reminded him that he had ordained me at the last session of the Ohio Conference, and told him that I had commenced my practice upon my colleague, Rev. Jos. Pownell.

"You," said he, "had a high beginning," and then, with a musical smile, added, "I had the privilege of beginning with a colored couple. When I was ordained deacon," said he, "I was appointed to Baltimore, and soon after was called on by a colored man to marry him. At the appointed time I went to the place, and found the man and woman sitting together. In a few minutes I requested them to stand up. As they rose she took fright, and breaking away from her affianced, rushed out of the back door and disappeared in the garden. The would-be husband pursued her, but after some time returned, saying that he could not catch her, and seemed greatly mortified. I returned home, but after an interval of some days the colored man returned, and requested me to come again, assuring me that she would stand now. I went, and to the great joy of the anxious man she stood until the ceremony was performed, and they pronounced man and wife. That," said the Bishop, with his inimitable smile, "was my start in that line."

During this year we had a camp-meeting at the forks of the Muskatatack, near Brownstown, which was numerously attended. A good religious influence pervaded the congregation from the beginning to the close of the meeting. Bishop Roberts was present, with his excellent wife, and during the meeting he preached several sermons of great power. He preached a sermon from the text "How shall we escape if we neglect so great salvation?" which had a thrilling effect on the audience. That mysterious exercise called the *jerks* prevailed to some extent. Saints and sinners both were affected by them. In fact it was not confined to the people, but dogs and hogs took them. I saw both dogs and hogs so exercised with the jerks, that as they passed around it could hardly be perceived that they touched the ground at all. This exercise was to us unaccountable. I have often, on that and other occasions, seen persons under the influence of the jerks go through exercises beyond all comprehension. It would seem impossible for any one to pass through such exercises and live. For example, women, under this influence, would remain upon their feet for hours, the whole form convulsed from head to feet, throwing the body to and fro, so that the head would almost touch the floor, both forward and backward. The hair would soon become disheveled, and the violence of the motions was such that it would crack like a whiplash. When, after hours of this kind of violent exercise, the influence passed off, they experienced neither soreness nor fatigue. My old friend Jacob Young, however, records a case where the neck of one of the victims of the jerks was dislocated, of course producing instant death. I simply add my testimony to the fact and strangeness of these phenomena, and shall not spend any time in speculating in regard to it.

Brother Pownell was also at this camp-meeting, and an incident transpired during it of special interest to him. During the exercises of the meeting one night, sister Pownell requested me to speak to her husband to come to her. They immediately retired to the house of brother Evans, near at hand, politely requested Bishop Roberts and wife, who had already retired, to accommodate sister Pownell with the use of the room and bed, and a few minutes thereafter they rejoiced in an addition to their family.

We had another excellent camp-meeting on Cooley's camp-ground, near Salem. This ground had been occupied several successive years, and commanded a large attendance of people. Rev. Samuel Hamilton, presiding elder, superintended the meeting. Revs. John Cord and Thomas Sewell, who had for many years been useful traveling preachers, were present and gave valuable service. Thomas Milligan, Peter and Christopher Monarchal, and brothers Jenkins, Andrews, and Harber—beloved brethren, held in high esteem for their work's sake—labored manfully for the success of the meeting. The result of the meeting was highly gratifying, many being awakened and soundly converted, whom I hope to meet in the kingdom of God.

The Blue River circuit then embraced Washington, Jackson, Orange, and Lawrence counties, and the county seats, Salem, Brown, Paoli, and Bedford, were preaching places. We had appointments in many other smaller towns, such as Bono and Orleans. Our strongest societies were at or near Salem, Paoli, Bono, and at the forks of the Muscatatack. It was a four week's circuit, and I performed the labor without a colleague. My salary was one hundred dollars, which was paid in full. Truly God was with us, and we had a year of success in our religious movements. At one time during the year some of our members, by some means, became tinctured with Pelagianism, and I had apprehension of a schism in the Church. We did, however, what we could in the way of doctrinal teaching and pastoral attention, and by the blessing of God the tide turned favorably, and our erring members returned to sound doctrine and evangelical experience. My predecessor reported five hundred and six members, and I had the pleasure of returning to the conference five hundred and eighty-nine—an increase of eighty-three.

The residence of Bishop Roberts in my charge, afforded me excellent opportunity of being posted in the general history of the denomination, and as the General Conference met this year, the denominational news was of unusual interest. The Conference held its session in the city of Baltimore, commencing May 1, 1820. Bishops M'Kendree, George, and Roberts were in attendance. Bishop M'Kendree, however, was so feeble in health that the Conference gave him virtually the privilege of superannuation, allowing him to do such work as in his own judgment he could safely perform. The matters which occupied the most of the time, and called out the most discussion, related to the mode of selecting the presiding elders; the adjustment of difficulties that had grown out of the war of 1812 between societies of the Methodist Episcopal Church and those of the Wesleyan body in Canada; the establishment of denominational schools; the transfer of the powers and duties of the quarterly conferences touching local preachers to a new body called district conferences; and instructions designed to control the manner of procedure in building houses of worship. Some of these questions elicited very earnest and, in some instances, impassioned debate. The Conference having ordered that presiding elders should thereafter be elected to their office by the Annual Conference, so violent was the opposition of the minority to that action that Rev. Joshua Soule, who had been a few days previously elected to the Episcopacy, declined to accept the office unless that offensive act was rescinded. He was obstinate, and Bishop M'Kendree favoring his views the Conference ultimately yielded.

The Rev. John Emory, one of the purest and ablest of our ministers, was commissioned to bear the fraternal regards of the Methodist Episcopal Church to the British Conference, and to secure such adjustment of the matters of difference between our societies in Canada as would promote harmony and the success of the common cause. He was happily successful in securing prompt and fraternal action on the part of the Mother Church.

The General Conference was much perplexed over the question of education. Repeated efforts to found liberal institutions had met with disaster, until those who had labored hard and sacrificed much in this direction were discouraged. But they determined to open the way and give official indorsement to efforts upon the part of the Annual Conference to found such institutions within their bounds as they might deem practicable. The district Conference arrangement was an olive-branch to the local ministry, many of whom thought that such a Conference would be promotive of great good. Though it failed to meet their anticipations and was afterward abandoned, yet it exhibited the disposition of the General Conference to meet the wishes of the petitioners, and in that regard, doubtless, allayed dissatisfaction, and for the time being promoted peace and harmony. In regard to the building of houses of worship, the Conference ordered that they should not be commenced until three-fourths of the amount necessary to defray the expense had been secured; and that they should be erected with free seats. Neither of these regulations, however, resulted in producing much practical change in these matters. The people of New England continued to rent their seats as usual, and the societies generally acted on their own judgment in regard to the financial management of the Church building.

CHAPTER VI.

MOUNT CARMEL CIRCUIT, ILLINOIS.

1820-21.

IN the month of September, 1820, the Missouri Conference met at the Shiloh meeting-house, in St. Clair county, Illinois, some ten miles from St. Louis. Bishop Roberts was the presiding officer. It would not be correct to say that he occupied the chair, because he was so sick as not to be able to sit up, and a bed being made for him in the church, his noble frame struggled with disease, while his masterly mind gave direction to the business of Conference. Arrangements having been made for camp-meeting in the adjoining grove, the work of revival went on while the business of the Conference was being transacted within doors. Preachers were detailed for the day services, while the whole Conference took part in the services at night. There for the first time I sounded the Gospel trumpet to an Illinois audience. The grove then echoed with the masterly logic of the commanding M'Allister, and with the eloquent and earnest appeals of Edward and Samuel Mitchell, David Sharp, Samuel Hamilton, and many others; but their voices are long since still in death, and, so far as I know, I am the sole survivor of the band whose voices were heard from that platform.

The following persons were received on trial: W. L. Hawley, Elias Stone, Samuel Bassett, Francis Moore, William Cravens, John S. M'Cord, W. W. Redman, H. Vredenburg,

David Chamberlain, George K. Hester, James Simms, Isaac Brookfield, Levin Green, Henry Stephenson, and Gilbert Clarke.

At the close of that Conference the following appointments were made for the great State of Illinois:

Illinois District—D. Sharp, presiding elder. Illinois circuit, Alexander M'Allister; Okaw, Hackaliah Vredenburg; Cash River, Francis Moore; Wabash, Thomas Davis; Mount Carmel, John Stewart; Sangamon, James Simms; Shoal Creek, Josiah Patterson.

With the prayers of our brethren, and looking to the great Head of the Church for wisdom and grace equal to our trials and opportunities, we sallied forth to find and occupy the fields assigned us. Every thing about us betokened that we should have to do with laying the very foundation of society. Illinois had been recently erected into a State, and her first governor, Bond, was serving his first term of office.

The stream of time has borne away on its rapid current nearly the entire generation of those who were engaged fifty years ago in laying the foundation of the social and ecclesiastical institutions of our State. Few of those whom I shall mention in these reminiscences now live to read them.

Mount Carmel circuit in 1820 and 1821 spread over the counties of Crawford, Lawrence, Wabash, Edwards, and White, embracing seventeen preaching appointments, and was what was called a "three weeks' circuit." And now, friendly reader, provided with a good horse, comfortable saddle, capacious saddle-bags, let us start on the round of the circuit. Our first Sabbath we spend in Mt. Carmel, preaching in the school-house, morning and night. Before leaving here it is proper to call up the reminiscences of the founding of this town which gave its name to the circuit. The original proprietors were Dr. M'Dowell, from Chillicothe, Ohio;

Judge Scoby Stewart, of New Jersey; Rev. Thomas S. Hinde—who used to be a contributor to our periodical press, under the *nom de plume* of Theophilus Arminius—and —— Stubbs, from one of the Carolinas. These gentlemen having purchased a large tract of land, and proposing to inaugurate a village enterprise, they employed as their financial agent Rev. William Beauchamp, a scholarly and eloquent Methodist preacher, of whom we shall have more to say hereafter. The proprietors being influential Methodists, and their agent being so extensively and favorably known by the Methodist public, it is not strange that the Methodist Episcopal Church had every encouragement in the town, and that the elements of a good society rapidly gathered there.

At the Hinde's, and Russell's, and Beauchamp's, and Stewart's, and Tilton's, and other houses, the itinerant felt that he had real sympathy and reliable backing in every good work.

Having preached in Mount Carmel on Sabbath and spent Monday in the pastoral visitations of the class, the circuit ride commenced on Tuesday morning. Ten miles down the Wabash, and at noon he finds at John Grove's a small congregation, to which he breaks the Bread of Life. He diverges a little from his course at this point to visit a strange community, under the leadership of Mr. Knapp. They were located at a place called Harmony, on the Indiana side of the river. Men and women lived separately, until the seventh year, when the family relation was acknowledged. They were distributed to the several useful trades and vocations according to the wisdom of their leader, who had such supreme influence over them, that in accordance with his teaching they thought eternal damnation would be the punishment that would overtake any one of them who abandoned their leader and the community.

I found them an honest and honorable people to deal with, and could always depend upon getting an article good in quality and reasonable in price. But we must hurry on to our Wednesday appointment, which is at brother Hamilton's.

We are here, only twenty-two miles from Mt. Carmel, and yet we already see cause for grave apprehension in regard to the spirit of the people. An aged colored man, emigrating with his wife, camped in this neighborhood for the night. They were harmless, well-behaved old people. Yet such was the hatred for free negroes that their camp was visited in the night, and he was shot to death in cold blood. Nor did the civil authorities regard it necessary to give any official attention to the matter. The conviction from that time became deeply seated with us, that, if Illinois is saved from the curse of slavery, the Methodist preachers and people have a work to do. The candid historian will be prompt to give Methodism due credit for doing a large measure of the work in preventing the establishment of slavery in this beautiful commonwealth.

Thursday, at noon, we are addressing a congregation twelve miles further on, in the residence of John Hanna, a Carolinian, possessing a large landed estate, and glad to open his mansion for the itinerant and the Gospel which he preaches. Having shared his hospitality for the night, and having but five miles to ride to our noon appointment at brother Withron's, we pass leisurely through the beautiful savannas. But, while we are delighted with its fertility and beauty, we are somewhat startled by the evidence of recent earthquakes. These deep cracks in the earth, which still look so ghastly, could they speak with their broad mouths, would tell of the terrors of many an ungodly man, and of the anxiety of many a lukewarm Christian, as they supposed that the great day of His wrath had come. In the congregation at Withron's we form the acquaintance of two valuable local preachers, Revs. Samuel and Charles Slocum. Though Samuel has identified himself with the movement to incorporate slavery into the organic law, he assures us that he regards this as the surest and speediest way of ridding the country of slavery. "Let us," says he, "spread it out so thin that it will exhaust itself and die." His motives are honest, but we can not subscribe to his logic.

A ride of nine miles, Saturday morning, brings us to our noon appointment at Henry Jones's. This is the extreme point of our circuit down the river, and is nearly fifty miles, by the route we have traveled, from Mt. Carmel. The kind family urges us to stay here for the night, but we have thirty miles to make by noon to-morrow, and we prefer to spend the night as near as may be to our Sabbath work. The scattered settlers will come together from a distance, and, as we will have a larger percentage of unconverted persons to address than we meet in our week-day appointments, we would be fresh and vigorous to meet the responsibility. Saturday night finds us at brother A. Driger's, and Sabbath at noon we are delivering a message from God to the people gathered at the house of brother George Mickles. Monday, at noon, four miles further north, we preach at brother Wheeler's. Though it is wash-day, the hungry people come together to get the Word of Life.

Tuesday, at noon, we are at brother Jacob Shrader's, fourteen miles from the last appointment. We shall henceforward always anticipate with pleasure the hospitality of this kind family. Here the itinerant *par excellence* finds a home. Brother Shrader gives his son John to the work, consecrates his house as a preaching-place, and, with an open purse and a warm heart, co-operates in every good work. In this neighborhood we form the acquaintance of the Scotch Curry family, of whom Rev. W. Beauchamp makes such eloquent mention in his notices of the triumphs of grace in the West. We shall have more to say of them, however, and of their son-in-law, Rev. John Scripps, when we come to speak of the camp-meeting, at which they find a home in the Church. Ten miles brings us to our Wednesday noon appointment, at James Ryan's.

Thursday we are in the saddle again, and, after ten miles' travel, reach the Ellison Prairie appointment, and at noon preach the Word to the people. Here the cotton-fields spread out in their whiteness. Vincennes, Indiana, looms up in the distance, and the landscape is one of surpassing loveliness. But we can not linger here, as we have to push forward twenty-two miles to our Friday noon appointment at brother Snipp's. We lodge at Rev. John Fox's, a superannuated member of the New Jersey Conference, and his counsel, and prayers, and sympathy do us good. The Saturday noon appointment is only four miles distant, at Union Prairie. On Sabbath we are at Palestine, eighteen miles from the last-mentioned appointment, and here, in the school-house, we deliver our message to a congregation of considerable refinement and pretensions.

Tuesday, at noon, we are twenty-five miles away, preaching at brother James Johnson's. This venerable man and his excellent companion, living twelve miles from Vincennes, on the road to Mt. Carmel, give us a welcome so cordial, and enter so thoroughly into all the works of the young itinerant, that we shall always feel toward them as did Paul toward the house of Onesiphorus. At noon on Wednesday we address the people in the next neighborhood, eight miles distant, at the house of an estimable local preacher, Rev. John Ingersoll, a brother-in-law to Judge Scoby Stewart. Thursday, at noon, we close our round of appointments, within four miles of Mt. Carmel, at brother Charles Riggs's.

He being an acquaintance of ours from Western Virginia, we enjoy the renewal of that acquaintance here, where mountains are out of sight and the atmosphere of freedom is about us.

Here, glancing backward, we find that during the past nineteen days we have preached eighteen times, besides leading the classes, marking the class-books, instructing the children, and visiting the people. We have swept over five counties, making a journey of between two and three hundred miles. We have enjoyed it immensely, but the repetition of these travels and labors every three weeks, when the Fall rains, and the Winter snows, and the Spring mud comes, will test our powers of endurance thoroughly. But it is an easy circuit in comparison with some we have traveled. We have a good horse, a comfortable saddle, a strong umbrella, a sublime mission, and we would not change places with the Governor of the State or the President of the Union. They are laboring for the commonwealth, backed up by a majority of the people; we for the kingdom of God, appointed and supported by him.

Our hopes for the year were fully realized. We commenced with one hundred and fifty members; expected to gather fruit while we scattered seed at every appointment. At the close of the year we reported three hundred members—an increase of one hundred per cent. One hundred of these had joined at the regular appointments, and fifty of them at the camp-meetings with which we wound up the year's labors. As these camp-meetings were among the grandest of their kind, we propose to give our readers our reminiscences of them.

The camp-meeting was an institution in those days greatly prized by our people, because greatly honored of God in carrying forward his work. During this year on the Mt. Carmel circuit I had two camp-meetings in two successive weeks, both of which proved to be meetings of great power and glory. The first one commenced the 20th of August, 1821, near Carmi, on the Little Wabash River, thirty-five miles below Mt. Carmel; the other commenced the 27th of the same month in brother Manlove Beauchamp's neighborhood, near Mt. Carmel.

Before I narrate the circumstances of these meetings, it may be interesting to the reader to obtain a general idea of the arrangements and regulations of camp-meetings in those days. In selecting grounds for camp-meetings we had respect not only to shade for the camp, water for the congregation, and pasturage for the horses, but also the character of the surrounding neighborhood, preferring a community that would appreciate the meeting, and assist in the maintainance of good order. The tents were mostly made by inclosing three sides and covering with boards, and leaving the side that faced the audience ground open, to be closed at night with blankets or sheeting. The grounds were lighted at night partly with fire-stands, which were elevated platforms covered with earth, and upon which a fire, fed with light, dry wood, was kept burning during the night, or until the hour appointed for retiring to sleep. In addition to the fire-stands, candles were fastened to the trees by the auger-hole candlestick instrument, and each tent was expected to keep one candle burning in front. The time of retiring to bed and of rising in the morning, also the time of taking meals, and of family prayers, and public service were all announced from the stand at the beginning of the meeting. It was explained how the trumpet would signal these things, that all might conform promptly to the order of the meeting. As the signal for rising in the morning the trumpeter marched around the camp, sounding the trumpet at the door of each tent; then, after giving sufficient time for dressing, the trumpet sounded from the stand for family prayers in the tents. The voice of song and prayer then rose from every tent at the same time, and sometimes the power of God descended, and the day commenced with the shout of a king in the camp. There was service at the stand at eight, eleven, three o'clock, and at "candle lighting," the intervening time being largely occupied with prayer-meeting at the stand or in the tents. At the blast of the trumpet calling the congregation to the stand for public worship, the occupants of the tents were expected to leave the tents and come into the congregation. The cooking was nearly all done at home before the meeting commenced, and all arrangements made, so that men and women could spend their time, not in serving tables, but in feasting upon the Word of God or ministering it to others. The meetings generally commenced on Friday and continued about four or five days. By commencing on Friday all that intended tenting arranged to be on the ground at the beginning of the meeting, and four or five days was about as long as food prepared at home would keep in proper condition for use. The attendance was not large as compared with the attendance on such meetings in older and more populous settlements, but as compared with the thin population of the country it was very large. At the camp-meeting on Mt. Carmel circuit in 1821, soon after the State of Illinois had laid off its territorial garments, the attendance was about one hundred on Friday, three hundred on Saturday, six hundred on Sabbath, three hundred on Monday, and one hundred on Tuesday, to hear the closing sermon.

At the meeting near Carmi, on the Little Wabash River, I was assisted by brother Wm. Beauchamp, Charles Slocum, and Samuel Slocum, and brother M'Henry. They all did good service and preached with a holy unction, but brother Wm. Beauchamp was the master spirit. He preached once each day. He was peculiarly blessed in the opening, and Sabbath, and closing sermons of the meeting. On the Sabbath his text was Romans v, 1–4: "Therefore being justified by faith," etc. It was a sermon never to be forgotten. The workmanship was masterly, and the power attending it was overwhelming. The expectation of the congregation had been elevated to a lofty pitch during the opening sermon of the meeting, but it continued rising. The members of the Church took advanced ground; the sons of Levi became mightily charged with the spirit of their station, and all labored together earnestly in the work. The closing discourse was on the "*inheritance of the saints,*" and was a fitting climax for the meeting. I had always seen brother Beauchamp great, but had seldom heard him soar with the soul-inspiring and heart-melting eloquence of that occasion. Many were awakened and converted during that meeting, and some *twenty* united with the Church on the ground; others carried the arrows of conviction deeply infixed in their consciences and hearts as they sadly returned to their places of abode; and as they have nearly all passed the bounds of probation long since, I fondly hope that they have entered upon the possession of that inheritance that fadeth not away.

The next Friday we commenced the other camp-meeting, near brother Manlove Beauchamp's, in the neighborhood of Mt. Carmel. It was also a quarterly meeting, and Rev. David Sharp, the presiding elder, was present, and took charge of the meeting. The preaching and prayer-meetings were attended with great power, and some *forty-five* professed conversion and *twenty-three* joined the Church. Of the number that joined was a Scotch family that is deserving of special mention. This family had lately emigrated from Scotland, and settled in the neighborhood of Jacob Shrader's. They had been educated in the observance of the

Sabbath after the strictest Scotch fashion, and now, having none of their own people with whom to associate, they commenced attending preaching at brother Shrader's. Previous to the quarterly meeting, according to our custom, I read the General Rules in each society, and once a year I read and explained the rules to the whole congregation. On one of these occasions this family remained to hear the rules read and explained. At the close of service they invited me to accompany them to their home. I accepted the invitation, and so enjoyed the opportunity of further conversation with them. Their home and its surroundings indicated neatness, industry, and thrift, while the family proved to be intelligent, serious, and very hospitable people. They volunteered to inform me that they approved of our General Rules and the exposition that I had given of them, and desired to form a more intimate acquaintance with our usages and people. During the conversation they startled me with the following question: "Would you regard it as proper to read the Old Testament Scriptures on the Sabbath-day?" Their education had been such that they had scruples of conscience on this point, and as they had seen professors of religion not only reading the Old Testament but secular books on the Sabbath, it had somewhat staggered them. I gave them such explanations of the law of the Sabbath and of appropriate Sabbath conduct as I thought proper under the circumstances. The family consisted of eight persons; namely, the parents, three daughters, two sons, and a nephew. The woman had professed religion in Scotland. The family attended the camp-meeting above described, and the remaining seven were converted. They were all bowed at the altar as seekers of religion at the same time, and within one hour all were soundly converted to God, and testifying of his wondrous grace. When the doors of the Church were opened they all came forward together and applied for membership.

Their application was received, and they welcomed amid the rejoicings of the people of God. Brother Curry and his family became at once efficient working Christians. The family was indeed a model family, and proved to be a valuable accession to the Church in that part of our Zion. Agnes Curry, one of the daughters, was afterward married to Rev. John Scripps, one of our able and popular preachers, and my successor on the Blue River circuit. I can not well pass the name of brother Scripps without digressing long enough to record my recollections of his peculiarities and excellencies. He was by birth an Englishman. As a minister of the Gospel he was emphatically a *Methodist*, every thing being done after the strictest method. When he started around a new circuit he would copy into his hand-book a complete list of the members of the Church, writing the names of the females with red ink and of the males with black ink. He would also map out on his hand-book the route from appointment to appointment, so that every cross-road or fork of the road were indicated. At each visit to each appointment he revised and perfected the class-book, making it and his own correspond, and when he left a circuit he left to his successor complete information in regard to every interest of the Church. He was once, if not oftener, a delegate to the General Conference—small in stature, but large in intellect, and valuable in labors.

But to return to the camp-meeting. It was a glorious winding up of the Conference year, scattered the hallowed fire all over the circuit, and left it in a blaze of revival. brother Beauchamp, and brothers Hinde, Ingersoll, and Sharp were among the honored laborers in this camp-meeting. A glowing account of these camp-meetings appeared in the magazine, from the pen of one of the ministers present on the occasion.

The result of the labors of the year were highly satisfactory. I had the honor of recording about one hundred and fifty names on the roll of Church membership, and have the satisfaction of believing that many of them are now rejoicing in the sanctuary above.

I had, during this year, a singular experience with a band of horse-thieves, who at that time were defying law and order in that whole region of country. As the narrative will be of interest, as throwing light on the state of society at that time, and show how the people rose to protect themselves when the ordinary officers and process of law seemed inadequate, I propose to give it in the next chapter.

I did not attend the session of the Ohio Conference in the Fall of 1820, but as I intend recording the names of all received on trial in that Conference, from year to year, I will here insert the names of those admitted at that session. This is the more proper as some of them will appear again in subsequent pages of the narrative. They were, Alfred Brunson, William Crawford, Charles Thorn, James Collord, Daniel Limerick, Charles Truscott, Nathan Walker, William I. Kent, William Simmons, Henry Knapp, Zarah Costin, James Havens, James Jones.

CHAPTER VII.

A HORSE-THIEF CHASED, CAPTURED, AND PUNISHED.

THE good people of Illinois and adjoining States were greatly harassed about the year 1819–20 with horse-thieves and counterfeiters. It was my misfortune to be victimized by one of the former, during the latter year. Sometime in the month of May I was spending a night at Jacob Shrader's. Observing that the shoes of my horse were loose, I took him to the shop and had them removed, and then put him in the stable. Next morning the stable door was bolted as usual, but my horse was gone, and we had no difficulty in reaching the conclusion that somebody, either angry at me on account of my denunciation of sinners, or covetous of my noble horse, or possibly influenced by both motives, had stolen him. As the horse was shod behind, sharp, and without shoes on his forefeet, there was no difficulty in following the track. I immediately started on foot, and followed some miles, when the track suddenly disappeared. I made out finally that the thief had taken the back track, and that he had been maneuvering by grazing the horse along the fence corners, to make any one who might pursue him think that the horse was loose, and rambling at his pleasure. After operating in that way for some time, he left the fence, went out into the prairie, and performed some circling, as does a honey-bee before it takes its course. He then took his course toward the Wabash River, which was some ten or twelve miles distant.

Following on I found that he had reached the ferry a little before daylight, for the dogs having aroused the ferryman he ascertained that some stranger had taken the boat and ferried over, and then sent the boat adrift. It was now evening; I had been pressing on all day, and at night found myself where the thief had been before daylight in the morning. I halted for the night at the house of brother Armstrong. He entered into full sympathy with me, and in the morning brought out two of his best horses. I mounted one and he the other, and we started on the track again. After crossing the river, instead of following the track we commenced investigating whether the thief had recrossed the river above or below the ferry. After satisfying ourselves that he had not, we immediately struck across to White River to see if he had crossed that. We, however, spent the whole day without getting any information. We now saw that we had committed a great blunder in not sticking to the track and following it in all its meanderings. We put up for the night much discouraged, but not in the least inclined to give up the chase.

Next morning we tried to make a bee-line for William Hawkins's ferry on White River, going much of the time through the forest. As we were jogging along through the woods, reflecting how much the thief had the start of us, and the strong probability that he was already beyond our reach, we would at times become despondent, and had about concluded that if we should get no further information against night we would abandon the hunt. Suddenly, in the midst of our gloom, and here in the pathless forest, we struck upon the well-known track of the stolen horse. It was indeed a sudden transition from despondency to hope. Our horses, that had appeared as dull as ourselves, caught the contagion, and pranced along with new life and vigor. A few miles brought us to a house where we obtained valuable information in regard to the object of our search. In answer to inquiries, the man informed us that "last night, just as the stars were beginning to shine, a stranger rode up and inquired if there would be any chance of crossing the river below the ferry. I told him the river was high, and it would be dangerous to attempt it. He said he could swim his horse by the side of a skiff or canoe, but I advised him," said our informer, "to go to Hawkins's ferry, as it was only three or four miles distant, and told him that if he hurried he might reach there before the ferryman had retired to bed." He said the man left in haste in the direction of the ferry.

We were greatly encouraged; the thief evidently thought that he had outwitted his pursuers, who were only one day behind him. Providence seemed to favor us; we thanked God and trotted on cheerily. We soon reached the ferry, and from the ferryman obtained full information in regard to the name, description, and plans of the thief. His conduct on reaching the ferry had been such as to excite suspicion at first, and then the ferryman recognized him as an acquaintance, and drew out of him, without appearing to have any design in the matter, his destination, and the route he intended to take. The information he gave us was about as follows: "About bed-time a man rode up and sat on his horse near the ferry for a time, as though he was half inclined to take a ride on his own account. After a little he rode up the river a short distance, hitched his horse, and then came down near the house and stood listening, perhaps to ascertain whether we were awake in the house. He then returned to his horse, mounted it, and rode down to the ferry and called for the ferryman. I asked him" said the ferryman, "if he could make change. He said he had nothing smaller than a five-dollar bill. I told him to come in and have it changed. He alighted from his horse and came to the door, but as soon as the door opened he recognized me and darted back, saying that his eyes were sore and the light hurt them. He handed in the bill, keeping his face out of sight. I recognized him as one William Baker, of Powell's Valley, over the Cumberland Mountains. I told my family that I knew Baker, and that he always carried counterfeit money. I handed back the bill, telling him that I could not change it, but not intimating any suspicion of the money. Baker was urgent to get over, and offered me his jack-knife, for which I agreed to set him over the river. I called him by name, and claiming acquaintance, we entered into familiar conversation. I admired his horse, which was a splendid fellow, and he told me that he paid one hundred and fifty dollars for it. I inquired after his relations, with whom I was acquainted, and talked without any apparent reason, and in the course of the conversation I learned that he intended going to Owl Prairie to visit his uncle H., and thence to Mt. Sterling to visit his uncles O. and R., and thence to his father's residence in Powell Valley." Possessed of such minute information, though Baker was two days in advance of me, I was confident of success in capturing him. After thanking Mr. Foster for the information, Mr. Armstrong and myself hurried on to Washington, and put the matter into the hands of the sheriff of the county. Selecting two men as assistants, the sheriff started off in hot pursuit, and by traveling all night, they reached the residence of Baker's uncle H., just at the break of day. To their chagrin, however, upon inquiry they found that Baker had left there just at daybreak, twenty-four hours in advance of them. They reported that he had gone to Mt. Sterling, which agreed with his plan as given to Foster at the ferry. The sheriff returned to Washington where I had remained, and reported progress. Armstrong returned home. The citizens of

Washington furnished me another horse, and I started alone and pushed my journey until near midnight, when, in view of the darkness and my ignorance of the country, I was compelled to stop and wait for morning. I was in the saddle with the break of day, and at four, P. M., had got within twelve or fifteen miles of Mt. Sterling. I rode up to a house, and the occupant coming out at once recognized me as a preacher, and besought me to remain and preach for them that night. A plan immediately presented itself to my mind which I adopted and acted upon. The invitation was accepted, the congregation gathered, and a sermon preached. At the close of the sermon, I took the brother in whose house I preached to one side, and requested him to select out of his neighbors present four or five men whom he could trust, and bring them to me. He did so. I stated my case, and inquired whether we could not surround the house of Baker's uncles O. and R., before morning, and capture the thief. They all entered heartily into my interest and plans, and being acquainted with the localities, were sanguine of success. Soon after we started, however, the rain began to descend. It became very dark and muddy, and they advised that we put up till morning, and I consented. In the morning, when we came to one of those houses, we saw the fresh tracks where the horse we were seeking had just been taken from the stable. We were confident that the thief had not more than one hour the start of us. Our horses seemed to partake of our sanguine and eager spirit, and we anticipated swift success. Soon, however, the traces indicated that the thief was maneuvering to deceive his pursuers and cover his flight. And he succeeded so well that a whole day of hard work in tracing his route had only brought us four miles from where we struck the track first in the morning. We were now in the immediate vicinity of Mt. Sterling. The intelligence had preceded us to the village that we were in pursuit of a horse-thief. When we entered Esq. Asbury and one of the constables of the place met me and told me that a man and horse answering the description I gave, were seen at nine o'clock in the morning, fifteen miles on the road to Kentucky, by way of Mack's ferry, and eighteen miles below the falls. They proposed to me to remain and rest in Mt. Sterling, and they would go for the thief; and they said they would not return without him. "Rest easy," said they; "we will bring him back if we have to go to Nova Scotia for him." They were so hearty in the matter, that I consented, and they started. After they had gone I learned the reason of the maneuvers of Baker that had detained us so much. It appeared that during a visit he had made to this uncle not long before, he had attended a party dressed in women's clothes, and had committed misdemeanors, on account of which a State warrant had been issued, which was now in the hands of the constable. He had been notified of this fact, and that was the occasion of his maneuvering to cover his course. But to pursue the narrative as given by Esq. Asbury after his return. At Mack's ferry Baker had tried to pass a counterfeit five-dollar bill on the ferryman, but he detected it, and would not take it. He said he *must* cross, and took the shoes off the hind feet of the horse with which to pay his ferriage. They pushed on to Hardin, in Kentucky. He had been seen to enter the town, and the horse with the bobbed tail and roached mane had attracted attention, but no one could be found that had seen him go out of town. They were here baffled for a day; the shoes having now been removed from the hind feet of the horse, they could no longer track him as before. But after a day of delay and inquiry, a boy was found who had seen a man with such a horse go out through a certain alley while the people were at breakfast. From this time they had no difficulty in keeping his route. The bald-faced horse, carrying a high head, and tail bobbed and roached, had been seen all along the way. So on they pushed over the Cumberland Mountains into Carmel county. At Jacksboro, as they ascended an eminence, they saw a man down in the valley, off his horse, taking a drink. On seeing them he sprang into his saddle, and without putting his feet into the stirrups, moved off at full speed. They jogged on without appearing to notice or take any interest in him. Gradually his fears seemed to subside. Thus they jogged on some fifteen miles, sometimes near to each other, and sometimes further apart. They knew they were approaching a stream of water, and anticipated that his horse would want to drink there; and they planned to enter the water, one on each side of him, and when in right position to seize him. Their plan proved a success. Their careless manner had thrown Baker completely off his guard. As all the horses were drinking, their's stepped along until one was on the right and the other on the left. The iron grasp of one of the men took hold of the collar of the thief; the horses parted, and they came down together; the other man sprang over the stolen horse and lighted astride of the thief. Now a prisoner, he confessed his guilt. They pinioned his arms, tied him on the horse, and took the back track. At the first blacksmith-shop they reached they had irons put on to him, and then with all convenient speed returned to Mt. Sterling, the place where the party had left me.

By this time the whole region embraced in my extensive circuit had become aroused on receiving intelligence of my loss, and different parties had organized and started out in different directions in pursuit of the thief. The excitement extended to adjacent counties in my former (Blue River) circuit. The thief had passed through Paoli. As soon as it came to their ears, Mr. Linley, the sheriff, started in pursuit, and at the next county seat, Mr. Tucker, the sheriff of that county, joined in the chase, and they started together to Mt. Sterling to have an interview with me. I had found the long suspense too great to allow me to remain inactive, and had started on in that direction. They told me that they believed they could overhaul the thief before Esq. Asbury and the constable, at all events they would make the attempt. On they started, and were making good time toward the mountains, when, somewhere in Kentucky, they met the returning party, having the thief in irons. The four returned to Mt. Sterling in company. They paused in the suburbs of the village to prepare for an imposing entrance. One of them took off his red flannel shirt, tore it up, and made flags of it; then they marched into town with flying colors. They went to the tavern and ordered dinner, lodged the prisoner in jail, and then dispatched a messenger for me. The messenger soon concluded that I had gone further than they anticipated and they would not be able to wait until my return, so he returned and made his report. At a preliminary consultation, in view of the fact that the State of Illinois had no penitentiary, and the county in which the crime was committed had no jail, they decided to give him the benefit of an immediate trial and summary punishment. Calling in five other citizens, making nine in all, they organized a court, found him guilty of horse-stealing, and sentenced him to receive fifty stripes on the naked back. Eight of the men were to lay on five stripes each, and the ninth man to lay on ten stripes, making the fifty in all. A constable, who had in hand a State warrant for Baker, on account of the former outrage perpetrated by him in that community, volunteered to lay on the final ten stripes, and assured the court that it should be well done. About midnight they went to the jail, took the prisoner out, and conducted him about one mile from the village, stripped him of hat, coat, jacket, and shirt. "Now clasp your arms around that gum-tree!" He did so, and was securely tied in that position. Sheriff Linley was stationed by him, with a knife in one hand and a candle in the other. "William Baker, you have been convicted of the crime of stealing a horse, and sentenced to receive fifty lashes on your bare back. You are now to receive that punishment, and if you make any ado I shall cut your throat from ear to ear." The sentence of the court, as thus communicated, was brief but sufficiently emphatic. The sharp blade of the knife shining in the flickering light of the candle was significant of the stern purpose of the speaker. The other eight men were stationed about eight rods from the prisoner. At the signal one of them marched up and delivered his five stripes. The party exclaimed, "Well done; your elbow must have been well greased!" As this one returned to the party, he was met midway by the second, who received at his hands the cowhide. He advanced and delivered his five, and he too was applauded as having acquitted himself handsomely. As he retired, the third man met him, received the cowhide, and advanced to his work. The prisoner, writhing under the severe treatment, and not without good reason, thoroughly alarmed as to the probable result, had drawn his body partly around the tree, so as to be somewhat protected by a sapling that grew near it. A severe cut on the ankle with the cowhide, which the executioner said was not to be counted, brought him out of his fort, and the five lashes were laid on to the satisfaction of the listeners. They applauded as before. The prisoner had now received thirty lashes, beside the one not to be counted, when he suddenly got loose, and through the darkness made his escape. Whether the sheriff had been moved to pity by the severe punishment, and feared that the poor fellow would be killed outright and so cut him loose, or whether the prisoner broke loose, no one could tell. The attempt to recapture him was ineffectual, and thus, without hat, coat, jacket, or shirt, and with a bloody back, he reached his uncles, who lived near by, and by them probably was assisted in getting away. In the morning the company called on these uncles, O. and R., and inquired of them, "Have you seen any thing of a young man without a shirt, and with his hat in his bosom?" The parties inquired of were mum with alarm. "We had," rejoined the visitors, "an interview with such a young man, and he informed us that you are connected with the company of horse-thieves and counterfeiters that have been preying upon the people for this some time past, and now we give you just ten days to take yourselves beyond our jurisdiction. If you are within our reach at the end of that time you may expect similar punishment to that inflicted on your nephew." It proved to be a *moving* address. This duty performed, the party returned to town, and were received with demonstrations of the wildest rejoicing on the part of the citizens. The best carriage that could be obtained was brought out, and the four men who had brought Baker to town were seated in the carriage, and the jubilant crowd escorted them around the village with the most demonstrative enthusiasm. It had transpired that Baker was a kind of messenger among the thieving gang, carrying the implements of counterfeiting, and conveying intelligence from one place to another. It was hoped that his punishment and this demonstration would exert a salutary effect upon all concerned. At the conclusion of the triumphal march the sheriffs returned to their homes.

Soon after they had left the town I arrived. The town was still in a high state of glee. The crowd gathered about me and congratulated me upon the recovery of my horse, and Esquire Asbury and the constable narrated to me the facts of the pursuit, capture, return, trial, and punishment substantially as narrated above. They insisted that I should go with them and see where the punishment was inflicted. They showed me the tree where he was tried, the spot occupied by the eight men, and the hat, coat, jacket, and shirt of the prisoner, hung up by the road-side. I now came to look at my horse, and my gladness at his recovery was greatly marred by the evidences of cruel treatment he had received. When he was taken from the stable at brother Shrader's he was in full flesh, round, sleek, and full of life; now he stood almost a skeleton, jaded and downcast. Instead of the cheerful sign of recognition with which he was used to welcome me, he paid not the slightest attention to my caresses. Poor fellow; he had traveled five hundred miles—and, if the windings and maneuverings were counted, much more than that—in seven days, while his feeding had, in all probability, been irregular and scant. If the reader can fancy how much a young itinerant, without family, and hundreds of miles from home, with little property except his horse, and fortunate in having a superior one, prized his horse, he can fancy how I pitied the noble creature, as I stood stroking his flabby hide, which lay in wrinkles, not having had time to adapt itself, as yet, to his suddenly reduced flesh. I spent a few days at Mt. Sterling, resting my horse, and then returned to Mt. Carmel. I was received with a hearty welcome and many congratulations. When I started off on foot in pursuit of the thief some of my friends had said, "Stewart has perseverance, and he will not return without both horse and thief." It was my good fortune to sustain the opinion they had expressed. The horse rapidly recruited, regained his flesh and life, and for four years longer gave me excellent service.

This incident had thoroughly aroused the people, and

determined them to make common cause against the bands of lawless men known to be perpetrating crime systematically. A public meeting was called and a society organized. Certain men were appointed, whose business it was to start in immediate pursuit when any act of theft was reported; others were to attend to the work of these parties during their absence, and their expenses were all to be paid by the society. The organization increased rapidly, and its influence was extensive and salutary. Soon after this another society was formed, further north, that talked great swelling words, but gave unmistakable evidence that it was in sympathy with the opponents of law and order. The tide of popular sentiment, however, had reached such a pitch that the lawless began to quail before it.

The two months that remained of my year on Mt. Carmel circuit passed quickly and pleasantly. The quarterly conference, by formal vote, requested my return for another year; but, having accomplished the two years of frontier labor that I had volunteered to do, and having postponed a matrimonial engagement of several years' standing, I felt myself, both in honor and inclination, bound to return to Ohio. I therefore respectfully declined the invitation, and made my preparations for my journey to Conference.

CHAPTER VIII.

VINCENNES CIRCUIT, INDIANA.

1821-22.

THE thought of a reunion with loved friends at home relieved in great part the pain that I would otherwise have experienced in bidding adieu to those I loved so dearly on Mt. Carmel circuit. Turning eastward, I soon lost sight of the beautiful plains of Illinois, and making but a brief visit among my old friends of Blue River circuit, I swept rapidly across the growing State of Indiana, and on to the eastern limits of Ohio, in the valley of the Hockhocking. I found myself in the enjoyment of a hearty welcome from parents, and brothers and sisters, and old classmates. A few miles from my father's residence resided a pious young woman who awaited my coming, and I was not long in finding my way thither. When we entered into matrimonial engagement five years before, I had not then decided fully upon my life-work; even after I was enrolled among the itinerants in the field it was not certain that I would find it my duty to continue permanently in that work. The work had been arduous, and the pay, speaking after the manner of men, had been poor. It was not the hardness of the work, nor the poorness of the pay, that was to decide the question. The question was, "Is this my vocation?" "Will God make me the honored instrument in turning the people to God?" I could no longer hesitate in regard to this. The great Head of the Church had blessed me in every field I had been sent to cultivate, putting his seal to my ministry. These matters all talked over, on the 19th of August, 1821, with the full consent and approbation of parents and relatives on both sides, I led to the altar Miss S. Long, and we were united in the holy bonds of matrimony. A few days after our marriage we went to Lebanon, Ohio, to attend the session of the Ohio Conference.

The following brethren were admitted on trial: W. Hughes, James T. Donahoo, Richard Brandriff, George W. Maley, John Pardo, John Walker, William Tipton, William H. Collins, Robert Dobbins, Henry S. Farnandis, and Platt B. Morey.

I had expected Bishop Roberts, according to promise, to re-transfer me to the Ohio Conference. He regarded the demands of the work in the Missouri Conference so pressing, that he entreated me to consent to spend another year in that work. I promised to lay the matter before my young wife, and if she was willing I promised to go. She had given all to God and the Church when she married a Methodist preacher, and was ready to go wherever the authorities of the Church should appoint. In view of this unexpected return to the Missouri Conference, it would have been agreeable to me to have been returned to Mt. Carmel circuit, but as I had anticipated remaining in Ohio, I had recommended brother Robert Delap, a young preacher of my acquaintance, to that circuit, and he had already, by my suggestion, asked the Bishop for that appointment. I could not now honorably interfere.

From Lebanon we proceeded direct to Mt. Carmel, where we spent a month, attending camp-meeting, and going once round the circuit before the meeting of the Missouri Conference. The camp-meeting was a time of power, and the greeting of my friends, on account of my unexpected return, were refreshing to myself and wife. Leaving Mrs. Stewart at the hospitable residence of brother Scoby Stewart, Samuel Hamilton, David Sharp, and myself started to M'Kendree Chapel, Cape Girardeau county, Missouri, where the Conference was to meet. The preachers from these widely scattered fields came together, and ready to report progress and receive marching orders. As was not unusual in those days, a camp-meeting was held in connection with the session of the Conference. Divine power attended the preaching of the Word, and all that country round about realized that the times of refreshing had come from the presence of the Lord.

At that Conference the following brethren were admitted on trial: P. Randle, James Bankson, John Blasdel, A. W. Cassed, James Keyte, James Armstrong, James L. Thompson, Abraham Epler, Dennis Willey, John Granville, and Ebenezer T. Webster. The following persons were ordained elders at this Conference: Alexander M'Calister, John Wallace, John Harris, Job M. Baker, and myself. To me the solemn service of ordination was profoundly impressive, and in the depths of my soul I felt the "vows of God are upon me." The same day that I was ordained I was seized with sickness. Conference adjourned, and the preachers, with saddle-bags in hand, pronouncing mutual blessings on each other, were starting for their fields of labor. I could not bear the thought of being left behind, so rallying all the force possible I was placed in the saddle, and kept along with my company during the day. The night was one of terrible suffering. The fever was succeeded with a dreadful night-sweat. The tedious hours, however, wore away, and morning found me alive. It seemed almost madness for me to leave my bed, but when the horses were brought out for starting I called for mine, and I succeeded in keeping the saddle during the day. And thus, with the assistance of my traveling companions, and the blessing of God, I reached Mt. Carmel. Rest, the medical attendance of Dr. Beauchamp, the kind nursing of my excellent wife, and the prayers of God's people in my behalf, succeeded in throwing off disease, and in about a month after Conference I was able to report at the post of labor.

I was again in the Indiana district, Rev. Samuel Hamilton, presiding elder. The following plan of the circuit indicates my twenty-three appointments, their distance apart, the hours of preaching, the numbers in the classes, and the usual stopping places, or preachers' homes. This circuit embraced Knox and Davis counties, and large portions of Martin, Green, and Sullivan counties. The year before it had extended up the Wabash River as far as Terre Haute, but the upper portion of the circuit had been cut off and called Honey Creek circuit. I had remaining, however, as shown by the plan, twenty-three appointments, and a ride of one hundred and seventy-five miles every four weeks. Vincennes, the old territorial capital of the State, was one of my preaching places. It had been the residence of William Henry Harrison, commander of the Northwestern army in the War of 1812, the excellent Governor of the Indiana Territory, and afterward the honored President of the United States—a man equally honest and sincere whether fighting for his country, treating with the Indians, occupying the Presidential chair, or kneeling at a Methodist mourners' bench.

Methodism early gained a footing in that place. Among those who assisted in building up Methodism and Christianity there was D. Bonner, a merchant, doing a large business, and commanding the respect of the community far and near by his rectitude in business and his activity and consistency as a Christian. His noble wife, though reticent in her habit, was intelligent, discreet, devotedly pious, and a helpmeet for such a man. She was of the Reynolds family, of Urbana, Ohio, a family widely known and as widely esteemed. May their good name remain on our Church roll for many generations! David Brown, who lived near Vincennes, was a Methodist of the old Baltimore type, and devoted to the interests of the denomination. He was the most prominent steward of the circuit, and being a man of energy and excellent business ability, his influence pervaded the circuit, and he was regarded as a leading spirit among the hosts of our Israel.

Wesley Harrison, a man of fine education, extensive property, and, better than all, of deep piety, lived at Carlisle. He was emphatically a man of God. It is, doubtless, the duty and privilege of every Christian to pray without ceasing. Brother Harrison had learned this secret, and lived in a heavenly atmosphere. Between forty and fifty years ago he graduated from the school of Christ on earth, but his name is retained in affectionate remembrance, and is truly as "ointment poured forth." Rev. Samuel Hamilton married a sister, and Rev. Job M. Baker, a wife's sister, of brother Harrison.

Abraham Miller lived near Carlisle. His house was opened for preaching and for the entertainment of the traveling preachers. It was a charming home for the weary itinerant, and I regarded his as a model family. Rev. John Miller, long a laborious and faithful preacher, was a son of his. Hugh Ross, Esq., a good lawyer and acceptable local preacher, married one of his daughters.

Washington, the seat of Davis county, was about the center of the circuit. It was a pleasant and thriving town. We occupied the court-house as a preaching-place, and had a good congregation and society.

At Bethel, a little south of Washington, resided Rev. John Wallace, a venerable minister, long identified with the work, and much beloved. Every circuit that knew him was more than willing to have him as its preacher. He had raised a family that was an honor and blessing to him. In the same neighborhood lived the Jones family and the Horrell family, numerous, respectable, and influential.

While I can not call special attention to but a few of the many excellent families of that circuit, I must not fail to mention Wm. Hawkins, the owner of Hawkins's ferry, on White River. He was a man of great moral worth, a substantial member of the Church, and having been blessed of God with property, he had learned the secret of getting the largest amount of enjoyment from it; namely, by dedicating it to the Lord, and using it for the promotion of his glory. I have abundant reason to remember his kindness. He welcomed me and my wife to his home, and made it truly a home to us. There our first-born, John Wesley, was given to us. At the end of the year, when we inquired for our board bill, he assured us that we were welcome to all they had done for us. This favor was the more appreciated by us as we had not received one-half of our disciplinary allowance for the year. The year was one of new experiences, new trials, and new joys. Though I had not gathered as many sheaves as on some former charges, yet I had been sowing good seed, and I committed the matter to the Lord, in hope that he would water it, and another, if not myself, would gather the harvest.

It was definitely understood when I was appointed to Vincennes circuit that at the close of the year I was to be transferred to the Ohio Conference. We made our arrangements to return in time to attend the session of that Conference. Myself, wife, infant son, and a small packing-box stowed away in our gig, behind our famous horse, we bid tried and faithful friends good-by, and started on our long and tedious journey. It proved, indeed, more tedious than we had anticipated, and in several instances we found ourselves exposed to extreme peril, and but for providential interference should have met with disaster. I shall only have room to record two or three of these. We crossed the east fork of the White River above the falls at Hindustan. The bridge was below the mill, and the bank was very high and steep. To lighten the load I walked and led the horse. When about half way up the hill he stalled and commenced backing. On my right hand was a perpendicular precipice of fifty feet, and below this a depth of probably fifty feet of water. The terrible plunge seemed to be inevitable. Down and down with increased velocity rolled the gig to the very brink of the precipice. It seemed for a moment that my wife and child were doomed to perish, and no one can fancy the horror of that moment to me. But God stretched out his hand. He had in his plan work for that woman to do, and that infant boy was to have a period of probation before he should be called hence. Just on the brink of the precipice the wheel struck an insignificant bank, the horse gathered up, and we were saved. With hearts full of gratitude we pressed our boy to our hearts, and thanked God for his preserving care.

Dr. Austin lived about five miles from this place, and we were anxious to reach his house that night. The road was mountainous, and we were not without anxiety in regard to our success. By and by we came to a mountain so long and rugged that we both got out to walk up. About half way up the horse again stalled and commenced backing. The gig soon gained such velocity as completely to overmaster the horse, and turning aside it thundered down into a deep ravine, overturned and tangled the horse in the harness, so that he lay utterly helpless. I cut the harness, and with the assistance of my wife succeeded in getting the horse up, righted the gig, ascended the mountain, and after hard toiling at length reached the place for which we were aiming. Every day brought us nearer home, and at last we found ourselves again in the quiet valley of the Hockhocking, at home and happy.

As this chapter has introduced my companion to the reader, I propose in the next chapter to give an account of her early life and Christian experience. I think it fitting to do this for several reasons. For nearly half a century she has shared with me the toils and trials as well as enjoyments of itinerant life. Much of my success, during that time, as a pastor, has been attributable to her prudence, activity, and acceptability as a helper. In the good providence of God we have been spared to each other, and now, (1870,) both of us passed over three-score years and ten, are still striving to help each other to serve God and get ready to meet him. The narrative was communicated by her to my son, Rev. W. F. Stewart, at his earnest solicitation, in a series of letters some twenty years ago.

I will close this chapter with the plan of the Vincennes circuit, and as it is a fair specimen of the mode of making the plans in those days, I shall insert it in its original form, as handed to me by Rev. Job Baker, my predecessor on the circuit.

PLAN OF VINCENNES CIRCUIT.

No. of Preaching-places	Neighborhoods where preaching is held, and places to put up at.	Places where Preaching is held.	Times of holding preaching.	Hours of Preaching	Distance from one preaching-place to another	No. in Society—White and Black
1	Vincennes, D. Bonner	Court-House	Sunday	11	...	15
2	David Brown's	Barackman's	Sunday	3	5	11
3	Rest	Rest	Monday	...	...	...
4	George Garret's	Meeting-House	Tuesday	12	3	12
5	Thomas Jordan's	Thomas Jordan's	Wednesday	12	3	19
6	Tevebaugh's †	Solomon Tevebaugh's	Thursday	12	7	25
7	Capt. John Horrel's	School-House	Friday	12	11	21
8	Hawkens's Prairie	John Hawkens's	Saturday	12	6	19
9	Washington	Brother Cosby's, or Court-House.	Sunday	11	3	11
10	Father Wallace's	Bethel	Sunday	3	3	80
11	Rest	Rest	Monday	...	...	...
12	Father Stone's	Father Stone's	Tuesday	12	9	14
13	Ballow's	School-House	Wednesday	12	9	21
14	Mt. Pleasant	J. Hatten's	Thursday	12	12	10
15	Meriday's	Meriday's	Friday	12	13	8
16	Dutch Settlement	Mires's & Robertson's	Saturday	12	8	24
17	Owl Prairie	Slenker's	Sunday	12	12	14
18	Rest	Rest	Monday	...	...	...
19	Month of Eel River	Soalsburry's	Tuesday	12	20	14
20	Black Creek, Fullem's	School-House	Wednesday	12	20	12
21	Abraham Miller's	A. Miller's	Thursday	12	10	24
22	Judge Latshaw or M'Clure's.‡	Judge Latshaw's or M'Clure's.	Friday	12	7	No Class.
23	Bruceville	Richard Posey's	Saturday	12	14	6
	Back to Vincennes after three weeks' absence.				175	360

    Amount of quarterage..................................
    Number of Whites in Society...............352
    Number of Colored in Society.............. 8
    Distance round the circuit.....................175 miles.

† There is a dispute here where the preaching is to be held; you must fix it.
‡ If Judge Latshaw should refuse preaching, move it to M'Clure's.

CHAPTER IX.

LETTERS FROM MRS. SARAH STEWART TO REV. W. F. STEWART, CONTAINING AN ACCOUNT OF HER EARLY CHRISTIAN EXPERIENCE.

KANAWHA SALINES, VA.,
January 29th.

MY DEAR FLETCHER,—I received your very interesting and kind letter of the 15th on yesterday, and was much gratified with the majority of its contents. It brings very charming news. While I sympathize with you in your pulpit embarrassments, I have no doubt that it is all designed for your good. If you live humble and faithful, trusting in the Lord and looking to him alone, he will sustain you, and give you liberty in preaching, and in all the labors of your holy calling, when he sees it is for your good. I am praying that the Lord may make you a polished shaft in his quiver, and that you may be very successful in tearing down the strongholds of the Prince of Darkness, and in bringing many, very many souls, for whom Christ has died, into the kingdom of righteousness and peace. I am much pleased with your complimentary mention of the fine abilities of your excellent colleague. I hope the Lord will continue to bless, abundantly bless, your united labors in his vineyard. I rejoice to hear of the success of brothers Meharry and Webster. Well done for Bourneville! Amen! May the fire burn farther and deeper, wider and higher! I have to regret that I have no revival intelligence to give you. The preachers in this district, as all along the border of slave territory, now have serious obstacles to contend with. This is not at present a land of peace, but a field of war, if not in outward action, it is in feeling. Pray for us that the God of battle may direct our arms and get the victory to himself. There is but one symptom that gives me any hope of a revival here, and that is the unusual burden of concern that rests on my own heart and upon the hearts of some of my pious intimate friends. I conduct a female class in my own room at two o'clock on Friday, also a female prayer-meeting each week at the same place. Pray for me that my feeble labors may be blessed, and that my own poor heart may be filled with the perfect love of God. We have received but one letter from W. since Conference. He expressed much disappointment that you did not visit him during the Conference vacation, and some solicitude in regard to his moral condition. I believe the Spirit is working about his heart. Let us continue to remember him, especially in our "evening prayers." I would like to comply with your request in regard to the subject of our correspondence, but having never kept a diary, I should not be able to gather up any thing like a minute account of my experience. If, however, such an effort will prove of any advantage to one for whose happiness I have always prayed and labored, I feel willing to make the attempt. As I have no manuscript, and shall have to rely upon a faded memory, overgrown with the thorns of many sorrows, disappointments, and crosses, you will not expect more than a very imperfect account of my early experience.

Though I did not make a profession of religion until I was fifteen years of age, my religious impressions and purposes are connected with my earliest recollections. My parents, during my early childhood, were not members of any Church, or professors of religion; yet my mother always taught me to pray from the time I could speak. I was about seven years old when my parents both embraced religion and joined the Church. The family altar was erected, and morning and evening was it sprinkled with the tears of repentance and thanksgiving. My young heart was deeply affected, and I then resolved to be a Christian. My mother frequently and faithfully instructed her children in the knowledge of the commandments of God and their duty to obey them. These early lessons had made indelible impressions on my young mind and heart. I fully believed religion to be the most valuable treasure; the very word "religion" was a word of sweetest sound to my ear.

Now, my dear son, I have made a beginning. Write me a full letter as soon as you get this. Your father is now at Guyandotte, looking after the interests of the district. Neither of us in very good health just now. Remember your mother.
SARAH STEWART.

KANAWHA SALINES, VA.,
February 8th.

MY DEAR SON,—At your request I continue the narrative of my experience. "Religion," as I said in the closing of my former letter, was a word that sounded sweet to my ear. It suggested to my mind a beauty and richness which no pencil could paint or language describe. Yet I tremblingly hoped that it might be sought and found by me. Yet so deeply did I feel my unworthiness that it seemed almost presumptuous for me to hope that I could ever be the possessor of such a treasure. For weeks at a time I would regularly attend to secret prayer, and try to be obedient to my parents, and kind to my brothers and sisters. I was at those times very scrupulous about all of my conduct, lest I should do something to offend my Lord. I often enjoyed much comfort from the approval of conscience, and sometimes thought the Lord regarded my prayers. At one time, in particular, I thought I received an immediate answer. My oldest sister, Catharine, was enduring exquisite suffering from an attack of earache. Every means that we could use failed to relieve her, and such was her suffering that I feared she was going to die. I thought that God could help her; so I retired to secret prayer, and poured out my request to my Heavenly Father to cure her. I returned to the room and found her perfectly composed. O, how my young heart was filled with humble gratitude to God! I was then about eight years old, and took much delight in secret prayer. At some times I became much excited in that exercise. Once my father sent me to drive the birds out of the field. While in the field I kneeled down by a stump to pray. While praying I became so excited that my voice grew louder and louder, so that one of my sisters heard me and came to where I was. When I ceased praying and rose from my knees she stood by me weeping. I said, "O, sister Peggy, I am determined not to go to hell!" I then thought that God loved me, but I did not know that that was religion, and being uncommonly diffident, communicated my feelings to no one. We were living at that time in Hardy county, Va. The place where my parents attended class-meeting was some seven miles distant. They frequently took me with them, and at such times I was so exercised that I was sometimes afraid that I would cry out. I have no doubt that had I enjoyed the advantages and instructions now afforded to children, I should at that early age have been a happy Christian. I do not remember to have spoken to any one concerning my exercises until I was twelve years old, except to my sister at the time above referred to. When I was about ten years old my parents removed to Ohio, and settled in Athens county. In our new home we enjoyed better religious advantages, and in the course of a year or two a revival of religion broke out in our neighborhood. My oldest sister, Catharine, joined the Church. I was not at meeting when she joined, and not knowing that she was at all exercised on the subject, my mind was filled with strange feelings, sorrow mingled with joy. I rejoiced that she had started, but felt more than ever discouraged in regard to my own case. I had been trying all my life to get religion, and now my heart seemed harder than ever. My sister seemed to be so far in advance of me, though so far as I knew she had never been exercised on the subject before. I would then think of the many resolutions I had formed and promises made to be a Christian, but it appeared to me that I had gone backward rather than forward. My desire was to follow the example of my sister and join the Church; but then I thought every body will say I just did it because she did, for nobody knew any thing of my life-long mental exercises.

One night at the meeting I ventured to the mourners' bench, but to my surprise and mortification I found that my father was displeased about it. This was so entirely unexpected that it completely overwhelmed me with discouragement. He supposed that I acted under an impulse of feeling, and without proper thought and understanding. O how careful parents should be not to discourage their children in their early attempts to be religious! and how should they watch for the indications of the presence of the Spirit working with their children, and encourage them to accept Christ at once! Thought I, "My *father* has no confidence in my sincerity, and of course no one else has." It seemed to me that I was despicable in the eyes of every body, and almost hated myself. I ceased making any public effort to seek the Lord. At some times I prayed in secret, and then again relapsed into a measure of indifference. I got so far astray as to indulge in playing and hunting birds'-nests on the Sabbath. Again my convictions would return so powerfully that I would be afraid to go to sleep at night, lest I should wake up in hell. I now felt that I must engage more earnestly in seeking my soul's salvation. About this time there was a camp-meeting appointed to be held on the land of Moses Hewitt, near the present town of Athens. My father was persuaded to allow me to go. I went on Friday. David Young had charge of the meeting, and brother Isaac Quinn was preacher in charge. I was earnestly seeking, and Sabbath night was so exercised that I lost my strength, and was carried to the tent. My heart will always swell with gratitude when I remember the interest that good people now took in my case; for my soul was verily near the borders of despair. Acquaintances and strangers all appeared equally concerned for me. To encourage my hopes and reconcile me to leave the campground, they told me that the Lord could, and probably would, pardon my sins on my way home or at home, assuring me that the Lord was not confined to any place or circumstances, but that whenever and wherever I gave my heart to the Savior, then and there I should find him. After we reached home my father took great pains to encourage me, and, as I had unbounded confidence in him, I appreciated these attentions very highly. For about five days I gave myself almost continually to prayer. During that time some of the members of the Church visited me, and tried to comfort and encourage me. One good old sister, Mother Case, tried to persuade me that I already had religion if I only believed it, but I was scrupulously afraid of being deceived. I could not find any evidence that I had received pardon, or in any degree enjoyed the favor of God. I determined never to rest short of the evidence.

Every day I made frequent visits to the grove to pray. Sometimes hope would spring up in my heart, and then again I would almost despair. The thought that I had been seeking religion from early childhood, and was still apparently as far from God and as destitute of his favor as ever, very much discouraged me. But I knew that to give up was death and eternal ruin, and I was fully determined never to cease seeking. One day, as I was coming from the grove, perhaps more discouraged than at any former time, I was pouring over my lost and ruined condition, Satan whispered into my ear, "You are too insignificant and unworthy to attract the notice of the great and holy God of the universe." Just at that moment of the blackness of darkness another voice, a still, small voice, spake to my troubled heart, and in language sweeter than any thing that my heart had ever conceived, said, "God is just as willing to bless you as he is to bless the most refined and cultivated lady in the world." In an instant my soul was filled with joy unspeakable and full of glory. For some time I stood still; my soul, filled with awe and wonder, adored the condescension of that God who had stooped to take away my load of sin, while my heart bounded with strange and new joy, rich, yes, richer far than my feeble mind had ever been capable of contemplating. "O," thought I, "is this treasure mine?" My tongue was filled with praises. Every thing looked strangely beautiful. Gloom was all driven away by the brightness of the glory of God. I said, "Is this religion—the long sought treasure—the prize after which my soul has been aspiring so long?" O, what a sense I had of the approbation of God! It seemed that every thing on earth loved me, and that every thing on earth was smiling on my account. The world seemed new, and yet, when I reached the house, I had not courage to tell what the Lord had done for me. In a few minutes I returned to the grove.

Often had I prayed there and then returned with a gloomy heart, but now every thing there seemed to be smiling on account of my translation from darkness to light, and from the bondage of sin and guilt to the liberty of a child of God. For some time I prayed and praised. Every thing my eyes looked upon was clad in unearthly beauty. Every forest leaf and every spire of grass had a voice to tell the wondrous change that had passed on unworthy me. From the grove I went to the corn-field, when every stalk of corn seemed to join with me in wondrous praise to Him whose impress it bore. Thence I went again to the house. Father discovered in my countenance the change that had taken place in my feelings, and we praised the Lord together for what he had done for me.

The next Sabbath was the regular preaching day in our neigborhood. I joined the Church that day, and in that act God blessed, so that I shouted aloud the high praises of my Heavenly Father. For three months after that I could say,

> "Not a cloud doth arise
> To darken my skies,
> Or hide for a moment
> The Lord from my eyes."

I had constant communion and basked in the smiles of his face. The subjects of death and the resurrection were most pleasant to my meditation. I could sing,

> "*Now* I can read my title clear
> To mansions in the skies,
> And bid farewell to every fear,
> And wipe my weeping eyes."

Now, my son, with a mother's expression of sympathy with you in your work, and prayer for your success, I pause in my narrative, and will resume it in my next. May God bless you! is the prayer of your mother,

SARAH STEWART.

RICHMONDALE, OHIO,
December 13, 1847.

MY DEAR SON,—My last letter closed with an account of the happy state of mind consequent upon my conversion. When I joined the Church I found few persons of my own age as religious associates. There were but two unmarried persons in the neighborhood who were professors: William Stewart, an elder brother of him who afterward became my husband, and Lydia Bastow, a very pious young lady. I found, however, what I needed, nursing fathers and nursing mothers, to whom I shall ever be greatly indebted for the care they took in my spiritual education. I was early taught that the way of the cross was the way to the crown of life. It was the custom in that society for the female as well as male members to pray in the public prayer-meetings. In this way I was immediately called into activity. I often trembled much under the cross, but never dared to refuse to bear it, and in the bearing of the cross was often powerfully blessed. On these occasions sometimes my strength would be taken away, and such were the transports of joy that I experienced that I would shout the high praises of my adorable Lord and Master. These seasons of rejoicing were often succeeded by seasons of sore temptation. It would be suggested to my mind that I ought to have restrained my feelings, and that I had perhaps offended some of those present by my conduct. Thus would Satan buffet me until I would almost resolve never to give such expression to my feelings again; but so long as I attempted to carry out that purpose a cloud hung over my sky, and I failed of full enjoyment. But when again I would promise not to quench the Spirit, and it was again poured into my soul without measure, I would think that I would never again listen to the suggestions of Satan. At times I would open my heart in regard to this matter to the older members of the Church, and they would exhort me to resist the temptation of the adversary. They assured me that it was just as much the duty of a Christian to praise God when he filled the soul to overflowing with his Spirit, as it was their duty to pray for a blessing. I found that if I would enjoy the happiness springing from a sense of the Divine favor I must deny myself, take up my cross, and follow Christ through evil report as well as good report, and this I resolved, by the grace of God, to do. I had resolved that I would never refuse to pray when called on. It was customary in the society to give an opportunity for persons to pray without being called on by name. The leader would say "Will some brother or sister pray?" When I took up the cross upon such an invitation I hardly ever failed of a blessing, and it seldom failed to produce a powerful impression on the congregation. I told my class-leader, William Gamble, that if he would not call on me I would always pray voluntarily when I felt it to be my duty. "You *promise faithfully*," said he, "and I will not call on you." At first I thought the cross would not be nearly so difficult to bear, but soon found that it seemed to be my duty to pray even oftener than the leader had accustomed to call on me, but having promised I dared not shrink from it. Though I could deceive my leader, I could not deceive God, who reads the heart. I went back to my leader, and said to him "I rue bargain, and throw myself again in your hands, and I will try and be obedient to the order of those who have the rule over me." I found that the more I exercised in praying and speaking in public, in the class-meetings, prayer-meetings, and love-feasts the more I was blessed of God and strengthened.

I remember on one occasion when the cross was peculiarly heavy on account of the presence of a Mr. Farnsworth, a gentleman who had but recently moved into the neighborhood, and being accounted a man of superior intelligence, and a member of the Presbyterian Church, it was anticipated that he would criticise our exercises, as it was known that he disapproved of females praying in public. I felt such a shrinking from the cross that if I could have escaped from the house unobserved I should have done it, but that was impossible. As I sat trembling the class-leader called out, "Sister Sally Long, pray." As I kneeled before the Lord all fear left me; a deep solemnity came over my spirit, and as I realized the presence of the Lord Jehovah I lost all thought of the presence of any criticising mortal; there was a mighty power rested on the congregation, and I experienced wonderful enlargement of soul as I talked with God in prayer. At our next preaching meeting our Presbyterian neighbor came and requested the privilege of uniting with our Church. He said he had never believed that it was right for females to pray in public until he attended the meeting spoken of above. That meeting had removed his prejudice. He shook me cordially by the hand, and told me that it was through my instrumentality that he had been brought to see the right way. This humbled me in the very dust before God, and I resolved that I would never shrink from the cross again. In after experience I have learned that when the cross seems the heaviest then was it most important for me to bear it, both for my own good and for the good of others.

About two years after I joined the Church a powerful revival broke out in the neighborhood, which ran and spread until nearly all the young people were brought within the pale of the Church. He who afterward became my husband was one of the subjects of that revival. As soon as he became a member of the Church, the impression pervaded the members of the Church that it would be his duty to give himself to the work of the ministry. It was ascertained in a short time that already the Holy Spirit was making a similar impression upon his mind. In a few months he was called into official relationship to the Church, and thenceforward became a laborer in the great harvest-field.

During and after this meeting I was often astonished and humbled in the very dust on account of the attentions paid to me, not only by the young converts and those of my own age, but also by the aged and dignified. The circuit preachers frequently called on me to make the prayer after the sermon in the public congregation. Though I dared not refuse, and though I was often much blessed in bearing the cross on these occasions, yet I seldom escaped being severely tempted by Satan afterward. The limited circumstances of my parents had prevented them from affording me any educational advantages. I was painfully sensible of my deficiencies in this respect. When the Rev. T. A. Morris—now Bishop—had charge of the circuit, he appointed a female prayer-meeting in our neighborhood, and laid upon me the duty of conducting it. I had never attended such a meeting, and thought that my youth and want of experience, education, and ability all seemed to make it the height of presumption for me to attempt it. I plead to be excused, and nominated others, in my estimation better fitted for the work; but my excuses were of no avail. He took a vote of the society, which was unanimous in support of my appointment. I was sorely pressed in spirit. If the meeting had been appointed only for the young folks, the cross would have been heavy, for I regarded many of them as far in advance of me in qualification for such a duty, but the meeting was designed for the old as well as the young. I went to some of the older members of the Church and laid the matter before them, and they assured me that my misgivings were only the temptations of the adversary, and that I must say "Get behind me, Satan." I prayed much for courage, but after all, when the time for the meeting arrived, and I started to the place, feeling that it was more than I could bear, I tried to get sister Lois Stewart to take my place. She declined, but promised to take a seat near me, so that if I became so embarrassed as to be unable to proceed, she would assist me. The congregation was assembled, and I essayed to do my duty, and succeeded in reading a chapter, but when I attempted to read the hymn I became so embarrassed that the good sister had to come to my assistance. But by the help of grace divine I was enabled to meet the responsibility laid upon me, and the Lord came down among us in great power, and we had truly a time of refreshing from his presence. Heretofore I had labored to support myself and to assist in the support of my father's family, so that I had but little time to employ in mental culture. Finding an opening to teach a school of small children, I embraced the opportunity, and commenced in right good earnest, trying to improve my mind. I was well aware that all that I ever could be must be the result of my own efforts and the blessing of God. I deeply felt the importance of living near to God, and knew that to do this my time should be divided and my life regulated by rule. I therefore adopted the following rules for my religious life: Three times each day a portion of time was spent in secret devotion. One day in the week was set apart as a day of fasting and special prayer. All the social and public means of grace I attended punctually, not only for conscience' sake, but because I had a keen appetite for them, and found them to be to me more than my ordinary meat and drink. The companionship of Christians was exceedingly precious to me, and I desired no other society. Between the duties of my school and the privileges of the means of grace, I had the comforting assurance that I was getting some additional preparation to meet the responsibilities that might come upon me in future life. . . . .

Let these extracts suffice to record the early conversion and devotion of my dear companion, and I shall now return to my narrative.

CHAPTER X.

MADISON CIRCUIT, INDIANA.

1822-23.

THE Ohio Conference met at Marietta, Bishops M'Kendree and George present, September 5, 1822. I was welcomed back by my former Conference associates, and felt really that I had got home again. In an interview with the Bishop I stated to him the facts in my case. I had not only performed the two years' frontier labor for which I had volunteered, but, at the solicitation of Bishop Roberts, I had spent a third year in that work, and had now returned to work in the Ohio Conference. He urged me to consent to one more year in the Missouri Conference, but finally, after consulting with Bishop M'Kendree, he conceded that I ought not to be urged to return again. He transferred me back to the Ohio Conference, and the session passed very pleasantly to me. When, however, the appointments were read out, I found myself announced as preacher in charge on Madison circuit, Miami district, Indiana. The Bishop supposed that I had not moved from Vincennes, Indiana, and that an appointment on the western borders of the Ohio Conference would accommodate me. When he learned that I had moved my family and effects to my father's, in South-eastern Ohio, and would now have to move back several hundred miles, he explained the matter to me, so that I was disposed to bear without complaint what at first appeared to be an unreasonable requirement.

The following persons were admitted on trial: Billings O. Plimpton, John Crawford, Albert G. Richardson, Orin Gilmore, Solomon Manccr, John Jean, Aaron Wood, Jas. Rowe, Geo. Gatch, Jas. C. Taylor, N. B. Griffith, Levi White, Wm. Westlake.

The following brethren were elected delegates to General Conference: Chas. Elliott, J. F. Wright, G. R. Jones, M. Ruter, C. Waddle, J. B. Finley, J. Young, Jno. Sale, Jas. Quinn, John Waterman, R. Bigelow, D. Young, John Strange.

Soon after the adjournment of Conference we packed up again, and made our tedious journey of three hundred miles to Madison. The circuit was a large and strong one. There were thirty-one appointments to be filled in five weeks, and some eight hundred and ninety-three members to be looked after. The following constituted the round of appointments: 1. Madison; 2. Crooked Creek; 3. Cope's; 4. Mitchell's; 5. Overturf's; 6. Hiatt's; 7. Brown's; 8. Versailles; 9. Hukel's; 10. Cole's; 11. Frazier's; 12. Clark's; 13. Downey's; 14. Coiner's; 15. Allenville; 16. Oakes's; 17. Buche's; 18. Green's, or Quaker's Grove; 19. Davis's; 20. Cooper's; 21. Camel's; 22. Miller's; 23. Lee's; 24. Martin's; 25. Davis's; 26. Heddy's; 27. Vevay; 28. Ashe's; 29. Brown's; 30. Gray's; 31. Hulm's. In filling the appointments we arranged to spend two weeks in the neighborhood of Madison, and then a three weeks' tour visiting the more distant appointments.

Though the circuit had a large membership it had no parsonage, and to save expense it was proposed that the preacher's family should "board round" among the people. We consented to this arrangement, not without misgiving and reluctance. Though our family was small, we having only one child at that time, yet we knew that this mode of living would be far from desirable. My wife was especially anxious to enjoy more privacy for study and devotion, and better opportunity for educating her boy than she could have mixing in with so many family circles, some of whom took their turn keeping the preacher's family rather in the light of duty than otherwise. But we made the best we could of our circumstances, and tried to do the best we could for the cause of God.

Nehemiah B. Griffith was my colleague. He was a holy man of God, able and willing to do his full share of the work assigned to us. I was truly grateful that in the providence of God I was favored with such a helper in the work. His race in the itinerant work was short, but he made his mark, which will stand to his credit in all after time—yea, beyond the bounds of time he shall shine as a star forever and ever. Alexander Cummins was my presiding elder. He was a first-class man, clear-headed and sound to the core, and not to be excelled in the administration of discipline. He was at that time in feeble health.

As I call up the list of local preachers, I dwell upon their memory with great pleasure. Some of them were men of renown. In those days, growing out of the fact that the support of the preachers was so meager, many of the best preachers, who had families to support and children to educate, found it necessary to locate and go into some secular business. As a rule, however, they retained the spirit of the itinerancy, and co-operated with the traveling preachers cordially, and greatly to the advantage of the work.

Joseph Oglesby was a man of superior talent. He had settled in Madison, and engaged in the practice of medicine. As he had been successful and popular during his itinerant life, so was he now successful and popular as a practicing physician and local preacher. John Green had also traveled in the New England Conference. He was brother-in-law to Calvin and Martin Ruter. He was a dignified, devoted, and useful local preacher. He lived near Quaker's Grove. Old brother Woodfield, who had worn himself out in the itinerant ranks in Kentucky, lived near Madison, and was highly respected. Joel Havens also honored God, and worked faithfully for the Church as a local preacher.

The society in Madison had many strong men connected with it. Among them I call to memory such as Taylor, Comstock, Gale, Wallace, Wilson, Robertson, Basset, Green, Pew, Oglesby, etc., a host whose names are recorded in the Book of Life. No wonder that the Church has expanded and strengthened with years, and continues to be a power for good in that community. The good men were not all found in Madison, but they were scattered all over the circuit. As my mind sweeps round that vast three weeks' tour, starting north to Mitchell's, Versailles, down to Langhra's, Allenville, Jacksonville, Quaker's Grove, York, Vevay, and then down the Ohio to Madison, I call up the names of men and women of great moral and religious worth.

During my labors on this circuit I was much annoyed by the Baptists. They were constantly prating about the subjects and mode of baptism, and evidently regarded themselves so strongly fortified that their position was invulnerable. Their attacks upon the denominations who differed with them on these points were bold and severe. "Believing penitents are the only proper subjects, and immersion the only proper mode of Christian baptism." This they asserted constantly, and challenged contradiction. I determined to master the subject, and for this purpose spent several weeks in its thorough investigation. The result of my study was to settle my mind thoroughly in the conviction that infants, as well as adults, are entitled to the sacrament of Christian baptism, and that sprinkling and pouring are modes supported as fully by reason and revelation as is immersion. I went into the field of controversy, and delivered a series of sermons that were blessed by the Great Head of the Church in doing, as I trust, much good in the establishment and maintenance of sound doctrine. As the result of these discourses many came and cast in their lots with us who had been connected with them.

During this year my dear companion rendered good service to the cause, though the care of our son Wesley and our inconvenient manner of living embarrassed her a good deal. God greatly blessed her in the exercise of prayer and speaking in class and love-feasts, and in her intercourse with families her life was so conscientious and devout as to exert a silent but powerful influence in all places.

Sometimes she accompanied me to the distant appointments. On our way to the camp-meeting at Quaker's Grove we were traveling on horseback, and had to pass through the Beech Swamp. The road, for some distance, was almost impassable. At one time my horse floundered in the mud so that I thought he would certainly come down. Fearing that my son John Wesley, whom I was carrying in my arms, would be hurt, I selected with my eye a place where there was a soft bed of mud, and tossed him as far from me as I could. After getting my horse extricated I returned and found the child in position and apparently fully content with his location. The camp-meeting was attended with great power. It being also a quarterly-meeting occasion, the presiding elder, Rev. A. Cummins, took charge of the meeting. He was in such feeble health that he could not speak loud enough for a large congregation, but selected for himself the eight o'clock morning appointment. On one of these occasions, from the language of Jude, "Keep yourselves in the love of God," he preached a sermon of special unction; it was, indeed, melting and sweet. He was a man greatly beloved, and always preached a sensible and profitable sermon. This was probably one of the last camp-meetings that he attended. It fell to my lot, by his appointment, during the meeting to preach each day at his hour. My voice was then clear and strong, so that I could be heard at a distance of one and a half miles. My soul was fully in the work, and God blessed me greatly. We met at this meeting some who we had known years before in Ohio. This reunion was especially gratifying to my wife, and added greatly to her enjoyment of the occasion. These were the Ruters, and Greens, and Wellses—noble Christian families, whose influence extends down to this day.

We had another camp-meeting near Madison, which was attended with great success. Bishop Roberts was with us, and, as usual, preached with great power. On one occasion his text was, "If they hear not Moses and the prophets," etc. It was a sermon never to be forgotten. The slain of the Lord were many, and during the meeting a goodly number turned to God.

This circuit became very dear to me, and when, at the close of the Conference year, the people requested my return for another year, I should have gladly consented, had we not felt it our duty to return to that portion of Ohio where our large circle of family connection resided.

CHAPTER XI.

MUSKINGUM CIRCUIT, OHIO.

1823-24.

THE Conference met September 4, 1823, in Urbana, Bishop R. R. Roberts in the chair. The following were admitted on trial: Sylvester Dunham, George Waddel; True Pattee, John A. Baughman, Robert O. Spencer, Job Wilson, Thomas Beacham, Alfred M. Lorrain, Thomas Hewson, Elijah H. Field, James M'Intyre, Isaac Ellsbury, Robert Hopkins, Silas Colvin.

At this Conference we recorded the death of brother Charles Trescott. He was born at Sheffield, Mass.; joined the Ohio Conference in 1820. On Sabbath, October 6, 1822, he departed in triumph. He was a systematic preacher, earnest and successful.

During the session we presented our first-born, John Wesley, then an infant fifteen months old, for baptism. As the venerable Bishop took him in his arms and administered to him the solemn sacrament of the Church, and as that devout congregation of pastors and people made hearty responses to the prayers offered, with hearts thrilled with the deepest and tenderest emotions, we gave him to God, promising that we would try to bring him up in the nurture and admonition of the Lord.

My desire in regard to my appointment was gratified, as Muskingum circuit joined the one in which our parents resided. We went from Conference direct to our circuit, and established our home in Putnam, on the Muskingum River, opposite the city of Zanesville. My colleague, Rev. Thomas Beacham, was a young man of superior parts, self-possessed, and an admirable preacher. Unfortunately he allowed his mind to be burdened and divided with too many things, and so weakened his effectiveness.

The following list of twenty-four appointments, to be filled every four weeks by each of us, shows that our field was an extensive one:

PLAN OF MUSKINGUM CIRCUIT.

Made August 29, A. D. 1823.

Day of the Week.	Day of the Month.	Preaching-places.	Preaching Hour.	Distance in Miles.	OFFICIAL LIST.	
Sunday	Sept. 21	Putnam's	11–4	...	Alex. M'Cracken,	} Elders.
Monday	" 22	Rest	...	...	John Wilson,	
Tuesday	" 23	Headley's	12	5	Samuel Wilson,	} Preachers.
Wednesday	" 24	Simpson's	12	4	Samuel Aikins,	
Thursday	" 25	Rest	...	...	John Goshen,	} Deacons.
Friday	" 26	Rest	...	...	Martin Fate,	
Saturday	" 27	Rest	...	...	John Wilson,	
Sunday	" 28	Dickerson's	11	10	Thomas Ijams,	} Stewards.
Monday	" 29	Rest	...	...	Elijah Ball,	
Tuesday	" 30	Gard's	12	4	Sam'l Chapman,	
Wednesday	Oct. 1	Wiggenbottom's	12	4	John Jordan,	
Thursday	" 2	Sain's	12	6	Wm. Armstrong,	
Friday	" 3	Springer's	12	6	Wm. Heath,	
Saturday	" 4	Lenhart's	12	4	Elijah Collins,	
Sunday	" 5	Asbury Chapel	11	6	David Fate,	
Monday	" 6	Hitchcock's	12	12	Jona. Witham,	} Exhorters.
Tuesday	" 7	Teal's	12	7	Robert Aikins,	
Wednesday	" 8	Fate's	12	5	David Edwards,*	
Thursday	" 9	Chaplin's	12	12	David Butt,	
Friday	" 10	Harris's	2	12	Mann'g Putnam,	
Saturday	" 11	Hopkins's	12	6	David Sherad,	
Sunday	" 12	Aikins's	11	12	James Kelley,	
Monday	" 13	Sailor's	12	7		
Tuesday	" 14	Edwards's	12	5		
Wednesday	" 15	Wesleyan Chapel	12	8	Number of Members, 760.	
Thursday	" 16	Wilson's	10	6		
	" 16	Beall's	3	3		
Friday	" 17	Hamet's	12	6	* Recommended to the lo-	
Saturday	" 18	Butt's	11	5	cal conference for license to	
Sunday	" 19	Putnam again		6	preach.	

As the travel was extensive, so the heavy membership demanded a large amount of pastoral labor. We had seven hundred and sixty members, all of whom I expected to visit at their respective homes. My constant practice was to meet the classes after preaching, so that twenty-four sermons and twenty-four class-meetings, besides extra appointments and pastoral visiting, made it a protracted meeting the year through. About the middle of the year, at the request of the quarterly conference, my colleague was removed to another field, and assisted by a noble band of local preachers I kept up all of the appointments during the rest of the year.

It will sound strange to the present generation of Methodists to learn that so large a membership only paid the pastor one hundred and thirty dollars with which to support his family. Many regarded the word "quarterage" as indicating the amount to be paid by each member. To assist in meeting our current expenses, my wife opened a primary school, and between the labors of housekeeping, hospitality, the school, and her share of the care of the Church, her hands were as full as mine. As she commenced her school at eight o'clock in the morning, she had to do most of her cooking at night and washing on Saturdays. It would have been an easy matter for those seven hundred and sixty members to have afforded us a support that would have allowed us more home comforts, and my companion more time for purely evangelical labors; but we committed ourselves to the Lord and went forward in his name. The year, notwithstanding its severe toil and sacrifices, was withal a very pleasant year to us. We were sustained by noble men, who themselves labored gratuitously and endured many sacrifices for the cause of Christ. The names of some of these I propose to place upon record. Alexander M'Cracken gave us valuable assistance; talented and devoted to the work, he was held in high estimation, and his preaching did much good. John Goshen resided in Putnam, and was the father of Methodism in that place.

He possessed a strong mind, a strong will, and a large heart. Always ready to work for the Church with tongue, or hand, or purse, he was, nevertheless, so tenacious for the old forms, that he became sensitive in regard to innovations in religious forms or style of living to an extent that often disturbed his own enjoyments, and possibly sometimes diminished his power for good. When the Rev. Jacob Young—some years after the time of which I am now writing—was presiding elder on the Zanesville district, he took a house for his family residence in Putnam, and was neighbor to brother Goshen. Having been old-time friends, brother Young wondered that his old friend did not call on him. At last he determined if possible to ascertain the reason.

"Brother Goshen, why do n't you come to see me?"

"You have that thing they call a melodeon in your house, and I can't conscientiously come to see you."

"My dear brother Goshen, come," said the good elder, "and I will carry the little thing out into the shed while you are there."

But every body had unbounded confidence in the integrity of brother Goshen, and doubtless many will rise up in eternity to call him blessed.

George Fate was also a local preacher of talent and efficiency. John and Samuel Wilson, who were brothers and Irishmen, and brother Samuel Aikins were all passable local preachers. These three last mentioned, however, became infected this year with the leaven of the radical agitation, and suffered damage thereby. The radical excitement was now raging in the East, and was developing with a good deal of bitterness at some points in the West. Some, doubtless, were influenced by sincere convictions that the government of the Church was defective and needed modifying, and others disappointed in not receiving the promotion that they thought themselves entitled to, hoped to mount to a higher level on the waves of this agitation. Some suspected Rev. Cornelius Springer to be one of this latter class, and were not backward in declaring their opinions that elevation to the more desirable positions in the Church would have fully realized his views of reformation. It was thought that the fact that Samuel Hamilton, who had been associated with Springer in their early life and early ministry, had outstripped him, and was now occupying the post of presiding elder, was chafing to the feelings of Springer, and had much to do in inclining him to the side of the so-called reformers. As Cornelius Springer was preacher in charge at the time that I was licensed to preach, and recommended to the traveling connection, I had a high regard for him, and looked up to him with a good deal of reverence. This feeling, however, met with a severe shock some years after this, when he and brother Aikins came to visit me for the purpose of proselyting me to the new doctrine. I was residing at the time at Athens. They came with much confidence that I would unite with them, and so carry over to their standard a large portion of my circuit. When brother Springer opened to me his mission and expectations I was thunderstruck, as I was not aware that I had ever given any one ground to think that I was not in the completest harmony with our Church polity. Regarding brother Springer as my superior intellectually, I at first attempted to play off a little. Referring to the fact above stated, he reminded me in a pleasant way that "he had made me and had a claim to me." "But at that time you were a Methodist Episcopal preacher, and so far as you made me you made me a Methodist Episcopal preacher." I waxed bold to ask him a few questions, and soon found that he was weak like other men. The whole interview was conducted in good feeling, and we parted in friendship; and though we diverged in our Church path, he trying the new and I continuing in the old path, yet I hope that we will meet again at the end, where we shall see as we are seen and know as we are known.

But to return from this digression. Among the excellent of this circuit I must mention Mrs. Hamilton, mother of Rev. Samuel Hamilton, already mentioned. She was given to hospitality, a mother in Israel, making the weary itinerant always feel at home when under her roof. Mrs. J. Iames—pronounced Imes—daughter of Mrs. Hamilton, and sister to Samuel Hamilton, and former wife of Rev. Robert Manley, was a master-spirit of her sex, extensively known, loved, and esteemed by the denomination. Methodism in that region was greatly indebted to her.

At Putnam we had a good society, embracing such as Russell, Moore, Chapman, Manning, Putnam, Wilber, Mizer, and many others equally worthy of record. Thus memory crowds upon us, and we shall hope to be welcomed by them when after a little while we cross the river. I can yet hardly realize it, but I must be getting to be an old man, for now I remember that my son, Rev. W. F. Stewart, who, sixteen years ago, served Putnam station as its pastor, and who has been preaching the Gospel more than a quarter of a century, was not born until the year after I closed my labors on that circuit. Dear Father, give me grace that will qualify me to meet the responsibilities of old age, and secure to me a peaceful evening, a calm sunset, and an abundant welcome to the skies!

The Conference sat in Zanesville, on the opposite side of the river from my home, and I requested to remove to another charge, which request was granted. Removals usually occurred at the end of one year; and though my circuits had almost invariably requested my return, thus far I had preferred to spread the Gospel in the regions beyond. At the close of the Conference the venerable Bishop

Roberts, in company with Rev. Martin Ruter, visited us to give us tokens of affection, and to give his blessing to our boy that he had baptized the year before.

On the first day of May, during this Conference year, the General Conference met at Baltimore. Our Conference was represented by the following brethren, viz: Charles Elliott, John F. Wright, Greenbury R. Jones, Martin Ruter, Charles Waddel, James B. Finley, Jacob Young, John Sale, James Quinn, John Waterman, Russel Bigelow, David Young, and John Strange. This large and able delegation took an influential part in the proceedings. The presiding elder question, which had met with such a sudden interruption by the stand taken by Joshua Soule in 1816, was again brought forward, and the proposition to make the office elective was defeated, and Soule was again elected to the episcopacy. This difficulty now being out of the way, he accepted, and he and Rev. Elijah Hedding, after a sermon by the venerable Bishop M'Kendree, were solemnly set apart to the work of general superintendency. The question of admitting lay delegates to the Conference was also discussed; but while the memorials asking for that change in our economy were answered by a respectful and candid address, the Conference, with much unanimity, declined the proposition.

CHAPTER XII.

MARIETTA CIRCUIT, OHIO.

1824-25.

BISHOP ROBERTS presided at the session of the Conference which met at Zanesville, Ohio, September 2, 1824. He was assisted by Bishop Soule, who had just been elevated to the general superintendency by the late General Conference. As we had all been familiar with the fact of his election four years before, and his declination, as stated in a preceding chapter of this work, we were anxious to see and hear him. Our impressions were decidedly favorable, and we welcomed him with great cordiality. The class of probationers received at this Conference was not large, but embraced some who have rendered the Church long and valuable services, as will be seen from the following list: John Chandler, Arza Brown, Jacob Delay, Augustus Eddy, Wm. C. Henderson, Homer J. Clarke, David Dutcher, Andrew F. Baxter, Wm. Runnels, Joab Ragan, Jos. S. Barris. Of several of these I shall have frequent occasion to speak more hereafter.

The Committee on Memoirs reported on the death of two of the preachers, Rev. A. Cummins and S. Baker. I have had occasion to speak in former chapters of Rev. A. Cummins. I was intimately acquainted with him, and entertained, as did the whole Conference, an exalted opinion of his piety and ability. He was born in Albemarle county, Virginia, September 3, 1787. He entered the traveling connection in 1809, and made full proof of his ministry until the time of his death, which occurred September 27, 1823.

Rev. Samuel Baker was born September 13, 1793, in Baltimore, Maryland, and died September 26, 1823, obtaining his crown just one day in advance of brother Cummins. He had been a faithful itinerant about seven years, and closed up his career with the triumphant exclamation, "Glory! glory to God and the Lamb! There is victory in death!"

Bishop Roberts favored me with an appointment still nearer to our parents and family connections. In fact, Marietta was the circuit from which I started, though since the time of my starting the Athens circuit had been organized, taking that portion of the original territory in which my parents lived. As the Rev. Daniel Limerick was returned to the circuit for the second year, I was associated with him as junior preacher. He was a man of fine preaching ability, and was both popular and useful on the circuit.

After the adjournment of Conference I lost no time in packing up and moving to my new work. An incident occurred on the journey, which illustrates what strange providences sometimes attend the founding of societies and the salvation of souls. In accordance with the usual customs of hospitality in those days, I had furnished me a list of places where I would be welcomed along my route. Among these was the name of Mr. Sawin, a Presbyterian, whose house was always open, with ungrudging hospitality, for the preachers and their families of either of the Churches. It was about 11 o'clock, A. M., the day that we reached his house. As soon as I introduced myself he gave me a cordial welcome, and requested us to make ourselves fully at home. After dinner he informed me that there was a lady in another room, who had been bleeding at the nose for several days, and as there was no hope of her recovery, or even of her being able to be removed to her home, he desired that I would converse and pray with her. I had been walking all the forenoon over a mountainous road, and found myself so reduced in vitality that I did not feel at all prepared to perform such duty properly. It would not do, however, to decline, under the circumstances. He conducted me to the room, where I found her indeed in a sad condition. Several of the neighbors were about her couch. I talked with her, and then we kneeled in prayer. I had no freedom in prayer, as I thought; seemed embarrassed both in thought and expression. I was deeply mortified, and thought that they would never desire to see me again. I bade them good-by, and went on my way. About a week after that, just as I was getting settled in my new home, Mr. Sawin came to see me, and told me that there was great anxiety in his neighborhood that I should send them an appointment, and come and preach for them, and said that those who were present when I prayed for the afflicted woman thought they had never heard so powerful a prayer. I was greatly surprised at this, and authorized him to publish an appointment for me.

At the appointed time I went and found a large congregation, to whom I preached as best I could; and, indeed, the Word was not bound, but had free course and was glorified. I never had greater liberty in publishing the Gospel. At the close of the sermon I proposed to speak to each person, as I was accustomed to do in the class-meetings of my denomination, but gave opportunity for any to retire who might not wish to be conversed with in regard to their salvation. Nearly, if not all, remained. We had a time of deep feeling, and, after speaking with each one, I explained to them our mode of organizing societies, read the rules to them, and then invited all who were disposed to join the Methodist Episcopal Church on trial to signify it by giving me their hands and names. Some thirty-three responded to the call, among whom was Mr. Sawin, his excellent wife, and several members of his family. The new society was at once incorporated into our circuit, and I enjoyed many seasons of refreshing with it during the Conference year. Brother Sawin afterward removed, with his family, to Illinois, and settled in the neighborhood of Quincy, where they were ornaments to the cause of God and Methodism.

This singular introduction to part of the territory over which I should travel during the year was very gratifying to me, and I regarded it as evidence that my appointment was providential, and as an earnest of a gracious harvest. As the preacher in charge occupied the parsonage at Marietta, I obtained a home for my family at Waterford. Brother Parks let us have part of his house, and his family greatly endeared themselves to us during the year by constant acts of kindness.

The following list of appointments indicates how extensive the bounds of the circuit still remained, notwithstanding the formation of Athens circuit. Commencing at Marietta, we had appointments at Nixon's, Lynch's, Goss's, Rainbow, Sprague's, Featherstone's, Callahan's, Miller's, Palmer's, Smyth's, Lake's, Barlow, Forks of Hocking, Daniel Goss's, Decatur, Newbury, Belpre, Moore's, Bridge's, and then back to Marietta. It was a four-weeks' circuit, and our time was fully occupied in preaching, class-meetings, pastoral visitation, and extra appointments, such as the one referred to above. In one view it seemed to be routine work, repeating itself over and over again from the year's beginning to its end, but it was not monotonous. It was full of interest, life, and enjoyment. Friendly faces crowded our congregations and attentive ears drank in our sermons, and as in the class-meetings we recounted our hopes and fears, instructing and exhorting each other, we learned each other's cares, and were enabled to bear each other's burdens. We felt Christ's yoke to be easy and his burden to be light.

One of the special pleasures of the year to me was found in the privilege of mingling with my early associates in Christian fellowship. The memory of my conversion and recommendation to the ministry, and the counsel, and prayers, and co-operation of those who had encouraged me when a penitent, and had assisted in bringing me into the work, made it a year of unusual interest. Such was the enjoyment of the year, and such its success, that, for the first time in the history of my life as a traveling preacher, I desired to be returned for another year. For reasons, however, which were not explained or known to me, this desire of mine was not gratified. At this I did not murmur. I heartily indorsed the itinerant feature of our economy, and I knew that in its workings changes must often occur that could not at the time be pleasant or even understood by those affected by them. I knew that He who stood at the helm could see and control all its workings, and that through all its workings he would have an eye to my good and to the good of the Church. Neither then nor ever since then have I been tempted to take my cause out of his hands. A long experience and extended observation has satisfied me that those ministers who interfere least with the established machinery of the Church in regard to their appointments are, as a class, the most contented and successful.

There was a band of working members on this circuit both in the laity and officiary, of great worth. Among them I might mention the powerful James Whitney, whose influence was not only felt in Port Harmar, where he lived, but extended to the outermost boundary of the circuit.

John Crawford, a local preacher, residing at the same place, excited a wonderful influence for the building up of the interests of the Church. Though they have passed away from earth, their influence still lives to honor God and bless his Church. Brother Daniels, a local preacher, residing in Marietta, honored his relation, and was highly esteemed. And now the names, and friendship, and deeds of scores of God's dear ones, who then labored and suffered for him, but who now rest and reign with him, come crowding upon my memory. The Gosses, and Guthries, and Knowleses, and Hoaglands, and M'Glochlins, and Kidwells, and Smiths, and Palmers, and Buels, and Lynches, and Protsmans, and Lakes, and those of like spirit and worth, were there—yea, blessed be God! I shall hail them by and by in the kingdom of God.

During this year our second son, William Fletcher, now a member of the Rock River Conference, was born. We gave him to God in Christian baptism at a quarterly meeting at Newberry, Rev. John Brown officiating.

At the close of the year I was seized with typhoid fever, and for weeks, at my father's house on the Hockhocking, my life trembled in the balance.

The plan of appointments for the year, which we give on the next page, will show the reader how fully the time of the preacher was occupied.

PLAN OF MARIETTA CIRCUIT.

DAY.	HOUR.	PLACE.
Sunday	10, A. M.	Marietta.
"	Night	Port Harmar.
Tuesday	12, M.	Nixon's.
Wednesday	2, P. M.	Lynch's.
Thursday	12, M.	Goss's.
Friday	2, P. M.	Rainbow.
Saturday	2, P. M.	Sprague's.
Sunday	11, A. M.	Featherstone's.
"	4, P. M.	Watterford's Landing.
Tuesday	12, M.	Callahan's.
Wednesday	12, M.	Miller's.
Thursday	2, P. M.	Palmer's.
Friday	12, M.	Smith's.
Saturday	3, P. M.	Lake's School-House.
Sunday	11, A. M.	Barlow.
Thursday	1, P. M.	Forks of Hocking.
Friday	12, M.	Daniel Goss's.
Saturday	12, M.	Decatur.
Sunday	11, A. M.	Newberry.
Monday	2, P. M.	Belpre, Ann's School-House.
Tuesday	12, M.	Moore's.
Wednesday	12, M.	Jacob Bridge's.

CHAPTER XIII.

GUYANDOTTE CIRCUIT, VIRGINIA.

1825-26.

THE Conference met at Columbus, October 12, 1825. Bishops George and Roberts presided. We had an interesting session. The Bishops of the United Brethren Church attended, hoping to make arrangements by which the class-meeting of the Methodist Episcopal Church should be open to the members of the United Brethren Church. Our Bishops, however, not having the power to change our rules, nothing could be done in that direction in the Annual Conference.

The following preachers were admitted on trial: John Hill, Absalom D. Fox, John W. Clarke, William B. Christie, Samuel P. Shaw, John C. Havens, John Ferree, Henry O. Sheldon, John W. Gilbert, Philip Strawther, and John W. Young. In this list the reader will discover the names of some who afterward became princes in our Israel, and whose memory is embalmed in a multitude of hearts, but the indefatigable Clarke, and the eloquent Christie, and the pathetic Ferree, and others of them have graduated to their rest above.

We recorded the death of Nathan Walker. He was born in Montgomery county, Maryland, October 20, 1795, and died August 26, 1825. He was received on trial in 1820. His last charge was Deer Creek circuit, and he died at the house of Mrs. Butler, at Oldtown. He was diligent and faithful as a preacher, and left a clear and honorable record. At this Conference I received my appointment to Guyandotte circuit, Virginia. The Kanawha district had just been formed, mostly of circuits which, by a change of Conference lines, had been transferred from the Kentucky to the Ohio Conference. The appointment was by no means a desirable one, in view of my prostration from sickness. As soon, however, as I was able to venture out of the house, we packed up and started for our field of labor. By the persuasion of our friends we left our oldest son, John Wesley, to spend the Winter with our parents. My horse was full of life and very restive, and I had so little strength that it was with the greatest difficulty that I could manage him. We reached the Ohio River in the midst of a severe storm of rain and snow. The ferry-boat was half full of water and snow; the horse was frightened, so that we had to get out of the carriage and stand on the wet ground nearly two hours, while the ferryman was getting his boat in order to take us across the river. My wife, with our youngest child in her arms, and he a very delicate babe, was severely chilled, and weak as I was it was a severe draft on my vitality. In process of time, however, we found ourselves comfortably seated by a cheerful fire in the tavern, on the Virginia side. The kind hostess felt great anxiety in regard to our health, and especially in regard to the delicate babe. She would walk the floor, back and forth, so excited that she really thought that the child was dying. We enjoyed, however, a comfortable bed, a good night's rest, and, by the blessing of God, in the morning found ourselves none the worse for our exposure. The landlady was greatly gratified, and fell so much in love with the babe that she went and purchased several presents for him before we left the house.

After prospecting my work I found nothing to change

the gloomy impression I had received in regard to it. I had before me a rugged ride of two hundred and fifty miles each round of my circuit, through a wild and mountainous region, about twenty-five preaching places, no parsonage for my family, but few rest days in the year to spend with my family, and a prospect of a very meager support. My wife, who had never faltered in meeting any of the duties or sacrifices incident to our work, now passed through a severe ordeal of temptation. Her loneliness in view of the absence of one of the children, her solicitude in regard to my health, her dread of being so much alone, and surrounded by a slave population, all combined to throw a dark shadow for the time along the path of the future.

The search for a house resulted in the offer by an excellent brother, Dr. Paine, of the log-cabin about a mile from Guyandotte, which he had formerly occupied, but which for years past had been occupied as a sheep-fold. It seemed to be the best that, under the circumstances, could be done. So the sheep were turned out, that the shepherd might be turned in. After days of cleaning, scrubbing, and fixing we were settled in our new home, and my excellent companion, determining to make the best possible out of existing circumstances, proposed to open a school for children, and so assist in gaining a support for the family. And it was well she did, for while that great circuit gave us but sixty dollars quarterage during the year, she earned eighty dollars in her teaching, and putting both together we succeeded in keeping the wolf from the door.

The following is a brief outline of the route of my circuit: From Guyandotte, the starting point, I went up the Guyandotte River to Barboursville; then on to Mopin's tavern and Black's tavern; thence to Miller's, in Tey's Valley; then on to the mouth of Coal River, on the Big

Kanawha. Pushing on up the Coal River some distance, I crossed over to Mud River; thence across to the falls of Guyandotte River; thence over to Twelve-Pole; thence over to the Big Sandy River, which I followed down to its mouth; then I followed up the Ohio River to the mouth of Twelve-Pole, and on up the Ohio to Guyandotte town, at the mouth of the Guyandotte River.

The people received me with great cordiality, and treated me with marked kindness, as they always did their preachers. Though they lived in a rough country, and many of them were rough in their style of living, yet they had warm hearts, were proverbial for their hospitality, and seldom failed during the year to develop an affection as between pastor and people as made each loath to say good-by to the other when the year's work was accomplished. Nor were the people all rude and uncultivated. There were at different appointments of the circuit many families of culture that would have adorned society anywhere. I had on my list of local preachers some persons of marked ability, men devoted to the doctrines and discipline of the Methodist Episcopal Church, and who were a tower of strength in her counsels and in her pulpits. Among these I would mention Burwell and Stephen Spurlock. They were brothers. Burwell was the ablest and most popular pulpit man, but both were men of great influence and acceptability. William M'Comas, also, was an influential local preacher. He had been a leading and popular politician, having represented the people both in the State Legislature and the National Congress. He had a son, William Wirt M'Comas, a young man of great promise, who was afterward licensed, and recommended to the Ohio Conference, under my administration. I prized the counsel and friendship of these very highly, and profoundly regret that, in the prosecution of this narrative, we shall have to find these same persons marshaling with the bitterest foes of the Church, and in the interest of American slavery preparing the minds of the people for rebellion against the supreme power of the State. Had any one then suggested the possibility of such a state of things, both they and myself, with equal indignation, would have said, "Is thy servant a dog, that he should do this thing?"

During the last half of this year we lived at Barboursville. There was but one member of the Church at that place—an old colored brother—and the place abounded in iniquity; but there were a few families there solicitous to secure the services of my wife as school-teacher. As they offered her an advance on the wages she was receiving, it was thought best to make the change. Mrs. Ladeley, the wife of a respectable lawyer of the place, was chiefly instrumental in bringing about this arrangement; and though she did not at that time profess to be a Christian, she proved to be a good neighbor, and used her influence to encourage the establishment of preaching in the place. We rented part of a large brick tavern, which well accommodated us for both residence and school-house. The tenants in the other part of the house were at first quite disgusted with the idea of a Methodist preacher so near, but they soon dismissed their prejudices and became good and pleasant neighbors.

There was one feature of our new residence that was any thing but pleasant to us. The public whipping-post was directly in front of our door, and not unfrequently we there had demonstration that the way of some transgressors even in this world is hard. This mode of punishment was not confined to negroes and the most degraded classes of criminals. There was a man who had been regarded as honest and respectable convicted of theft, and sentenced to be put in jail for a certain length of time, and once in so many days to receive a complement of stripes on his naked back with a rawhide at the hands of the sheriff of the county Sheriff M'Ginnis, though a generous and warm-hearted Virginian, yet when as the executor of the commands of the people, it might be said of him in truth he bore not the cowhide in vain. But it was horrible to see a man tied up to the post and bared to the skin, and the blood following the rapidly descending strokes. Usually the crowd of idlers gathered to witness the spectacle, but in the case of the one referred to above, in view of his previous good standing, the people seemed to sympathize with him and to avoid adding to his mortification by their presence.

A merciful Providence attended us during the year, and though we entered upon it with many misgivings and in great physical weakness, we found ourselves at the close of the year in good health, and had the consciousness that our labor had not been in vain. We commended the people to God and the word of his grace, when the year's work was done, and turned our faces toward Ohio again.

CHAPTER XIV.

DEER CREEK CIRCUIT, OHIO.

1826-27.

THE Conference which met at Hillsboro, commencing October 4, 1826, was presided over by Bishop Hedding. A gloom was thrown over the whole Conference in consequence of charges brought against the moral character of one of the most popular preachers of the Conference, Rev. Charles Waddle. He had been honored in the pulpits of the Conference, and had been elected by his brethren as one of the delegates to the General Conference of 1824. The charges were sustained and he was expelled.

The following persons were admitted on trial: George W. Walker, Wesley Browning, Cyrus Carpenter, Benjamin Cooper, Adam Sellers, James Callahan, Adam Poe, John Ulin, Amos Sparks, David Whitcomb, Stephen A. Rathbone; a class some of whom became men of might in the Church.

We recorded the death of Rev. John Walker. He was born in Hampshire county, Va., February 28, 1797. He entered the traveling connection in 1821, and was a faithful laborer until the close of his life. As he stood on the borders of the spirit-world the veil seemed to be drawn aside, and with his expiring breath he exclaimed, "I have fought a good fight."

My appointment to Deer Creek circuit was altogether agreeable to my feelings. The travel was less laborious than the mountain circuit on which I had labored the past year. This was one of the oldest and strongest of the circuits. It was organized in 1808, and though its original boundaries have been curtailed from decade to decade as circuits and stations have been separated from it, it has for more than sixty years maintained its identity and honorable record on the Conference roll. As I shall have occasion to return to this circuit again far down in the narrative, when I shall preach the Gospel to the grandchildren of those who are my hearers in 1827, I will postpone to that time what I have to record in regard to the history of the circuit. In 1827 I found the following list of appointments: Waugh's, Riley's, Salem, Knight's, Hayes's, Inglish's, Upper Egypt, Lower Egypt, Brown's, Fisher's, Rector's, Littleton's, Dry Run, Oldtown, Moberry's, Ely's, Given's, Bethel, Buckskin, and Durflinger's. My colleague was Rev. John Ferree, a young man of deep and uniform piety whose whole soul was consecrated to the work of soul-saving. He was indefatigable in the prosecution of such studies as would better prepare him for his work, and his pulpit ministrations were characterized by a simplicity and tenderness that seldom failed to reach and move his hearers. All ages respected him, and I found him to be a most valuable fellow-worker.

Our presiding elder this year was Rev. Russel Bigelow, one of the grandest men ever associated with the Methodist pulpit. His powerful ministrations gave wonderful interest to our quarterly meetings and camp-meetings. Many persons of education and refinement who had little acquaintance with the Methodist Episcopal Church, but who were strongly prejudiced against both our doctrine and usages, abandoned their prejudices after hearing a sermon from this mighty man.

On a certain occasion a young man of culture and fine

moral sensibilities was importuned to attend a Methodist camp-meeting. He utterly refused, regarding such gatherings as pernicious, and having a horror of Methodism. He was induced, however, to go to see a patient on the camp-ground. Before he was ready to leave the ground the horn sounded for public service, and he sat down to listen to a discourse. We extract the account which he afterward gave of the man and the occasion:

"I dreaded," says he, "the occasion, but had always been educated to venerate religion, and had never seen the day when I could ridicule or disturb even a Mohammedan at his prayers or the pagan at his idol. In the pulpit were many clergymen, two of whom I knew and esteemed—the one a tall and majestic man, whose vigorous frame symbolized his noble mind and generous heart; the other a small, delicate, graceful gentleman, whom nature had fitted for a universal favorite. Had I been consulted, one of them should have occupied the pulpit at that time.

"All was stillness when the presiding elder stepped forward. Never was I so disappointed in a man's personal appearance. He was below the middle stature, and clad in coarse, ill-made garments. His uncombed hair hung loosely over his forehead. His attitudes and motions were exceedingly ungraceful, and every feature of his countenance was unprepossessing. Upon minutely examining him, however, I became better pleased. The long hair that came down to his cheeks concealed a broad and prominent forehead; the keen eyes that peered from beneath his heavy and over-jutting eyebrows beamed with deep and penetrating intelligence; the prominent cheek-bones, projecting chin, and large nose indicated any thing but intellectual feebleness, while the wide mouth, depressed at its corners, the slightly expanded nostrils, and the *tout-ensemble* indicated sorrow and love, and well assorted with the message, 'Come unto me all ye that labor and are heavy laden, and I will give you rest.'

"As he commenced I determined to watch for his faults, but before he had closed his introduction I concluded that his words were pure and well chosen, his accents never misplaced, his sentences grammatical, artistically constructed, and well arranged both for harmony and effect, and when he entered fully upon his subject I was disposed to resign myself to the argument and leave the speaker in the hands of more skillful critics. Having stated and illustrated his position clearly, he laid broad the foundation of his argument, and piled stone upon stone, hewed and polished, until he stood upon a majestic pyramid, with heaven's own light around him, pointing the astonished multitude to a brighter home beyond the sun, and bidding defiance to the enemy to move one fragment of the rock on which his feet were planted. His argument being completed, his peroration commenced. This was grand beyond description. The whole universe seemed animated by its Creator to aid him in persuading the sinner to return to God, and the angels commissioned to open heaven and come down to strengthen him. Now he opens the mouth of the pit and takes us through its gloomy avenues, while the bolts retreat, and the doors of damnation burst open, and the wail of the lost enters our ears. And now he opens heaven, transports us to the flowery plains, stands up amid the armies of the blessed, to sweep, with celestial fingers, angelic harps, and join the eternal chorus, 'Worthy, worthy is the Lamb!'

"As he closed his discourse every energy of his body and mind were stretched to the utmost point of tension. His soul appeared to be too great for its tenement, and every moment ready to burst through and soar away as an eagle toward heaven. His lungs labored, his arms rose, the perspiration, mingled with tears, flowed in a steady stream upon the floor, and every thing about him seemed to say, 'O that my head were waters!' But the audience thought not of the struggling body, nor even of the giant mind within, for they were paralyzed beneath the avalanche of thought that descended upon them. I lost the man, but the subject was all in all. I returned from the ground dissatisfied with myself, saying within me, 'O that I were a Christian!'"

That young man afterward sought admission into the Methodist Episcopal Church, was called to the work of the ministry, was elevated from one post of responsibility to another, until he occupied a place on the Episcopal Board, and became honored and loved throughout the whole denomination.

But to return. It is not at all strange that, with such pulpit ministrations, our quarterly and camp-meetings were looked forward to with large expectations. But there were other circumstances that gave the quarterly meetings of those days decidedly the advantage of those of the present. The circuits then extended over a large scope of country, and the majority of the societies had preaching only once in two weeks, and then on a week-day! A Sabbath and sacramental service had powerful attraction, and they thronged from these distant appointments to spend two or three days in their spiritual Jerusalem. Then, the presiding elder not having more appointments than he was able to attend in person, he was able to be present at four quarterly meetings on each charge each year. We had on Deer Creek circuit, at this time, nearly a thousand members scattered through some twenty-odd oppointments. The reader may fancy, then, what a moving there would be toward the place of quarterly meeting after they had once enjoyed the ministrations of Russel Bigelow.

The parsonage on this circuit was in a country place, on

Dry Run. It was a hewed log-house, and embowered in a beautiful maple forest. The nearest neighbors were about a quarter of a mile distant, so that, except when the forest was stripped of its foliage, we were entirely out of sight of any other human habitation. The neighbors were constant and lavish in their attentions to my family, sending in supplies almost daily of what was needed for our comfort, and usually some one of the neighbor girls would come to stay with the family at night when I was absent on the circuit. On Sabbath, too, some one of the neighbors would call to assist the family to church. But, with all this kind attention, the isolated location of the parsonage caused us much inconvenience.

On one occasion, in my absence, my companion was waked at midnight by the difficult breathing of our second son. She found that he was suffering with a very severe attack of croup, and before it was possible for her to prepare any such remedy as was within reach he appeared to be gasping in the very embrace of death. It was impracticable to send to any of the neighbors. But, by the blessing of God on her endeavors, the violence of the disease was arrested, and the child recovered.

On another occasion, while the little boys were playing in the forest near the house, one of them by accident severely wounded the other with a tomahawk. The screams of the boys, one of them screaming with fright and the other with pain, soon called my companion to the place. She carried the wounded one in her arms to the house, and held the mangled member tightly in her hands, so as to prevent as much as possible the flowing of blood, until the oldest son, a little boy only six years old, ran to the nearest neighbor, a quarter of a mile distant, and obtained assistance. The spring from which we obtained water was about eighty rods distant, and when we were without older company to care for the little ones, their mother made this arrangement with them to prevent them getting into danger in her absence to get water: The oldest boy was put at the cradle, with instructions to rock the cradle, and the second boy took his station by the side of a chair, to which he was tied with a string. He became so well accustomed to this performance that as soon as he would see his mother get the water-pail, he would hurry to hunt up the string and place himself in position for his temporary imprisonment. It was impossible for me so to arrange my plan as to avoid being absent from home very much of the time. In this retired place our third son, Daniel Asbury, was given to us, a lovely babe, but destined to be soon transferred to the companionship of the blessed above.

About the middle of the year my wife was taken down with typhoid fever. One of the most skillful physicians attended her, and was most faithful in doing all that he could do, but she grew worse and worse, until the physician despaired of her recovery. He said that he had never read of but one case of recovery where the symptoms were so bad as hers. He left expecting that she would die that night.

The impression had been strong upon her mind from the beginning that she would not recover, and being exceedingly happy in the presence of the Savior and the hope of heaven, she was much averse to taking medicine. At her request the children were brought to her bedside; she embraced them, and gave her dying counsel and charge to the boys, then gave me directions in regard to her burial. She requested that brother Bigelow should preach, and selected as the text, "Be ye therefore also ready," and sent as a message to her parents and friends the triumphant language of Paul, "I have fought the good fight, I have finished my course," etc. Ah who can tell the feelings of my heart!

Now I had no place to go to but to the great Physician. His eye was upon me and upon these little ones. He could sanctify the most simple remedies for the accomplishment of the most wonderful cures, or he could work independent of means. And if in answer to prayer he raised up Paul's friend lest he should have sorrow upon sorrow, why should he not hearken to me? He did, and that night she began to amend. The physician learning that she was still living returned to see her, and she recovered rapidly, so that in a few weeks she was able to resume the care of her house again. But before she was thoroughly recovered, the infant was seized with cholera infantum. Dr. Denning, the noble-hearted and skillful physician at Oldtown—now Frankfort—invited us to bring the child to his house, where he could give it more constant attention. We did so, but it pleased the Lord that little Daniel Asbury should be transferred to a better home than he could have on earth. On the day that he would have been nine months old we laid his remains away in the village cemetery. And now we realized a pang incident to our itinerant vocation that we had not known before. The forms of our loved ones are destined to be *scattered*, and we shall not have the sad privilege of often visiting the graves of our loved ones. But then, thank God! there will be a resurrection of the dead, and the fragments of the family shall be gathered again in that great day.

Dr. Denning, the physician above referred to, who attended us in sickness, gave us the freedom of his house, and spared no pains or expense to alleviate our sufferings and add to our comforts, was an able and valuable man and physician. I had the honor and unspeakable pleasure of leading him to Christ, and of recording his name on the roll of the visible Church. Some years after this he removed his family to Lafayette, Indiana, where he died. Before he died he requested that a chair should be left standing at the head of his grave. Could it be my privilege to visit that grave methinks I could spend hours in profitable meditation, as I would recall the memories of the past, and dwell upon the brevity and vanity, the dignity and sublimity of life.

Among those that I received into the Church during that year, besides the one above-mentioned, and who proved to be valuable accessions to the Church, I recall with peculiar pleasure the names of Tillman Rittenhouse, who afterward served his country faithfully and honorably on the judicial bench, and David Reed, who afterward became an able and popular minister in the Ohio Conference. How my heart swells with gratitude to God, now while I am writing, that the great Head of the Church put such honor upon me as to give me such men as my spiritual children! But all three of them have outstripped me in the race and have landed on the other shore.

The following local preachers were on the plan of my circuit, and gave me assistance during the year: Rev. Joseph Hays had been an able and efficient traveling preacher, but his wife having died, he found it necessary to give more of his time to the care and education of his children. He remained a widower, and brought up his children with great respectability. Brother Atherton followed school-teaching as a profession. He was a scientific man; his preaching was of an intellectual type, and was listened to with much interest. William Hughey was a good preacher and much appreciated by the people, but he committed the great mistake of running with the radical excitement and connecting himself with the so-called "reformers." John Jenkins was also infected with this excitement, so as to damage both his enjoyment and usefulness for the time being, but in after years he settled down, and spent the evening of his days feeling at home in the Methodist Episcopal Church. When many years after this, my son, a stripling boy eighteen years of age, was sent on to the Frankfort circuit, he found a hearty welcome and valuable encouragement at the house of brother Jenkins. Rev. Jesse Bowdle was of a large and respectable family, and as a Christian and minister he was sound to the core. Stephen Timmons had been in the regular work, both in the East and in the West. He was father of Rev. F. A. Timmons, of the Ohio Conference, who came into full connection in the Church under my administration that year. He had marked peculiarities, and the country was full of amusing anecdotes setting forth his eccentricities. He greatly admired humility, and detested any thing that looked like pride in the traveling preachers. In 1814 H. B. Bascom was the junior preacher on the circuit, and on the occasion of one of his visits to brother Timmons, the latter brother is said to have adopted the following mode of taking the starch out of the clothes and the blacking off the boots of the young preacher. Just before time for the preacher to get ready to go to his appointment, brother Timmons turned his horse into a large corn-field, when a muddy chase of an hour after the frolicking horse, in a field full of burs, effectually did the work as far as outward appearances were concerned. Rev. Reuben Roe had been in the regular work, and was a valuable and acceptable preacher. Brother Maddox was also a good worker, loyal to the Church and esteemed by the people.

Then among the laity there were the M'Neils, and Rittenhouses, and Browns, and Bowdles, and Withgots, and Hursts, and Crabbs, and Waughs, and Robbinses, and Blacks, and Augustuses, and Shepherds, and Rectors, and Littletons, and Hossletons, and others, a noble host, never to be forgotten.

We had a grand camp-meeting near the close of the year, in the neighborhood of Oldtown. There was an immense gathering of the people and an able corps of preachers, and the meeting resulted in much good. Rev. Zachariah Connell preached a very able sermon on, "Is there no balm in Gilead?" etc. Rev. E. G. Wood preached a valuable sermon on "The Highway." Rev. H. O. Sheldon gave efficient help, and manifested much ingenuity in his mode of reproving the rowdies. As they were so boisterous one night as to prevent sleep, the people were called up at midnight for preaching, and brother Sheldon took the stand. Pointing with his finger as though he had his eye on some one in the distance, he exclaimed, "Friend, how camest thou in hither, not having a wedding garment?" He said there was an old tradition that in the beginning of our race the Creator, having made a number of bodies, put them out to dry preparatory to furnishing them with souls, and that a few of them ran away in that unfinished state. He then suggested the query whether those persons that were howling through the forest, to the annoyance of sensible people, might not be descendants of those unfortunate soulless people.

The Conference met September 19, 1827, in the old Stone Chapel, in the city of Cincinnati, Bishop M'Kendree presiding, assisted by Bishops George and Soule. It was the time of the quadrennial election of delegates to General Conference. We received on trial John Wood, Gilbert Blue, Jesse Roe, Frederick Butler, William T. Snow, and James Armstrong. We elected the following brethren to represent our Conference in the General Conference, which was to meet at Pittsburg the first of May next: Jacob Young, David Young, J. B. Finley, J. F. Wright, R. Bigelow, G. R. Jones, James Quinn, John Collins, Moses Crume, Leroy Swormstedt, John Brown. We recorded the death of Rev. John Sale. He was a native of Virginia. Entered the traveling connection in 1796. He died at the house of brother French, near Troy, Ohio, January 15, 1827. He commenced his itinerant labors in the North-west in 1803, and had the honor of laying the foundation of Methodism in many places. By some, the honor is attributed to him of forming the first society in Cincinnati, but we have gone with what seems to be the main current of evidence in giving that honor to Rev. John Collins.

I was returned to Deer Creek circuit, with Rev. Adam Sellers for my colleague, and Rev. John Collins for my presiding elder. My colleague proved to be a faithful preacher, and a superior business man. The presiding elder, though not the intellectual giant that his predecessor was, yet as a man of power among the masses of the people, had few equals, and, perhaps, no superiors. He was emphatically a "son of consolation," and it might be said with equal emphasis that he was a "son of thunder." He had a remarkably sweet voice, a prepossessing appearance, was full of incident which, in the most simple and happy manner, he wove into his sermons. Whenever becoming animated in his discourse, he would throw his massive head to one side, and begin to shrug his right shoulder, then those who were acquainted with him expected to hear some of his overwhelming bursts of eloquence. The effect of his happiest efforts was wonderful beyond description. As he had traveled Deer Creek circuit some years before, and his labors had been greatly blessed, his return as presiding elder was hailed with delight by the people.

During this year I lived in Greenfield. My family had more society, and we had a pleasant and profitable year on the circuit.

The General Conference, as before stated, met at Pittsburg, the first of May, 1828. The session was an exciting one. The question of greatest interest related to the demand for changes in our Church polity, and the proper course to be pursued with those who were thoroughly committed to the proposed changes, and whose efforts were constantly employed in agitating the Church on these questions. In the bounds of the Baltimore and Pittsburg Conferences the agitation had already reached a crisis, and some of the leaders in the agitation had been dealt with by the authorities of the Church. Rev. Nicholas Snethen, a local minister of great eloquence and intellectual power, became the leader among the agitators, and Rev. Thomas Bond, a local preacher also, became a leading champion of the existing polity. When the matter came before the General Conference it was very thoroughly discussed, and the voice of the Conference was not only emphatically against the innovations, but indicated with equal clearness that the policy of the Church would be to bring discipline to bear against persistent agitators. We expected that the agitation would lead to secession in many places, as it also came to pass. Many ambitious and disappointed men went out regarding themselves as not appreciated, and many good and conscientious members separated themselves, thinking that the position of the General Conference was wrong and severe.

CHAPTER XV.

MIAMI CIRCUIT, OHIO.

1828-30.

SEPTEMBER 18, 1828, the Conference met at Chillicothe, only a short distance from my field of labor. In view of this, I had arranged to hold a camp-meeting near Oldtown during the session of the Conference. The membership of the circuit was all aglow from the effects of the camp-meeting just closed, and came up to this one with enlarged expectations, and well prepared to do battle for God. Able and earnest members of the Conference came out each day to assist, and the Word was attended with great power, and a multitude witnessed to the efficacy of the blood of Christ to save. Among those who joined at this meeting was William R. Anderson, who afterward became a standard-bearer, and for many years stood shoulder to shoulder with the honored members of the Ohio Conference. The meeting, like its predecessor, was a grand success. In consequence of attention to this meeting I could not give much attention to the business of Conference. Bishop Roberts presided, full of grief at the recent death of Bishop George; and the following persons were received on probation, namely: Jacob Hill, Thomas Thompson, Thomas Simms, Joseph Hill, William Herr, Leonard B. Gurley, Alvin Billings, James W. Finley, George Huffman, Joel Dolby, Joseph M. Trimble, Henry Colclazer, and David Cadwallader. The names of several of these have long been as household words in our Zion. At this Conference I first heard the voice of J. M. Trimble, one of the foregoing list. He followed one of the preachers in exhortation, and inspired both preachers and people with large expectations of his usefulness as a standard-bearer.

Considerable excitement occurred at this session on Freemasonry. A Mr. Morgan, who had declared himself a member of that fraternity, and had revealed what he declared to be the "Secrets of Masonry," had suddenly disappeared, and popular rumor claimed that the Masons had inflicted upon Morgan the penalties of the order. What became of Morgan is a mystery to this day, many still believing that he was murdered, and others thinking that the whole procedure was a shrewd mode of advertising his book, and that he enjoyed pecuniary profit from the excitement that resulted from his sudden disappearance from his home. The excitement that pervaded the country reached the Conference, and resulted in a "compromise," in which the Masons pledged themselves to abstain from attending the lodges, except on very special occasions, and the "antimasons" pledged themselves to cease their bitter assaults upon the fraternity. The excitement passed away after a few years, and neither party seemed very conscientious in keeping the pledges of the compromise. At different times since then this controversy has been measurably revived. There have been enthusiastic Masons, who have appeared to give Masonry and the lodges the place in their thoughts and affections that belong to Christ and his Church. On the other hand, there have been enthusiastic antimasons, who have regarded the institution as antichristian, and its members antichrist. Between these extremes, however, the great mass of Christians and citizens have been content that individuals should make it a matter of individual conscience as to their personal connection with societies of the kind. As it has been charged by the extremists first named that the majority of the clergy are connected with such societies, the mass of intelligent people have concluded that that fact, if a fact, was presumptive evidence that the society neither taught doctrines nor practiced ceremonies that Christian ministers could not subscribe to and participate in. And if a word from an aged minister of the Gospel, now nearing my four-score years, and expecting soon to be done with all of this life, could tend to remove the trouble of any on this subject, I would say that I have been acquainted with Masonry for nearly half a century, and while I have never been so wedded to the institution as to incline to neglect any religious duty or Church privilege to visit lodges or associate with Masons, yet I can cheerfully record my belief that the principles and teachings of the order emanate from the Scriptures, and that any man living up to those teachings, and his promises, will be a good moral man and a good citizen. And I will further add, that I have never known Masonry to be employed for the purpose of influencing Conference action, or the matter of appointments of the preachers. And now to return from this long digression.

I was appointed to the MIAMI CIRCUIT, with Rev. Wm. Simmons for my colleague, and Rev. Greenbury R. Jones, presiding elder. As brother Simmons was on the circuit the year before, and now returned for the second year, he was very properly preacher in charge. I found him to be a competent, zealous, and enterprising Christian minister, commanding the confidence of the Church and people, and proposing no compromise with the world, the devil, or the Pope. I moved into the parsonage at Chester, where the people received me with great kindness. The circuit in those days, as compared with others, was regarded as rather a small and easy circuit, but as compared with the circuits of the present day, it was a vast field of labor. We had twenty-eight appointments, embracing a membership of nine hundred and twenty-nine, and occupying all the territory between the Miami Rivers, from the Ohio River back to Lebanon, except Cincinnati and Hamilton stations. The following is a list of the appointments: Chester, Spring Meeting-house, Monroe, Pisgah, Palmyra, Union, Price's, Penton's, Montgomery, Reeder's, Madison, Armstrong's, Salem, Weatherby's, Wood's, Spark's, Blue Rock, Brown's, Cleves, Ebenezer, Cheviot, Shaw's, Williams's, Gregg's, Wood's, Maddox, Liberty, and Columbia.

We had a prosperous year; the attendance on the public and social means of grace was good. If any proved delinquent, we exercised the discipline promptly, but kindly, and generally succeeded in restoring the delinquent to duty and enjoyment.

We closed the year with a camp-meeting seven miles back of Cincinnati. A multitude of people attended. We had also an abundant supply of able ministers, whose hearts were in the work, and the meeting proved to be a success. We carried up a good report to the Conference.

September 3, 1829, the Ohio Conference met at Urbana, Bishop Roberts presiding. The following persons were received on trial: Thomas D. Allen, Joseph A. Reeder, William Sutton, Adam Minear, Jesse Prior, Elijah H. Pilcher, Amos Sparks, Samuel A. Latta, Henry E. Pilcher, Homer J. Clarke, Wesley Wood, Elmore Yocum, Erastus Felton, William Sprague. Some of these are still ably working for God. Homer J. Clarke had been admitted several years before, but had retired to secure an education, and now came into the work again fresh from the university.

I was returned to Miami circuit, with Rev. G. R. Jones continued as presiding elder, and Rev. James Laws as my colleague. I had regarded brother Laws as somewhat self-opinionated, and feared that he would be dissatisfied to labor as second preacher on the circuit, especially as he was my senior both in age and in the ministry. But he entered upon the work with me, and exhibited great versatility of talent, and proved to be an efficient co-worker. He was ready as a preacher, spirited in exhortation, powerful in prayer, a sweet singer, and almost unsurpassed in his power of endurance. The membership was in good working order at the beginning of the year, and continued so during the year.

Near the close of the year my circuit proposed to unite with the churches of Cincinnati in holding a camp-meeting. The proposition was accepted, and ground on Mill Creek, about three miles from the city, selected. Extensive preparations were made, and a general interest was felt in securing the success of the meeting. Revs. J. B. Finley and W. Browning, the pastors in the city, brought out their working host, and our membership well represented the several appointments on the circuit. Curiosity moved the great mass of population, and the attendance was very large indeed.

We were unexpectedly favored with the services of the Rev. Stephen G. Roszel, of the Baltimore Conference. He had come West to visit his son, then a student at Augusta College, Kentucky, when, being invited to visit Cincinnati and attend this meeting, he consented to do so. His reputation was sufficiently known among the preachers to excite large expectation; and then his giant and commanding physical proportions, as soon as he entered the pulpit, excited similar expectation upon the part of the vast multitude. He announced his hymn, which was sung with spirit. We kneeled in prayer, and his commanding voice seemed to penetrate the very heavens as he led in a prayer of wondrous power. When he arose to announce his text, every eye and ear was fixed in attention. It was soon apparent to all that an intellectual giant occupied the pulpit. For about two hours that vast multitude was held spell-bound. Shocks of divine power accompanied the Word, and, at times, the more spiritual in the audience, overcharged with the heavenly electricity, would give vent to their feelings and make the grand old woods ring with their rejoicings. Seldom has a congregation been so profoundly stirred under the preaching of the Word. The work went on steadily, and that Saturday night was a night of power. It was generally expected that Roszel would preach again on Sabbath, and expectation had reached the highest pitch. He filled the appointment and fully met expectation. Again, for more than two hours, he held the mighty mass of humanity and swayed them as the wind sways the forest. In the midst of the intense excitement, he called the congregation to their knees before God. O, my soul! what a sublime bowing before the Lord was that! For some time the congregation lingered before God, thrilled with the shocks of power that had accompanied the preached Word. I had witnessed many demonstrations of power before, but I had never witnessed any thing superior to this. We placed upon the muster-roll of the militant Church, before the meeting closed, the names of between three and four hundred who purposed to enlist for the war. I trust, when the war is over, and the conquering legions are called home, that I shall meet many of them, to talk over the victories of that great camp-meeting.

There were many valuable men in the laity, as well as in the ministry, on Miami circuit. Joseph A. Reeder was then working at his trade, as tailor, in Montgomery, and keeping the post-office. He had very great influence over the masses of the people, both in and out of the Church, which influence he used wisely. During this year we licensed him to preach, and he soon became an effective traveling preacher. William Parish, then a private member, resided in West Chester, and carried on a tannery. He was a man of sterling Christian character. He had taken strong hold of the confidence of the people, and promised large usefulness in the Church. He was afterward licensed to preach, and did the Church valuable service.

James Conrey, of a numerous and very respectable family, lived near West Chester. He was the father of Rev. Jonathan F. Conrey, and was at that time in a sad state. He was in a state of despair as regarded his prospects of salvation. He said that there had been a time when he might have been saved, but that time had passed forever. He recognized intellectually the importance of salvation, but said that he had passed the boundaries of feeling, and was left without concern. His neighbors, feeling deeply interested for him, besought me to put forth some special effort in his behalf. I entered into his case, and determined to do all I could to foil the devil in his attempt to ruin this man. The tempter had done with him as he has done with so many others. For years he had said to him, "Time enough yet, time enough yet," and had thus robbed him of years of his term of probation; and now he had turned upon him and said, "It is too late now; you have rejected so long that there is no mercy for you now." I visited him frequently, and urged him to commence reading the Bible and praying, and assured him that, though he might experience no feelings of tenderness at first, it could do him no harm, and I had faith that the spirit would visit him again. He undertook to follow my advice. After days of effort, he said that he had no feeling as yet. We urged him to persevere in the effort. He did so, and in less than a month he began to feel encouraged, and before three months had passed the snare of Satan was broken, and he was rejoicing in God his Savior. He developed into a useful and exemplary Christian, was licensed to preach, and for more than thirty years witnessed a good profession in the Church and before the world.

Danforth Weatherby and Aaron Burdsal were neighbors, living some eight miles back of Cincinnati. They were local preachers of good standing, and used their talents to advantage for the cause of the Master. About eight miles west of Cincinnati lived brothers Biddle and Gosling, who were local preachers, both from New Jersey, and both highly appreciated in their relation to the Church. The names of a great many members of the Church scattered over that large circuit still linger in my memory and my heart. There was Price, and Vantreese, and Conrey, and Elliott, and Flinn, and Williams, and Short, and Cline, and West, and Shaw, and Brown, and Reeder, and Ward, and White, and Sackett, and Williamson, and Wood, and Maddox, and Dr. Beach, and Legg, and such. But out of nearly a thousand members, the great mass of whom were living Christians, I shall not be able to go through the enumeration of their names.

It was during this year that God gave us our first daughter, Sarah Jane, a child destined to be a joy in our household for a few years, and then to precede us to the heavenly home.

CHAPTER XVI.

OXFORD CIRCUIT, OHIO.

1830-32.

SEPTEMBER 8, 1830, the Ohio Conference met at Lancaster, Bishop Soule presiding. There was a full attendance of the preachers, and many of them came up in the fullness of the blessing of the Gospel. God blessed them in their pulpit ministrations, and a precious revival broke out about the third day of the Conference, which increased steadily until the close of the meeting. Some of the preachers regarded it as one of the most spiritual Conferences they had ever attended. The following were received on trial: Bradford Frazee, John M. Goshorn, William M. Sullivan, Herbert Bayard, John C. Hardy, Joseph Leedom, Bernard A. Casset, Levi P. Miller, William Morrow, William Young, Ebenezer B. Chase, James Gurley, Allen D. Beasley, Asa B. Stroud, Ebenezer Owen, Charles C. Lybrand, Noah Hough, Abram Millice, Benjamin Boydston, Elnathan C. Gavitt, Elam Day, Ezekiel S. Gavitt, and Leonard Hill—a good class, that has rendered long and valuable service to the Church.

I was appointed to the charge of Oxford circuit, with Rev. G. R. Jones presiding elder, and Rev. A. D. Beasley for my colleague. The following was my list of appointments: Oxford, Owen's, Dover, Loop's, Riner's, Deem's, Miltonville, Draper's, Marsh's, Harrison, Swearingen's, New Haven, Venice, Lehigh, Youman's, Stewart's, Alhand's,

Fay's, Dickinson's, Brown's, Hazleton's, Ebenezer, Butler's, and Woodruff's. These twenty-four appointments occupied an extensive territory, but we had upon the whole a pleasant field of labor. My colleague was a worker in the pulpit and out of it, and we labored together in harmony and affection. The people gave us a warm welcome, and we had the gratification of seeing the pleasure of the Lord prosper in our hands. The greatest drawback to my enjoyment was the want of a parsonage for my family to live in. Brother Charles Stewart gave us the use of an unoccupied house on his farm, and though it was not a very comfortable place, yet the great and constant kindness of that noble Christian family went very far to reconcile us to the discomforts of the house until we could do better. With the approbation of the official members of the circuit, I opened subscriptions for the erection of a parsonage at Oxford. The people responded cheerfully, and the house was built and put in order, ready for myself or whoever should serve the charge the next year.

The Conference met at Mansfield, Ohio, September 8, 1831, Bishop Hedding presiding, who preached a sermon of great power on the Conference Sabbath. The following persons were admitted on trial: James F. Davidson, Elias M. Daley, Joseph M. Matthews, Adam Miller, Benjamin L. Jefferson, George Elliott, Charles W. Swain, Michael Marley, Henry Turner, Thomas Wiley, Jesse Prior, John G. Bruce, George C. Crum, Jacob Martin, Lorenzo Bevans, Philip Wareham, Benjamin Allen, Stephen M. Holland, and David Kinnear. This, too, was a good class, and some of them rose to great prominence and became widely known as able representatives of Methodism.

We recorded at this Conference the death of the venerable Michael Ellis. He was one of the grandest of our pioneers. He was ordained deacon at the same time that

Bishop Asbury was ordained Bishop. Having spoken of him more at large in another part of this narrative, I shall not enter upon any detailed account of this man of God in this place.

As the General Conference was to meet the first of May next, we elected our delegates at this session, and the lot fell on the following brethren: David Young, Russel Bigelow, J. Quinn, J. F. Wright, L. Swormstedt, W. H. Raper, A. W. Elliott, J. B. Finley, Z. Connell, Curtis Goddard, John Collins, W. B. Christie, Charles Holliday, and G. R. Jones—a very large and a very able delegation.

I was returned to Oxford circuit, and associated with a new presiding elder and assistant. Of my new presiding elder, Rev. James B. Finley, I have already spoken at large in a former chapter. I was sorry to separate from brother Beasley, who had proved to be such a faithful assistant. My new assistant, however, Rev. James F. Davidson, though just entering the life of an itinerant, was well received, and fulfilled his duties creditably to himself and satisfactorily to the people. I moved into the new parsonage at Oxford, and was much better situated, both for family comfort and for the advantages of personal improvement. The Miami University, one of the State institutions, being located at Oxford, its influence pervaded the whole social atmosphere, to a greater or less extent. So much did I become exercised on the subject of education myself, that could I either have set myself back in age a few years, or had my sons been old enough to enter upon the prosecution of a collegiate course, I believe that I would have entered the University, and abandoned the itinerant field until I should have secured a liberal education. As it seemed impracticable under all the circumstances for me to gratify my desire in this direction, I resolved to make what proficiency my opportunities should afford me, and to lay my plans to secure to my sons the advantages of a thorough education.

During this year our fifth and last child, Ruth Eliza, was born, and now our family consisted of two sons and two daughters with us on earth, and one son with our Father in heaven.

Rev. Moses Crume, that venerable and precious man of God, who had worn himself out in the Master's work, was now on the retired list, residing in Oxford. I valued him as a friend and counselor. Danforth Weatherby and Colbreth Hall were both acceptable local preachers, belonging to the society at Oxford. Joseph A. Waterman was licensed to preach, and recommended to the traveling connection from this charge this year. He became an intellectual giant, and, had he been a well-rounded man and fully imbued with the spirit of the itinerant work, inferior to very few in the denomination as a Methodist preacher. Brothers Merrell and Stout were appreciated by the people as faithful local preachers. They both lived on the college lands. Brother Aaron Powers was an active and valuable local preacher, living in the neighborhood of Charles Stewart's. After I left the circuit he became infected with the Mormon vagaries, and going to their community consorted with them for awhile, intending to unite with them. After a short time Jo. Smith, having learned that Powers had property, informed him that he had a revelation from the Lord directing that he should give to the Church one-half of his property. "When," inquired Powers, "when did you have have this revelation from the Lord?" The so-called prophet mentioned the time. "Then," responded Powers, "I have had a revelation from the Lord since then that I should do no such thing." The brothers Comstock, senior and junior, were both respected local preachers and practicing physicians, and exerted a healthy influence in the communities where they were known. Rev. John Deem, at that time an acceptable local preacher, afterward entered the traveling connection. Brother Lincoln, in Harrison, and brother Kitchen, of Oxford, were also local preachers, acceptable and worthy, and by me much beloved. Matthew and William Morehead were veterans in the cause of God. George White and Peter Butler, and Russel, and Bartlett, and Youman, and Turner, and Melone, and Marsh, and Riner, and William Crume, and a host of others, are dear to me, whose works will praise them in the gate.

Near the close of this year we had a camp-meeting near Charles Stewart's. It proved to be a grand gathering of the hosts of the Lord; and though Satan came also, and attempted to distract the work, yet God was there in power. Many were awakened and converted, and the saints went to their homes strong to do and suffer for the Master.

It was during this year that I first came in contact with Mr. Kidwell, a noted champion of the doctrine of Universalism, and editor of the Star of the West. Our controversy was brief, but spirited, and occurred on this wise: Having occasion to notice the doctrine of Universalism in one of my discourses, I had stated that if the teachings of that doctrine were true that God had seemed to show partiality toward the wicked. He had swept the wicked inhabitants of the antediluvian world suddenly into heaven, and had left the few righteous to be shut up in the ark, tossed upon the waves of the flood, and to remain for years longer sufferers in this world of disappointment and afflictions; and suggested, further, that if the teachings of that doctrine were true, it might be a work of benevolence to massacre all who were in any circumstances of want or suffering here. Such an act would immediately introduce those massacred to heaven, and though men might call it murder, it could in no way jeopardize the salvation of the murderer. Kidwell became excited, and answered me in his paper, and challenged me to meet him in public debate. He said that if he believed as Stewart did, that all dying in infancy are saved, he should esteem it an act of benevolence to kill off all the children in infancy, so that they might not come to years of accountability to hazard their salvation. Believing that public controversies seldom resulted in much profit, I had intended to treat his challenge with contempt. Sometime after this I casually met him, and was introduced to him in the post-office by Rev. Moses Crume. I then told Mr. Kidwell that I had not seen his paper, but that I had heard of his strictures, and of the challenge that he had extended to me, and said, "I intended to pay no attention to your challenge; and as regards the massacre of the innocents, consistently with your doctrine you can murder them and not endanger your salvation, but I can not." He stammered for an answer, but was taken so by surprise that he left the office in confusion. A gentleman present complimented me by saying, "You certainly took the bull by the horns."

CHAPTER XVII.

BELLEFONTAINE CIRCUIT, OHIO.

1832-33.

THE Conference met at Dayton, Ohio, September 19, 1832, Bishop Emory presiding. This was the first and only time that he presided at our Conference. He was a first-class presiding officer, and made a most happy impression in all his intercourse with us. We received on probation Obadiah Johnson, F. A. Timmons, L. L. Hamline, Daniel G. Dector, John Kinnear, Luther D. Whitney, Daniel Poe, Robert Cheny, Samuel G. Patterson, Joseph M. M'Dowell, Edward Thomson, Marcus Swift, Eliakim Zimmerman, Peter Sharp, David Reed, Edward D. Roe. H. M. Shaffer, John Hasty, Andrew Dixon, William Westlake, H. Dodds, George Smith, Arthur B. Elliott, Zachariah Games, William P. Strickland, Benjamin Ellis, and William S. Thornburg. Two of this list have since been promoted to the episcopacy, and many of them have accomplished their ministry and gone to their reward, and others of them are still doing valuable service. Two of them I had received into the Church and was happy to meet them here.

When the appointments were read out, I learned that I not only had a long move to make, but one of the most laborious frontier circuits to serve. Bellefontaine circuit had at that time some thirty appointments, a membership of twelve hundred and thirty-six, and a territory of vast extent. Rev. William H. Raper was my presiding elder, and

Revs. J. G. Bruce and Peter Sharp my colleagues. Though I would not have desired that appointment, yet I was in the strength of manhood and felt no disposition to complain. As promptly as practicable I moved my family within the bounds of the circuit. There being no parsonage I secured the best temporary shelter for my family that could be found, and addressed myself at once to the work. After prospecting the field, I reported to the presiding elder that if he had suitable work elsewhere for one of my colleagues I would rather reduce the work to a four weeks' circuit than to run the awkward machinery of a six weeks' circuit. He approved my suggestion, and transferred brother Bruce to another work. Brother Sharp was willing and efficient, and during the year, by the blessing of the Lord, we each preached over thirty sermons each month, besides meeting the classes, visiting the people, and responding to extra calls for ministerial service.

Our closing camp-meeting, which was held in the neighborhood of brother Messick's, was an occasion of great interest and uncommon power. Added to the ordinary attraction of such an occasion, it had been announced that brother Syms, the missionary among the Wyandott Indians, would attend with a detachment of the converted Indians, so an immense concourse of people gathered. The missionary and the Wyandotts came as was expected, and added greatly both to the interest and profit of the meeting. These recently converted children of the forest had thrown away the tomahawk and the scalping-knife, and now, with the greatest simplicity and fervency, worshiped God and rejoiced in his salvation. Their prayers, and songs, and exhortations, and shouts made an impression never to be lost by many who, perhaps, would not have been reached by any ordinary instrumentality.

Among the local preachers whose co-operation and friendship I remember with pleasure were Rev. David Kemper, then a single man, diligently applying himself to study to secure a proper qualification for the life-work in which he has since been honored and blessed; Rev. John M'Gruder, more advanced in years, and efficient and respected in his sphere of labor. Brother Casebolt also did good and acceptable service as a local preacher.

Among the private and official members there were many noble spirits. There was George Messick, whose name deserves to be recorded in golden capitals. He had "a soul as big as all out-doors." The latter half of the Conference year he brought my family and divided his house with us, furnished us with a cow, and, indeed, there was no end to the kindness of himself and family to the preachers. May the blessing of the great Head of the Church rest upon his posterity forever! Joseph Bowdle, whose name I recorded among the good men of Deer Creek circuit, had settled near Roundhead, and contributed liberally of money, labor, and influence to extend the borders of Zion about his new home. Noah Z. M'Culloch, the clerk of the court in Bellefontaine, was a solid member of the Church, a man of unflinching integrity and devotion to the cause of God. Then there were the Balies, and M'Farlands, and Carters, and Pools, and Brookses, and a great many more of kindred spirit and worth whose names are graven on preachers' hearts, and I trust also in the Book of Life.

The following is the list of the principal appointments on the Bellefontaine circuit: 1. Bellefontaine; 2. Richard's; 3. Roundhead; 4. Rutledge's; 5. Brooks's; 6. Richardson's; 7. Timber; 8. Parkerson's; 9. Liberty; 10. Monroe's; 11. M'Farland's; 12. Fine's; 13. Gregory; 14. Stephens's; 15. Salem; 16. Robertson's; 17. Antioch; 18. Musselman's; 19. Sidney; 20. Laramie; 21. Harden; 22. Hathaway's; 23. Burdett's; 24. Quincy; 25. Newman's; 26. Messick's; 27.

George's; 28. Powell's; 29. Wood's; 30. Spry's; and a few others the names of which have gone from my memory.

Our proximity to the Indian Mission, as referred to in preceding pages, had drawn out our sympathies this year much for that people; and the attention of the whole denomination had been aroused in behalf of Indian evangelization by an incident that occurred this year laying the foundation of our missions beyond the Rocky Mountains. A deputation from the Flathead Indians had made a journey of between two and three thousand miles from their home near the Pacific Ocean, and presented their plea to Mr. Clark, the Indian agent in St. Louis, for knowledge of the white man's God and religion. The Advocate and Journal published the account, accompanied with a cut of one of the heads of the strange people. Jason and Daniel Lee volunteered to go as missionaries, and such was the influence of the movement that the missionary collections for the year nearly doubled the amount for the previous year.

CHAPTER XVIII.

TROY CIRCUIT, OHIO.
1833-34.

AUGUST 21, 1833, the Conference met at Cincinnati. Bishop Roberts presided. As the cholera had been prevailing in Cincinnati, many of the preachers declined attending the session. The following persons were received on trial: Joseph A. Waterman, John Alexander, William H. Lawder, Benjamin F. Myers, James Parcels, Cyrus Brooks, Samuel Harvey, Granville Moody, F. H. Jennings, Henry Maynard, S. A. Rathburn, Samuel Allen, Joseph Newson, Samuel Lynch, William H. Brockway, Duncan McGregor, David Burns, James Wheeler, Paul Wambaugh, James B. Austin, Robert Graham, Richard Lawrence, T. A. G. Phillips, Philip Nation, John Donalson, Alexander Morrow, J. W. Cooley, Lester Janes, Lorenzo Waugh, Henry Whiteman, Charles R. Lovell, Henry Camp, James Webb, John C. Hardy, James Courtney, Zephaniah Bell—a large class, some of whom are among the most valuable workers in our Zion at this day. We recorded the death of Rev. John Ulin. He was a man of brilliant parts, and was stricken down suddenly with cholera, July 13, 1833. He had been successful and was much beloved.

The Troy circuit, to which I was appointed, was organized at this Conference out of part of the Piqua circuit. I regarded it as a small and very easy circuit, it having only nineteen appointments—one-third less than my last circuit.

Rev. W. H. Raper remained on the district, and Rev. J. G. Bruce was my colleague. He was the same young man who was appointed with me to Bellefontaine circuit, but having been removed, as stated in my narrative heretofore, I had not formed his acquaintance to any great extent. He proved to be a man of fine preaching ability, well adapted to and faithful in meeting the responsibilities of the work. I was well pleased with my appointment and associate, and anticipated a pleasant year.

Soon after Conference I was comfortably settled in the parsonage at Troy, and enjoyed a hearty welcome from a whole-souled membership. The cholera had been sweeping many into eternity, and still lingered to some extent, but the violence of the dreadful visitation had passed before we came to Troy. I had for my nearest neighbor in the pastorate Rev. Arza Brown. He was at Piqua, and was then in his prime—a man who never failed to endear himself to the people that he served, and who left his mark in the person of living witnesses, raised up, through his ministry, to declare the power of the Gospel to save.

Though myself and colleague applied ourselves industriously to our work, we did not realize the revivals and in-gatherings that we had hoped for. This failure to realize our expectation was not traceable to any Church difficulties or any want of co-operation on the part of our membership. I have learned, however, both by experience and observation, that present visible success does not always attend the most faithful and anxious labor. There are times when the spirit of awakening pervades whole districts and continents, and the Word runs and is glorified without much apparent effort on the part of ministers. The pool seems to be troubled; times of refreshing are come, and the conviction penetrates all hearts, "Now is the day of salvation." There are other times when labor, however faithfully performed, yields no immediate visible fruit. It is, however, the duty of each laborer to sow good seed, and to sow it in abundance; to sow it in the morning and to sow it in the evening, as he knows not which shall prosper most, this or that, or whether both shall prosper alike. He must trust God for the increase, who can give thirty-fold, sixty-fold, or a hundred-fold. He has promised that our labor shall not be in vain in the Lord, and though we go forth weeping and bearing the precious seed, we shall doubtless return again, rejoicing, and bringing sheaves with us.

Associated with us as supernumerary was Rev. Richard Brandriff. He was living in Troy, in impaired health—a good preacher and much respected by the people. He afterward committed the great mistake of quitting the Church of his choice and uniting with the "True Wesleyans." They made much of him, but I am inclined to think that his latter days were neither as cheerful nor useful as they would have been had he remained in the communion in which he had spent his strength. Brother D. Dyke was also living in the bounds of the circuit. He had been a useful traveling preacher, and exerted a good influence among the people. Brother J. Goddard was a good local preacher. Very humble in his own estimation, he had a high place in the esteem of his brethren. Brother J. Mitchell was also an acceptable local preacher, and was listened to by the people.

Among the lay members at Troy, D. Sabin and Levi Hart stood very prominent. The former was an able and successful medical practitioner. He was a thorough Methodist, able to grasp the whole economy of the Church, and to defend it against any adversary. He was thoroughly posted, and a man of great mental power. The preachers found in him a steadfast friend, and he always extended to them faithful professional services, free of charge. Brother

Hart was active in meeting the responsibilities of his official relations, and did his work intelligently and thoroughly. In fact the official board of the Troy circuit, as a whole, was a very dignified, strong, and efficient body. Such was my attachment to them and the people generally of the charge, that I would gladly have remained another year. There were other reasons, too, why it would have been agreeable to my family to have remained another year. My oldest son, John Wesley, had commenced learning the printer's trade, in the office of brother Tullis, who published and edited the "Troy Times," and we would have been gratified to remain, so that he could have still been a member of our family and under our influence. We, however, submitted to the order of the properly constituted authorities.

As I omitted to record the list of appointments in the proper place, I will insert it here: 1. Troy; 2. Crisman's; 3. Mahuron's; 4. Chambersburg; 5. M'Fading's; 6. Pisgah; 7. Lee's; 8. Gearheart's; 9. Mitchell's; 10. Bethel; 11. Leffel's; 12. Sim's; 13. Rector's; 14. Arney's; 15. Spring Meeting-house; 16. Crary's; 17. Clarke's; 18. Lamb's; 19. Carlisle.

CHAPTER XIX.

ADELPHI CIRCUIT, OHIO.

1834-35.

AUGUST 20, 1834, the Conference met at Circleville, Ohio, Bishop Soule presiding. The following persons were admitted on trial: Joseph O. W. Cloninger, David Kemper, Charles R. Baldwin, Reuben S. Plummer, John Morey, Lorenzo Davis, John Rodgers, John F. Gray, Edward Estell, Jonathan E. Chaplin, James Brooks, Moses A. Milligan, Richard Haney, William Morrow, James A. Kellam, Stephen P. Heath, McKendree Thrapp, Frederick A. Seborn, David Warnock, George Armstrong, Daniel M. Conant, Robert F. Hickman, Zachariah Wharton, Alanson Fleming, Dudley Woodbridge, Robert S. Kimber, John T. Kellam, John Bronaugh, Wesley Rowe, Hiram Gering, Orin Mitchell, William I. Ellsworth, Sylvester F. Southard, Mark Delany, Sheldon Parker, Lucien W. Berry, Wesley Brock, Richard Doughty, James Wilkinson, John W. White, Wesley C. Clarke, J. A. Brown, William B. Bradford—43. Some of these I have recently met in the great North-west, occupying leading positions in their Conferences, and some of them are known throughout the denomination.

During the past year two of our preachers had been transferred from the Church militant to the Church triumphant; namely, Thomas F. Sargent and James Callahan. Brother Sargent had occupied a high position in the East, and was transferred to the Ohio Conference and stationed in Cincinnati. He died December 29, 1833, before the close of his first year among us. He was a man of diversified and extensive attainments, and was lamented by a large circle of admirers and friends. Brother Callahan died of pulmonary consumption at the residence of his father-in-law, brother Burlingham, near Marietta, Ohio, November 9, 1833. His father, Rev. George Callahan, had given him to God early in life. He embraced religion early, entered the traveling connection in 1826, and his talent, devotion, and success, during the few years of his ministry, had given promise of great usefulness. But He who sees "the end from the beginning" transferred him to the brighter clime above.

My removal from Troy, as intimated in the last chapter, was contrary to my wishes, and, as I had reason to believe, contrary to the desires of the members of that charge. It was not only contrary to our mutual wishes, but altogether unexpected. When the Bishop had made his address, and commenced reading out the appointments, I sat easily in my place, expecting to be returned, but when he reached that appointment he read: "Troy, J. *Laws*, W. I. Ellsworth. *R. Brandriff*, sup." The thoughts of my sick wife, my boy just commencing to learn a trade, and all the embarrassments in the way of a removal, flashed through my mind and I was somewhat disconcerted. But I yet hoped that I might find myself stationed on some adjacent charge. The Bishop read on and finished that district, and on through the third, and the fourth, and fifth, and sixth, and seventh, and eighth, and at the last appointment of the eighth district read: "Adelphi circuit, John Stewart, J. W. White." A move of about one hundred miles, and a large, rugged four weeks' circuit of twenty-eight appointments was before me. I was driven to my wits' end to be reconciled; but I never had rebelled, and I determined to go to my work and not let any body know that it was not just the work that I desired. I never asked any explanation of brother Raper, the presiding elder, and he never volunteered to give me any, so I do not know to this day why the change was made. Since then, however, my experience in the Bishops' cabinet has instructed me that changes sometimes need to be made for the reasonable relief of individuals, or to secure the general interest of the work, that could not be anticipated, and that could hardly be explained to all the parties concerned so as to appear altogether satisfactory to them. The system of Methodist Church polity is one of mutual sacrifice, to secure in its ultimate results mutual advantage and the largest amount of efficiency with a given amount of men, and means, and labor.

PLAN OF ADELPHI CIRCUIT.

Day of Service	Preaching-Places	County	Distance	Hour	Number in Class	Class-Leaders
Sabbath	Adelphi	Ross		11 A. M.	51	George Will, A. Cartlich.
Tuesday	Widow Low's	"	4	11 "	21	Pastors.
Sabbath	William Dawson's	"	4	Night	10	"
Wednes	Dowd's	Athens	30	3 P. M.	29	Bro. Westcoat's.
Thursday	D. Culbertson's	"	5	11 A. M.	12	D. Culbertson.
Sabbath	McArthurstown	"	3	11 "	56	James Johnson.
Monday	Loving's	Jackson	5	12 M	23	A. Horton.
Tuesday	S. Redfern's	"	5	11 A. M.	27	S. Redfern.
Wednes	Comer's S. H.	Ross	5	11 "	30	Brother Comer.
Saturday	Londonderry	"		3 P. M.	57	A. Gordon.
Sabbath	Concord	"	6	11 A. M.	85	David Gundy.
Monday	S. Hanson's M. H.	"	4	11 "	23	John Gundy.
Tuesday	Rout's	"	3	11 "	15	Brother Rout.
Wednes	Bookwalter's S. H.	"	5	11 "	24	Pastors.
Friday	Monett's M. H.	"		5	11 "	29	J. Monett.
Sabbath	Tarlton	Pickaway	6	11 "	74	J. Shoemaker, Brother Roby, A. Lybrand.
Tuesday	Jesse Cartlich's	Hocking	20	11 "	48	George Fate, I. Cartlich.
"	David Fate's	"	3	3 P. M.	16	Pastors.
Wednes	Woodward's S. H.	"	7	11 A. M.	20	Bro. Woodward.
"	Mannie's	Athens	3	3 P. M.	10	Bro. Bieggerstaff.
Thursday	Aaron Young's	Hocking	10	2 "	14	James Young.
Friday	Webb's M. H.	"	3	12 M	37	Thomas Webb.
Sabbath	Logan	"	5	11 A. M.	61	S. S. Bright.
"	Pitcher's	"	3	3 P. M.	36	Brother Sellers.
Monday	Brown's	"	10	11 A. M	55	Brother Conrad.
Tuesday	Cave's		7	11 "	23	M. Caves.
Friday	Thomas's	Pickaway	5	2 P. M.	22	Brother Wheeler.
Saturday	Rice's M. H.	"	4	11 A. M.	48	William Rice.

The following names were reported as exhorters, local preachers, and circuit stewards: *Exhorters*—John Dressback, Isaac Cartlich, Dr. Hibbard, A. Cartlich, J. Dressback, F. Fate, and D. Fate. *Local Preachers*—D. Culbertson, S. Redfern, D. Dutcher, J. Monett, John Rodgers, Joseph Starling, Aaron Young, Thomas Webb, Nathan Brown, and Henry Brown. *Circuit Stewards*—George Will (recording steward), John Patterson, James Johnson, A. Gordon, Geo. Binkley, S. S. Bright, and William Rice.

This is the plan as given to me by my predecessors, Rev. William Westlake and Philip Nation. The only addition that I have made to the plan is to add the counties in which the appointments were located. In a few instances, where they were located near the county lines, I may not be entirely correct. It will be observed that the circuit extended into five counties, and embraced a membership of nearly one thousand.

The first year that I traveled the circuit, Rev. Augustus Eddy was my presiding elder, and John W. White was my colleague. The second year, Rev. John Ferree was my presiding elder, Wesley Rowe my colleague, with all of whom my associations were both pleasant and profitable. Of the presiding elders I have already spoken in former chapters. My colleagues were both young men just entering the work, and both gave unmistakable promise at the outstart of extensive usefulness in the Church. Brother White had a lively imagination, a ready utterance, a large share of magnetism in his nature, and his ministrations were much blessed to the people. Brother Rowe was prompt to duty and reliable in every relation. He had great social power, and was an interesting and profitable preacher. His sermons were brief, practical, and often pathetic. They have both fulfilled the high hopes that I entertained of them, the former still standing on the walls of Zion, and the latter having passed on to the Church triumphant.

I had some difficulty in finding a house to live in, as the circuit had no parsonage. The best we could do for some months was to occupy an old house connected with a tannery, in the suburbs of Adelphi, which, according to popular rumor, was the resort of "spooks," and therefore a great terror to the young. We had some difficulty in educating our children to overcome the timidity occasioned by these stories. After a few months brother Monett invited us to occupy a vacant house near him on his farm, where we were very pleasantly associated with his excellent family. I addressed myself, however, to the work of providing the circuit with a parsonage, and had the privilege of occupying it in Tarlton my last year on the charge. In each of these neighborhoods my family had the attention of first-class Methodists, and we and the people of the charge became mutually greatly attached. Each Conference year wound up with a glorious camp-meeting. The one at the close of the first year was held in the Concord neighborhood, on Walnut Creek. It was an immense gathering, and proved to be a meeting of large results. Among those whose ministrations were greatly blessed at that meeting were Rev. Augustus Eddy, the presiding elder, then in the strength of his physical manhood and the palmy period of his pulpit power; Rev. David Lewis, full of love and zeal and faith; Rev. Evan Stevenson, of Kentucky, a man of lofty enthusiasm and almost consuming zeal; Rev. Philip Nation, one of the sweetest singers and most powerful exhorters; and J. W. White, my colleague, of whom I have already spoken. The great altar was at times crowded with penitents, and as the converting power descended we witnessed some scenes thrilling and grand beyond description. It was at this meeting that my son, who afterward became a minister, joined the Church. He was a lad but ten years of age; while the call was being made for volunteers, he stood back in the congregation, leaning against a tree, weeping. One of the ministers on the platform saw him, and conjecturing his feelings, approached. "Bub, do you want to join the Church? If you do, you may." And without waiting for an answer, he gathered the child up in his strong arms, and pressing him to his great warm heart, he literally carried him into the visible fold of Christ.

The camp-meeting which closed the second year on that circuit was held in the neighborhood of Logan, and about one mile from the falls of Hockhocking. It, like the other, was a powerful meeting. As the circuit was this year attached to Marietta district, Rev. John Ferree, presiding elder, was present during part of the meeting, preaching with his usual unction on such occasions. Rev. David Lewis was again with us doing efficient service, but as the meeting was distant from any other pastoral charge, we had but few ministerial visitors, and myself and colleague had to perform a good deal of the pulpit labor. I was much blessed preaching on Sabbath night on "Surely I come quickly."

As the time drew near for me to leave this circuit I found that the bands that bound me to the dear people of my charge were very strong. They had given me a warm welcome and hearty co-operation, and the most liberal support that I had ever received. I received this year two hundred and forty dollars, which was forty dollars more than I had received on any other charge.

At that time Adelphi circuit was blessed with a very able and efficient corps of local preachers. Among them I would mention the venerable Jesse Cartlich, a good man, possessing a large fund of useful knowledge, and a rare facility in communicating in a most interesting way that knowledge, either in the social circle or the pulpit. Four of his sons became preachers, two of whom, Abraham and Isaac, served the Church as acceptable members of the Conference. Rev. David Dutcher had been a man of popularity and power in the regular work. While he performed the labors of a circuit, one of his sons took charge of home interests and supported the family. The sudden death of that son by accident had necessitated the location of brother Dutcher. But while local in form he itinerated in fact much and very usefully to the Church. Brother Solomon Redfern was a useful local preacher, and gave a son to the traveling ministry, of whom much was anticipated, but the Master soon called him to the rest above. Of brother Monett I have already spoken. He was a minister highly esteemed by all who knew him, and was blessed of God with a model family. His descendants have inherited his spirit, and some of them are known among the excellent of the Church. Before the close of my time on the circuit, he removed with his family to Marion, where he made fortunate investments in lands. Rev. Nathan Brown, venerable for years and prized for his moral worth, was still abundant in every good word and work. He also gave two sons to the ministry, John, long a valuable member of the Ohio Conference, and Henry, who was an acceptable local preacher on this circuit. There, too, were brothers Rodgers and Starling living at Tarleton, both doing good service as local preachers. We had a working class of exhorters, too, whose names appear in the "plan" of the circuit, several of whom afterward became preachers. The Cartliches, and Dressbacks, and Fates are all deserving of honorable mention. We had an able board of stewards. Will, Patterson, Johnson, Gordon, Binkley, Bright, and Rice were men devoted to the cause of God and Methodism. The recording steward, brother George Will, was a man of remarkable executive talent. I have seldom known his equal in efficiency as a steward, and it was to me a source of profound grief when, under temptation, he withdrew from the Methodist Episcopal Church. But he afterward united with another branch of the Church. I hope to meet him and many of his excellent family where there are no partition walls and no tempter.

I will close this chapter with a reference to the session of the Conference which occurred at Springfield, Ohio, August 19, 1835, at which Bishop Andrew presided. I should have mentioned it sooner, as it was from this Conference that I was returned to the circuit for the second year.

Among the matters of interest at this session was the visit of Rev. H. B. Bascom. He had started in the Ohio Conference, but for many years had been absent from us, laboring in other parts of the work. He now appeared among us like a blazing meteor, and electrified the Conference and audience with his amazing eloquence. His sermon on Sabbath from the Scripture, "The law shall go forth from Jerusalem," etc., brought the audience to their feet, and held them spell-bound during the delivery of the discourse.

We received on probation the following persons: Silas H. Chase, Wm. T. Hand, Werter R. Davis, William Metcalf, Andrew Carroll, Rufus F. Blood, Augustine M. Alexander, Thomas Barkdull, John O. Conway, Larmon Chatfield, William Nast, Uriah Heath, Joseph A. Morris, John Blanpied, Jehiel Porter, Thomas Hesson, John H. Pitezel, Washington Jackson, Solomon Howard, Harvey Sweney, Abraham Buckles, John W. Young, Thomas Dunn, Wesley J. Wells, John Quigley, Henry Wharton, Jonathan Anthony, James Hooper, David Gray, Osborn Monett, Michael G. Perkhiser, Lewis Smith, John Reed, Martin

P. Kellogg, James Frees, Stephen F. Conrey, Robert Triggs—37.

On this roll are the names of men who were destined to be giants in our Israel, and whose names will be handed down through all the history of the Church as men greatly gifted and honored of God.

When the Committee on Obituaries came to read their report, it appeared that the great Head of the Church had called from labor to rest and reward some of the most princely and saintly men of our Conference. Philip Gatch, William Page, and Russel Bigelow, had accomplished their ministry and gone up on high. Brother Gatch commenced itinerating in 1773, and had done the work not only of a pioneer, but of a hero, and had almost been honored with the crown of a martyr. He settled near Cincinnati in 1798, and from that time until the 28th of December, 1835, the time of his death, he labored as an itinerant local preacher. He did much work and did it well.

Brother Page was born in Monmouth county, East Jersey, September 2, 1772; joined the traveling connection in the city of Philadelphia at a Conference held in 1793. In 1814, having previously located, he removed to Ohio and settled in Adams county. He re-entered the traveling connection in 1820. He was a valuable and esteemed minister of the Gospel, and after a long and useful ministry died peacefully November 15, 1834.

I have spoken of that peerless man, Rev. Russel Bigelow, at length in another part of this narrative.

We elected the following brethren as delegates to General Conference: Thomas A. Morris, Jacob Young, David Young, W. H. Raper, Leroy Swormstedt, John Ferree, J. B. Finley, W. B. Christie, James Quinn, J. F. Wright, A. Eddy, J. H. Power.

CHAPTER XX.

ATHENS CIRCUIT, OHIO.

1836-38.

THE Conference met at Chillicothe, September 28, 1836, Bishop Soule presiding. The following persons were admitted on trial: Daniel Wainwright, John Steele, O. C. Shelton, George Fate, Maxwell P. Gaddis, William H. Fyffe, James Brooks, Jeremiah Hill, John Hasty, David Kinnear, John W. Stone, Joseph Gassner, Mighill Dustin, Evan Stevenson, Martin Wolf, William R. Anderson, Justus Brewer, Ancil Brooks, Jos. W. Smith—19—not as large a class as the one received a year ago, but the list contains some valuable and well-known names.

We recorded the name of one dear brother, William Philips, as having died August 4th, 1836. During the few years he had belonged to the Conference, he had exhibited a diversity and strength of talent which inspired the Church with great hope. In the pulpit or the editorial sanctum he was equally at home. His work exposing the errors of Campbellism gave proof of his ability in the department of polemical divinity. His death was a great loss to our Conference.

From this Conference I had my appointment to Athens circuit, with Rev. J. Ferree for my presiding elder, and Rev. Mighill Dustin for my assistant. Brother Dustin was a devoted and faithful itinerant worker, and rapidly gained the confidence and affections of the people. He was a man strong in his convictions and uncompromising in the maintenance of what he regarded as right and duty. He has been gradually rising in,influence in the Church ever since that time, and now occupies a high position among his brethren in the Cincinnati Conference.

I experienced mingled emotions when my appointment was announced. I was both pleased and embarrassed— pleased to return to my home and worship with my parents and former associates, embarrassed in view of the responsibility of becoming the pastor and teacher of those who had been my teachers, and who had known me from my childhood. During the twenty years that I had been in the itinerant work, I was accustomed to visit home usually as often as once a year, and had so kept up acquaintance with the people generally. They had continued to call me familiarly "John," and among them I always regarded myself as a boy. My parents and my wife's parents were all living, and the associates of my boyhood were there. So soon as I reached the circuit, however, the people gave me such a kind and hearty welcome that my embarrassment soon left me, and I spent two years on the circuit, which were among the most pleasant and successful, in some respects, of my ministry.

At that time Athens circuit embraced twenty-six appointments and had nearly eight hundred members. Its quarterly conference was composed of able and valuable men, such as Hon. Calvary Morris—brother to Bishop Morris— J. Reynolds, A. Cooley, Jonas Smith, Enos Thompson, Stephen Pilcher, John Minton, George Bean, John Walker, Isaac Humphrey, Elijah Pilcher. They received me as God's messenger, and gave me cordial moral and material support.

For a brief sketch of the founding of Methodism within the bounds of this circuit, the reader is referred to the first chapter in the narrative. The name of the circuit and its boundaries had been changed from time to time. At the time of which I now write, it extended along the Hockhocking a distance of forty miles, from Meeker's Bottom to the mouth of the river. The preaching-places were as follows: 1. Daniel Stewart's; 2. Elmore Rowel's; 3. Mouth of Hocking; 4. Coolville; 5. Bethel; 6. Lotridge's; 7. Frost's; 8. Denmore's; 9. Veit's; 10. McCulm's; 11. Gates's; 12. Center Stake; 13. Woodyard's; 14. Dickson's; 15. Runion's; 16. Harris's; 17. Walburn's; 18. Bolen's; 19. Leetown; 20. Minton's; 21. Reynolds's; 22. Wolf's Plains; 23. Ross's; 24. Athens; 25. Canaan; 26. Harrison Long's. These twenty-six appointments were regularly filled by each of the preachers every four weeks, thus securing regular circuit preaching to each society every two weeks. Then we had a noble band of local preachers and exhorters, who supplemented our labor so as to secure service every week to the most important points. I hardly dare commence putting the names of the excellent spirits of that circuit on the record, because while it will be impracticable to transfer the whole roll, I may seem to be partial in my selection. I will mention a few as a sample of the many: Justus, Isaac, and Eli Reynolds were brothers and men of Christian influence; two of them were local preachers of respectable talents and efficiency. Then there were the Cooleys— Simeon, Asahel, Caleb, and Herman—all men and Christians of the first order. Asahel was one of the most excellent exhorters. John Minton was a man of great power in exhortation. He was listened to with profound interest, and hundreds of slumbering consciences have been thoroughly aroused by his thundering appeals.

The Conference met September 27, 1837, at Xenia, Ohio. Bishops Hedding and Soule presided. One of our preachers, Gilbert, was convicted of immorality and expelled.

We received on probation William Parish, Solomon Howard, David Smith, Ebenezer Owen, James L. Grover, John Fitch, Alfred Hance, Matthew Scovel, Madison Hansley, Jesse M'Mahon, Andrew Murphy, Richard Doughty, George W. Bowers, Jonathan F. Conrey, Jedediah Foster, Jonathan Anthony, Calvin W. Lewis, Benedict Hutchinson, Elijah V. Bing, Luman H. Allen, Randolph S. Foster, Thomas Chesnut, Joseph S. Brown, John Kiger, John W. Weakley—25—a good class, furnishing material for all the departments of ministerial labor. From it have been taken men to preside over important stations, and districts, and institutions of learning, and it may yet have its representation in the Board of Bishops.

We this year recorded the death of Rev. John A. Waterman and Erastus Felton. Brother Waterman was one of our ablest ministers. He was licensed to preach at Athens, O., and joined the Conference in 1814. When the Pittsburg Conference was organized he fell into it, where he traveled until 1832, when he was transferred back to the Ohio Conference. He was one of the ablest metaphysicians, and obtained the rank of a first-class pulpit orator. He died peacefully at Oxford, O., August 6, 1836.

Brother Felton entered the Conference in 1829, and died on Roscoe circuit, June 25, 1837. He was a preacher of great zeal and fidelity. He professed, illustrated in his life, and preached to the people the doctrine of perfect love. Death found him fully prepared, and when he heard the call he mounted the chariot and ascended to his mansion home on high.

In accordance with my preference and the desire of the charge, I was returned to Athens circuit. Rev. Samuel Hamilton succeeded brother Ferree as presiding elder. I loved them both. Brother Hamilton and myself had volunteered in 1819, as heretofore narrated, for Western mission-

17

ary work together, and by long acquaintance and sympathy, were closely united to each other. He was a man of more popular pulpit power than brother Ferree, but they both had the power of reaching the human heart. The influence of the Gospel, as preached by brother Ferree, came gently as the dew; but it continued to come until the minute particles accumulated into dewdrops, and every spear of grass, and bud, and flower, and leaflet, bowed its head with its burden of tears. When Hamilton became fully aroused in a sermon, his burning words and glowing imagery swayed the audience with wondrous power. He, too, had his melting moods. Thousands who have enjoyed his ministry, remember his sermon on the "prodigal son." When the young man began to contemplate a return home, he wrote to his father. And then the preacher represented the father's anxiety about his absent profligate son. The father receives at the hand of a messenger a letter—the preacher takes up a letter—opens it, puts on his spectacles, and commences reading. His heart is moved with the penitence of his unhappy boy. Glancing over the spectacles, he looks down the lane and sees an object approaching; it is a man— familiar in his movements—is it not my son? He starts; they meet and embrace. The whole scene passed before the audience so natural and life-like, that the result was overwhelming.

My colleagues this year were Rev. W. R. Anderson and Matthew Scovel. The former, a young man of rare promise, shone as a bright light for the few years that he stood on the walls of Zion, but he was transferred early to the paradise of God. Brother Scovel was subject to seasons of great depression, indicating a tendency to mental disease, but he was a man of sterling piety and worth, and commanded the sympathy and respect of the people. He retired from the regular work after a few years.

The principal importance of Athens was found in the fact that the State had founded a University at that place. As a perpetual endowment for the support of this institution two townships of land were set apart and called college lands. These lands were to be appraised and then leased; the lessees were to pay six per cent. on the valuation, and that was the revenue to belong to the University. Deacon Wyatt, John Brown, and Daniel Stewart were appointed by the Legislature to appraise the lands, which they did. As the lands were occupied the revenue developed, and the school extended its reputation and efficiency. Able men have had charge of the institution, such as Jacob Lindley, Dr. Wilson, Dr. M'Guffey, and Dr. Sol. Howard. Hundreds have been educated there who have proved to be valuable workers in the different honorable departments of life. Some have attained to eminence. Among its early graduates was Thomas Ewing. He was a poor boy; paid for his board at first as an errand boy; then alternated between the salt-works of Virginia and the school, working awhile, and then going to college until his money was gone. "Tom, the Salt-boiler," was afterward, when he appealed to the people for their suffrages, a soubriquet that gave him great popularity. Whether as a lawyer, a judge, a senator, or member of the President's cabinet, he was eminent in every position. In after years, one looking at his aristocratic residence and surroundings, would hardly believe that he commenced his career in the obscurity of poverty, reading on the cabin floor by the light of the blazing fire. But such is the genius of our country, and such the aids that it extends to its youth, the child of poverty may climb to sit among princes and presidents. In the ministry of our Church, Rev. E. R. Ames, now one of the Bishops; Joseph M. Trimble, D. D., late Assistant Secretary of the Missionary Society of the Methodist Episcopal Church, and who has faithfully and honorably served the Church in the various relations of Professor of Mathematics in Augusta College, Kentucky, pastor of the most important city churches, and presiding elder for many years; Rev. E. W. Sehon, for many years an eloquent and favorite preacher in the Ohio Conference, and for years past among the leading ministers of the Methodist Episcopal Church South; Rev. William Herr, for a long time one of the agents of the American Bible Society; Rev. Homer J. Clark, for a long time editor of the Pittsburg Advocate, and President of Alleghany College at Meadville, Penn., and a long list of valuable men came forth from the halls of the Ohio University at Athens.

At the time that I traveled Athens circuit, Dr. Wilson was President, Rev. Dr. Daniel Reed and Dr. Ryors were professors, and Dr. Andrews had charge of the preparatory department, and Rev. M. Marvin of the English grammar school. For many years the University was under the control of the Old School Presbyterian Church, and served all the purposes to them of a denominational school. After the Methodist Episcopal Church had founded the Ohio Wesleyan University at Delaware, and demonstrated the success of the enterprise, it was suggested by some not satisfied with the management of the State institution at Athens, that it would be advantaged by getting the Methodist Episcopal Church in some way more closely allied to it. Leonidas Jewett, Esq., and others began to agitate the matter, and my son, Rev. W. F. Stewart, stationed in Athens at that time, interested himself, and nominated as suitable persons for professorships Rev. Dr. Joseph S. Tomlinson, and Professor J. G. Blair, and brother O. M. Spencer. The Legislature elected some new trustees favorable to the influence of the Methodist Episcopal Church; the board sent up a formal request to the Ohio Conference at its session in

Zanesville, to extend its patronage to the institution. Thus the University became entirely friendly to the Methodist Episcopal Church. Afterward, Solomon Howard, D. D., a scholar of great moral and ministerial worth, whom I had the honor of welcoming to the Methodist Episcopal Church when traveling the Miami Circuit, was made President and practical manager of the institution.

CHAPTER XXI.

FELICITY CIRCUIT, OHIO.

1838-39.

THE Conference met at Columbus, Ohio, September 26, 1838, Bishop Waugh presiding. We received on trial the following persons: Peter Schmucker, John Miley, Andrew Irvin, A. B. Wambaugh, Jeremiah B. Ellsworth, Samuel Maddux, Samuel Bateman, O. P. Williams, Joseph Baringer, Isaac N. Baird, Juba Estabrook, and Isaac Cartlich—12—a small but good class.

James W. Finley had died during the year. He was the son of Rev. John P. Finley; had entered the traveling connection when about twenty-one years old, and had traveled usefully about nine years, when he was summoned to pass over the river. He was a young man of much promise, and left the example of a Christian life and a triumphant death. On the 11th of June, 1838, he expired, with exclamations of "Glory! glory!" upon his lips.

I had spent my full constitutional term on Athens circuit. My sons, John Wesley and William Fletcher, had commenced a course of education in the University, and I was anxious to be appointed to some charge where they could prosecute their studies without interruption. With this in view, I had an interview with Bishop Waugh, and requested that he would either transfer me to the Kentucky Conference, or give me an appointment as near as might be to Augusta College. He promised to consult with his cabinet, and make such arrangement as they should recommend. The result was I was sent to Felicity circuit as second preacher. Rev. William B. Christie was my presiding elder, and Rev. E. B. Chase, preacher in charge. The arrangement suited me well. I was relieved from the responsibility of the administration of discipline, and was near enough to my family to spend part of my time at home. I moved my goods one hundred and twenty miles, from Athens, Ohio, to Augusta, Kentucky, with wagons, and my family in my private conveyance; bought a house on the banks of the Ohio River, in Augusta, and got my family comfortably settled as soon as possible after Conference. My two sons entered college, and my two daughters entered the Female Seminary. I seemed about to realize my hopes in regard to the education of my children, but, alas! I little knew what trying scenes I should pass through during my short sojourn on the shores of the Ohio River.

Augusta College was then in its meridian popularity. Rev. Joseph S. Tomlinson, D. D., was the President. He was a man of extensive and varied scholarship, and a popular pulpit orator. Rev. H. B. Bascom was Professor of Moral Science and Belles Lettres. He stood peerless as a pulpit orator at that time, and, attracted by his national fame, the young men of wealthy and ambitious families came from distant States to be under his care. Rev. Joseph M. Trimble, son of Governor Trimble, of Ohio, was Professor of Mathematics, and abundant in labors, and exceedingly popular as a preacher of the Gospel. Rev. Burr H. M'Cown was Professor of Languages, and though not equal to his colleagues in pulpit power and popularity, he was an excellent preacher, a very competent teacher, and in every sense of the word a Christian gentleman. Rev. Josiah L. Kemp had charge of the preparatory department. The halls were well crowded. The reputation of the College at home and abroad was such as to be creditable to the denomination. Unfortunately the College was founded on the wrong side of the Ohio River—on slave instead of free soil. Had it been otherwise, perhaps to-day, instead of its blackened walls being desolate and forsaken, it might have been taking rank with the oldest and best institutions of the land. But it did a noble work in its day, and the labors of its illustrious line of professors, Ruter, and Durbin, and Fielding, and Finley, and Tomlinson, and Bascom, and Trimble, and M'Cown, and Johnson, and Elliott, and others, have not been in vain. It more than repaid to the Church and the country all that was expended upon it. In the ministry of our own Church we have its Foster, and Boring, and Smith, and Locke, and Fee, and Chalfant, and Lyda, and Stewart. Some of the superior lights of former days, such as Christie and Kavanaugh, were from its classes, and in all departments of honorable life it has its honorable representatives. It may be said of old Augusta College, though dead, it speaketh yet.

The appointments on the Felicity circuit were as follows: 1. Felicity; 2. Concord; 3. Childs; 4. Neville; 5. Moscow; 6. Buckhannon's; 7. Calvary; 8. Fred's; 9. Bethel; 10. Clover; 11. Rounds; 12. Hamersville; 13. Leming's; 14. Foor's; 15. Higginsport; 16. Yates's; 17. Mt. Zion; 18. Wesley Chapel; and 19. Goodwin's—in all nineteen appointments. The membership was one thousand five hundred and thirty-nine, it being one of the strongest circuits, numerically and otherwise, in the Conference. It had long been known by the name of Whitoak circuit, and after this year returned to its old name.

My colleague, Rev. E. B. Chase, was a very efficient man, efficient in many departments; he excelled in singing, prayer, exhortation and preaching, and he worked well to the pastoral and business interests of the charge. It was a great satisfaction to me to see the charge of the work in such competent and faithful hands. There were several men on this charge, both ministers and laymen, whose names already have an honorable place in the history of the Church and country. Hon. David Fisher had emerged from obscurity through the religion of the Lord Jesus and the Methodist Episcopal Church. He developed a giant mind, and whether in theological discussion with Kidwell, or in political discussion with his opponents on the stump, or in the halls of Congress, he proved himself a great and a true man.

Holly Raper, brother to Rev. W. H. Raper, was an influential layman, filling with dignity and popularity places both in Church and State to which his fellow-citizens and the authorities of the Church had called him.

John Patterson, living on the hill near Higginsport, was an original character and a very good man. He used to relate with deep feeling his checkered experience at home with his family. His wife for years was not in sympathy with his religion, and for some time made active and persistent endeavors to annoy him and so induce him to abandon his religion. When he would commence his family prayers, she would mix with the sound of his voice the clang and rattle of chairs, and pots, and dishes. He endured it with great fortitude until patience seemed to promise no victory. He changed suddenly his tactics, and commenced praying earnestly that God would convert his wife, or if she would not be converted, to kill her and take her out of the way. She heard the prayer with dismay, and could hardly believe her own ears. But clear and distinct as a man would converse with his friend, he still pleaded, "O God, convert her or kill her." The prayer was answered. She was seized with a sudden sickness, and then she began to call lustily for mercy. Her husband prayed for her.

She was at last powerfully converted, shouted the high praises of God, and ever after proved to be a faithful Christian, and seemed to enjoy it to hear her husband tell in love-feast how grace had triumphed.

He was an eccentric, good man, and many were the incidents that were current in regard to his singular exercise. He was connected with the founding of the Methodist Episcopal Church at Augusta, Ky. It seems that while he was living at Augusta, working at his trade, in his early life, he went off to attend a camp-meeting and was greatly blessed. He requested one of the preachers to send an appointment by him to preach in Augusta. The preacher consented, and Patterson came home and published the appointment. A short time before the preacher came, Patterson went to James Armstrong, a merchant in the place, and said to him, "Mr. Armstrong, the Lord sent me to tell you that a Methodist preacher is to preach here, and that you are to go and hear him and join the Church." Armstrong was thunderstruck, but when the day came he went, and heard, and joined. The result was the organization of a class and the establishment of a preaching appointment at Augusta. Sometime after this James Armstrong put his head into the door of Patterson's shop and said, "John, the Lord sent me to tell you to go down street, and gather all the men you can find and meet me at"—a point that he mentioned, on the banks of the Ohio, in the upper part of the village. John, without gainsaying, did as he was requested, and soon had the available male force of the village at the spot designated. "Now," said Armstrong, addressing them, "I intend that a house shall be built for the Lord on this spot, and I want you to help me prepare for the foundation." They went at it with a will, and a neat brick church rose on that spot which served the people for more than a quarter of a century, and where, in after years, Durbin, and Bascom, and Tomlinson made some of their mightiest efforts, and where scores of students found mercy in the blood of Jesus.

After brother Patterson had settled on the hill near Higginsport, he became interested for the building of a church in that village. One day, putting on his coat and taking his ax, he said, "Boys, get your axes and come with me." The boys did as directed, and followed their father into the forest, wondering. After fixing his eye upon a tree that would make a beautiful stick of building-timber, he laid his ax at its root and kneeled down. He told the Lord that if he would promise him to convert some of his neighbors in it, he would build him a house in Higginsport. The Lord promised, and he and the boys went to work. With what assistance the people were disposed to give, he pressed the work to its completion. The Lord redeemed his promise the first meeting that was held in it. Good brother Patterson was satisfied, and often assured the wondering people not to be alarmed at him, for he was "compos mentis," and felt as if he could "rake the stars and kick the planets." I might fill many pages with anecdotes of this kind, but let these suffice. He commanded the respect and confidence of the people widely, and did much good in his day and generation.

CHAPTER XXII.

GEORGETOWN CIRCUIT, OHIO.

1839-40.

SEPTEMBER 18, 1839, the Conference met at Cincinnati, Bishop Soule presiding. The following persons were admitted on trial: A. W. Musgrove, John Barton, Edward Williams, Lorenzo D. Huston, Thomas Hurd, James H. M'Cutchen, Lovell F. Harris, Luther M'Vey, William Hays, Thomas Perkins, William M. D. Ryan, James T. Holliday, John Longman, Jacob G. Dimmitt, Noah Hough—a small class, some of whom have since been heard from in important positions in the Church.

Death had been making unusual ravages in our ranks during the past year. No less than five of our traveling preachers had passed to their long home; namely, Frederick B. Butler, Dudley Woodbridge, William D. Barrett, Moses Crume, George Fate.

Brother Butler was born in Prince George county, Va., July 22, 1803; joined the Ohio Conference in 1827, and fell asleep in Jesus March 5, 1839. He was an earnest advocate of the doctrine of holiness, and feeling its power in his own soul, his ministry was abundantly successful. To a friend who visited him near his end, he said, "My body is fast sinking and will soon be housed in the tomb; but as it respects the state of my mind, all seems to be about right. My faith is the same, my hope is the same, my love is the same. My prospect is clear, and whether you see me die or not, you may know that when I am gone all is well."

Brother Woodbridge was born in Marietta, O., and educated at the Ohio University, at Athens. Some time previous to his graduation, and during the memorable revival under the labors of brothers Farnandis and Spencer, he was converted and united with the Methodist Episcopal Church. He joined the Ohio Conference in the Fall of 1834, and died January 3, 1839. He was a young man of remarkable amiability, of spirit, and life. Talented, cultivated, and having come to us to give his life to the trials of the itinerancy, although his worldly prospects would have been much brighter in the denomination with which his parents were connected, he had found a warm place in our affections. That affection had constantly increased as we marked his singleness of aim and his great success in the work of the Lord. Though thirty years have passed since that young man was called from us, yet his memory in all that country where he was known is still as ointment poured forth.

Brother Barrett was of one of the pioneer Methodist families in Virginia. He became a traveling preacher in connection with the Virginia Conference in 1817. After traveling some years he located, emigrated to Ohio, and afterward, in the year 1830, joined the Ohio Conference, where he traveled until his death, which occurred February 22, 1839. He was an earnest and successful preacher, and pushed the battle to the very gate. He had just prepared to start to an appointment, when arrested with an attack that brought him down to the grave. He ceased at once to work and live.

I was associated with brother Crume when I traveled the Oxford circuit, as he was a superannuated preacher, residing there at that time. Having spoken of him in my narrative there, I will only repeat here my high appreciation of him as a man and minister of the Gospel. He lived to purpose, and, I doubt not, many will rise up in the great day to claim him as their spiritual father. He was converted in 1785 and died in 1839, having served God and his generation nearly half a century.

Brother Fate was born in Perry county, O., about the year 1808, and died August 28, 1839. He was admitted to the Ohio Conference on trial, at Chillicothe, in 1836. He had a good revival on his first charge, and completed the work the Master had for him to do on the second charge to which he was appointed. With almost his dying breath he exclaimed, "O, there is a great fullness in Christ."

Thus the great Head of the Church calls home the workmen—the gray-haired veteran, who has outlived his generation and labored until bowed beneath the weight of years, and the young man in his prime and strength. But while he calls his workmen home, he carries on his work.

We elected the following brethren as delegates to General Conference: W. H. Raper, W. B. Christie, J. Young, S. Hamilton, G. W. Walker, L. L. Hamline, J. F. Wright, and R. O. Spencer.

I was appointed to Georgetown circuit, with Rev. Jacob G. Dimmitt for my assistant. It would have been agreeable to me to remain another year on the former charge, but the Bishop had a little more difficult work which he desired me to do. So far as convenience of travel was concerned, Georgetown suited me about as well as Felicity. The only drawback and the circumstance that inclined me to shrink from going to Georgetown circuit, was that its last preacher in charge, Rev. Reuben Plummer, had been convicted of immoral conduct and expelled from the Church. A sad event of that kind never fails to bring disgrace on the Church and cause the people to look with suspicion upon other ministers of the Gospel for a time. The Bishop and his counsel selected me as the proper person to fill the gap, and I went to the work without murmuring. I had the utmost confidence in Rev. W. B. Christie, my presiding elder, and soon found that the Bishop had favored me with a most excellent fellow-worker in my colleague. He was a man who combined dignity, gracefulness, humility, eloquence, and diligence in an unusual degree for one just starting out in the itinerant field. He grew in my estimation during the whole year, and as I have watched his record now for thirty years, he has fully met the large expectations that I formed of him during that year.

As my family was located in our own house at Augusta, we did not have to move, so that I was at my work immediately after the adjournment of Conference. We had a membership of eight hundred and forty-six, distributed among the following nineteen appointments; namely, Georgetown, New Hope, Ross's, Taggart's, M'Quittie's, Newmarket, Sugar Ridge, Sloan's, Niven's, Collins's, Winchester, Davidson's, Davis's, Jennings's, Russelville, Ashridge, Moore's, and Fincastle. The people received us very kindly and co-operated with us heartily. If the people looked upon us with any suspicion, growing out of the misdoing of my predecessor, they concealed it from us, so that we did not realize embarrassment from that source as we had feared. We held protracted meetings in different parts of the circuit with much success. Many were converted and added to the Church, and the year was crowned with very cheering success.

At the close of this year we held a camp-meeting, which was made a blessing to many. In addition to the preachers of the circuit, we enjoyed the help of brothers Estill, Wharton, and Perkhiser. The last mentioned brother preached a sermon which made a deep and lasting impression on a multitude of hearts, from these words: "If I regard iniquity in my heart," etc.

Several valuable preachers have been raised up from this circuit, some of whom I have already referred to, and others of whom shall have honorable mention as we advance in the narrative.

The Conference met at Zanesville, Ohio, September 30, 1840, Bishop Hedding presiding. The following persons were admitted on trial: Isaac Elbert, Asbury Lowrey, Homer S. Thrall, George G. West, Joseph A. Bruner, Samuel Black, Addison Hite, James W. Southard, George Gonzales, John M. Howland, William O'Connor, Richard A. Arthur, John Dillon, jr., Joseph Brooks, John W. De Vilbiss, George A. Breunig—16.

Several of these in after time became tinctured with the leaven of slavery, and were finally swallowed up in the maelstrom of secession. But others stood true as steel to their Mother Church, and are now bright ornaments and influential laborers in her ranks. Some of them fought the battles of the Church bravely by my side in the mountains of Virginia, as the future of this narrative will show.

At this Conference we made a record of the death of two of our number; namely, Charles R. Baldwin and Jeremiah Hill. Brother Baldwin was born in Stockbridge, Mass., March 17, 1803, and died at Parkersburg, Va., November 9, 1839. Highly favored with such family connections, mental qualifications, and professional prospects as prophesied a brilliant future for him, he, nevertheless, counted all loss for Christ; and when he experienced the converting grace of God, he abandoned the law and devoted himself to the Gospel. He joined the Ohio Conference in 1834, and from that time until his decease his labors were in Western Virginia. His last charge was Parkersburg, where he not only performed the duties of preacher and pastor, but took charge of a seminary located at that place under the patronage of our Church. He labored successfully, but sank under the overburden of responsibility. He lived in a holy atmosphere and died in sight of heaven. He had enjoyed the blessing of sanctification for some six years, and from the very borders of the other world sent to his brethren this inspiring message: "Tell the preachers of the Ohio Conference that the blessing of sanctification which I have enjoyed and preached to others now sustains me in death."

Brother Hill was born in the city of Providence, R. I., October 2, 1816, and died on Marion circuit, May 17, 1840. He was a faithful Methodist preacher, and died with the harness on. When informed by the physician that he must die, he calmly replied, "I am ready;" made arrangements regarding his funeral, etc., and then made the room vocal with his note of triumph as he anticipated the crown that glittered in his sight.

I was re-appointed to Georgetown circuit with Rev. Jonathan F. Conrey as my assistant, and Rev. William H. Raper for my presiding elder. I would gladly have retained both the elder and colleague of the former year, as they were greatly endeared to me and the people; but my new associates were excellent men, and were soon fully established in the affections of the people. Brother Conrey was a young man full of laudable ambition, and worked well and earnestly. Our ever-active Baptist friends agitated the public mind with their peculiar notions, until I found it necessary for the peace of our own Zion, that the question of baptism should be thoroughly discussed. The appointments fixed upon where these discourses should be delivered were "Nivens's," "Georgetown," and "Higginsport." As soon as the announcements were made there was an excitement. The Baptist friends sent for Rev. John Moore, their champion, to come to the rescue. He came and delivered himself on the subject, greatly to the comfort of his people, before the time of my appointments arrived. At my first appointment I was invited to occupy the Presbyterian church in the neighboring village, that there might be accommodations for the crowd that was expected. The house was crowded, and among those present were several Baptist preachers, prepared to take notes of my discourse. As I ascended the pulpit and looked upon the vast throng, a tremor ran over me, and I was not sure that my courage would be equal to the occasion. In spite of my best endeavors, my voice trembled somewhat when I began to speak, but in a few minutes I lost all feeling of timidity, and had remarkable freedom in the presentation of the subject. I had the profound attention of the whole audience, and the assurance that the arguments that I was presenting were establishing in the minds of the people a conviction of the truth of my main propositions. I received the hearty congratulations of my friends, who expressed the opinion that the eloquent sophistry of the Baptist champion had not only been neutralized, but that those who had been undecided were now convinced that, first, believing penitents and infants have a right to membership in Christ's Church and to baptism; and, second, that sprinkling and pouring are modes of baptism as well sustained by Scripture and reason as immersion. The next discourse was delivered at Georgetown. There, too, the audience was very large, composed of representatives of all the Churches; and here again I was highly complimented by my friends on the success of the discourse. The last discussion was at Higginsport. Here the Campbellite wing of the Baptist notions became much excited, and occasionally boiled over as I poured out hot shot upon their strongholds. I had abundant reason to think that these discussions were promotive of great good. Though the immersionists kept up a constant fire for some time, the people now had their eyes fully opened, and would not swallow the flimsy sophistries which aforetime had distracted them.

Near the close of the year we held another camp-meeting, which was attended with much good. The rowdies made some demonstrations, much to the annoyance of my excellent presiding elder, brother Raper. He was a man of very tender sensibilities and a high sense of honor. I shall never forget an appeal he made one day to that class of men. He showed them how unmanly, and unpatriotic, and mean such conduct was. He assured them that in 1812 he had gone forth to defend the rights of his country at the hazard of his life, and as he loved the Church of Jesus Christ even more than he did his country, he felt very much like showing such men that he could vindicate the cause of Christ against assailants with as much courage and as good conscience as he had fought the British.

This year was one of great affliction to me, and yet one of great spiritual comfort and profit. Our Heavenly Father saw fit to lead us through deep waters and fiery trials, and I never more fully tested the faithfulness and preciousness of his promises than this year. On the 25th of December of this year my venerable mother departed this life, in Athens, Ohio, at the age of sixty-seven years. Her life had been one of toil and usefulness, true to the Church of her choice and devoted to her children. I felt that I had sustained an irreparable loss, but was comforted with the assurance that I should meet her again.

During the following Spring our two daugters, Sarah Jane and Ruth Eliza, while students in the Female Seminary at Augusta, contracted colds from which they never recovered. For a time the physicians encouraged us that as soon as the weather should become warm and settled they would be able to throw off disease. The warm sunbeams and showers clothed the earth in beauty, but though buds and blossoms decked garden, and hill, and valley, the Autumn winds and frosts were doing their sad work with these lovely flowers of our family. Their disease baffled the skill of the physicians. At last the confidence of the physicians gave way, and they communicated to us their fears. Deep gloom gathered for a time about my spirit. I went to God for help, for I felt that vain is the help of man. He heard my cry and came to my assistance. He did not see fit to deliver us from the affliction, but he gave us grace to submit the case to his disposal, and to trust him that he would do right. But as day by day marked the slow, steady, sure progress of fatal disease, we were filled with anxiety and suspense. The girls themselves were the most composed and happy of us all. They fully realized their situation, and talked intelligently and familiarly concerning their approaching decease. On the seventh day of May the most beautiful month of the year, the clouds overcast the sky; it was a dark and rainy day. On that day our youngest daughter, then aged nine years, fell asleep in Jesus. O, how desolate our home appeared! And now the thought of burying her in a slave State, and then returning to Ohio, where we could but seldom have even the sad privilege of visiting her grave, distressed us. Added to this the thought of placing her remains, to us so lovely and so dear, in a cold and wet grave, was almost insupportable. We went again to God, and he tempered the winds and the waves so that we should not be crushed.

The next day the clouds were all gone, the sun rose in grandeur and beauty, and when we stood by the grave and looked down into it, I thought that I had never seen so beautiful a grave in all my life. We laid the lovely dust of our dear child there, to remain until the morning of the resurrection. From the grave we returned to our home to minister to the other daughter, who was evidently following her sister. While there is life there is hope, and we inquired, Is there any thing that we can do that will be blessed of God in sparing to us this dear child? The thought suggested itself to us that a change of air and scenery might do her good. The physicians encouraged the experiment. We shut up our now desolate home, crossed the Ohio River, and were soon in the midst of the dear sympathizing people of my charge. Never shall I forget or cease to be grateful for the great kindness of that people in the time of our deep affliction. This change and exercise for a time seemed to brace her up; and we were full of hope and cheerfulness. Then again the symptoms changed for the worse; and when we were at Newmarket, forty miles from home, she commenced sinking so rapidly that hope again fled. Every body seemed to be interested for us. Dr. Boyd volunteered his service, and sat anxiously by her side, to afford whatever professional relief he could ; the keeper of the village hotel urged upon us the best accommodations of his house, and the good people were constantly coming and going, anxious to do something to assist or comfort us. Now that we gave up all hope of her getting better, I thought that I would give all my earthly prospects for the favor of getting her home alive, that she might die in the same hallowed room where her sister had died. We now made that the burden of our prayer, and God heard and granted our request. Laying her on a soft couch in the carriage, we turned our face toward home. Three days of slow and careful moving brought us within sight of our cottage home. We thanked God, and felt that we could now leave the case submissively in the hands of our Heavenly Father. We crossed the river and entered our home; it seemed now more cheerful than when we left it. The physicians were attentive and full of sympathy; the neighbors flocked in to express their gratitude that we had reached home with her alive. Lydia Haws and Jane Phares, two maiden ladies of remarkable gifts in song and prayer, and whose praise was in all the churches thereabouts, came and remained with us, watching day and night with the now rapidly sinking sufferer. Their company and sympathetic assistance was valuable to us beyond all price. Brothers T. H. Lynch, J. L. Kemp, and B. H. M'Cown, of the Faculty of the College, were very attentive. A few hours before her death, as brother Lynch retired from the room, she said, "Pa, why did you not ask brother Lynch to pray?" I called him back, and while she was bolstered up in her bed, her parents and youngest brother, and the two ladies mentioned above, gathered around her bed, while the man of God conducted our devotions. She desired that he should not pray for her recovery, as she wished to go and dwell with her sister in their Heavenly Father's house. After singing a hymn we all kneeled down to pray. Brother Lynch had access to God in prayer. The frail dying girl was leaning forward in her bed, with her emaciated face in her little delicate hands, earnestly engaged in prayer. My eyes were upon her and suffused with tears; my ears were open to hear her tremulous voice, as with increased fervency she prayed. Now she fell back, and straightening herself in her bed, a tremor passed over her frame. I reached over and touched her mother, and whispered, "Sarah Jane is dying." The prayer ceased, and we all stood around the bed, supposing that she was now crossing the river of death. Her countenance indicated that there was a struggle within; suddenly her eyes opened, and her whole countenance was lighted up with such a heavenly glow as I had never seen before in human face, and she exclaimed, "O what a lovely place! I want to be there!" She seemed to be gazing right into the glory land. After awhile a cloud passed over her countenance, and it indicated the return of that inward struggle. Soon the cloud passed off again, and her countenance beamed as before, and again she exclaimed, "O let me go? I want to go!" Turning her eyes to sister Lydia Haws she said, "Sing." "What shall we sing?" "Sing,

> "What is this that steals upon my frame?
> Is it death? Is it death?
> If this is death, I soon shall be," etc.

Sister Haws, with her sweet voice always in tune, sang, while the rest of us joined in as far as our emotions would allow. Glory seemed to fill the room, and the young, happy spirit was anxious to be released from earth and to go home, but our Heavenly Father designed that she should linger with us another day. I thought then, and I have thought ever since, had I no other evidence of the truth of the Christian religion than what was furnished in the experience of that dying Christian child, I could never doubt. During all the next day, as she lingered in weakness and pain, she gave assurance that she expected to go home at night. In the afternoon she wished to be out of the bed and on the floor with pillows, and while she changed from side to side and from place to place, no word of murmuring or complaint escaped her lips. At night she said to me, "Pa, you are tired; go up stairs and rest." "No," said I, "daughter, I would rather stay with you." She yielded, and that night, August 9th, she calmly fell asleep in Jesus. So heavenly and triumphant had been the closing scenes of her life, that while we felt we had sustained an irreparable loss, we felt, too, that our lovely daughter was now safe from storm and sin. We determined that the residue of our days should be spent more resolutely and earnestly in working for the Master and getting ready to join those who had gone before.

In a conversation with her mother a few days before her death, she had expressed her wishes in regard to her own burial and that of the remaining members of the family. She desired that her body should be buried by the side of her sister's, then in Col. Payne's cemetery, at Augusta; that if possible her brothers, when they should die, should be buried together, and that her parents should be buried in the cemetery at Oldtown, Ohio—Frankfort—where little Asbury was buried. She thought it would be pleasant in the morning of the resurrection for them to rise thus. According to her request, we laid her remains by the side of those of her sister. We had altar-shaped monuments, with suitable inscriptions, placed over their graves, and both inclosed with a neat paling. Though my fields of labor have usually been remote from that place, I have made frequent pilgrimages to their graves. Now, since my age and failing strength have compelled me to desist from the responsibilities and labor of a regular charge, I have once more made the journey of a thousand miles to meditate and pray on the spot where their ashes lie.

The college edifice, which was once crowded with ambitious young life, is now a mass of ruins. The voices of the most of those eloquent professors who taught those students are now silent in the grave. The population of the village and country had greatly changed, but as I stood there by those graves, the past came back, and I lived again in the scenes of other years. O, that I, and my companion, and my sons may be as well prepared for our end and go as peacefully and joyfully to our long home as did those young disciples of Jesus! They were respectively six and eight years of age when they gave their hearts to God and joined the Church, at the camp-meeting near

Athens, Ohio, and they were respectively nine and eleven years old when they passed through death triumphant home.

The experience of this year was calculated to make a profound impression upon our lives, and the kindness of the people of Augusta and of our charge gave them a permanent place in our memories and hearts. Among the men eminent and useful I should record the name of Rev. John Meek. He was a man of great pulpit popularity, and had been among the earliest pioneers in planting the standard of Methodism in Ohio. Rev. Daniel Hare was a large, athletic, and earnest worker for the Lord, enthusiastic as a Methodist, and always ready to exhort or preach. He gave to the ministry his son, Rev. M. H. Hare, who afterward became one of the master spirits in leading on the hosts of Methodism in Iowa. Brothers Manker, Taggart, and Ramsey were useful local preachers. Among the prominent and valuable men in the laity, I would mention brothers Gaddis, Ross, and Grant—all names identified with the history of Methodism in Ohio, and the last of which has become national, and in fact, through the fame of his honored son, has been sounded to the ends of the earth. Brother Ross has one son in the Ohio and one in the California Conference, both honoring their parents, and brother Grant has a son sitting in the presidential chair of the nation. When I used to be at brother Grant's home in Georgetown, Ulysses was a student at West Point. When he graduated, my son, W. F., applied for the vacancy, but was providentially prevented from entering the military school. The voice of God was calling him to preach, but, like Jonah, he was endeavoring to escape in some other direction.

During this year we formed the acquaintance of a local preacher, then a young man, prosecuting a literary course at Augusta College, without fortune or patronage, except his willing hands and widowed mother's prayers. He worked his way through college, graduated with honor, joined the Ohio Conference, soon took an honorable position in that body, and was afterward transferred to the Rock River Conference, where he continues to labor successfully for God. In the several positions he has occupied, as educator, pastor, presiding elder, or financial manager of public charities, Rev. Ezra M. Boring has made himself felt and has been appreciated.

CHAPTER XXIII.

BAINBRIDGE CIRCUIT, OHIO.

1841-42.

THE Conference met at Urbana, August 25, 1841, Bishop Roberts presiding. The following persons were admitted on trial: Joseph Gatch, Thomas Gorsuch, Samuel Brown, Orin Stimson, Isaac Whitnell, Richard Walker, Frederick Merrick, Philip A. Mutchner, Levi W. Munsel, George L. Creager, John W. Kenaga, Frederick Humphreys, Alexander Meharry, Daniel Breckley, Jacob J. Hibner—15. Some of these I shall have occasion to speak of in the future of this narrative as we shall toil and suffer and triumph together.

We recorded at this Conference the death of Rev. R. W. Finley. He was born in Bucks county, Penn., June 9, 1750; was educated for and entered the Presbyterian ministry. In 1788 he emigrated to Kentucky, and in 1795, at the head of a company, he assisted in exploring the Scioto country, and in 1796 settled his family in the valley of the Scioto, near the present city of Chillicothe. He united with the Methodist Episcopal Church in the year 1800, and entered the traveling connection in 1811 or 1812. When the Conference judged him to be superannuated, and placed him on that list, he being well on to eighty years of age, his missionary spirit rebelled against the idea of superannuation. He mounted his horse and penetrated to the wild region of St. Mary's, where he organized a circuit and held a camp meeting. The next Conference sent a missionary to his aid. He was an able and earnest expounder of Wesleyan theology. He died at the residence of his son, Rev. J. B. Finley, in Germantown, Ohio, December 8, 1840, in the 91st year of his age.

I was appointed to Bainbridge circuit, with Rev. Michael Marlay, for presiding elder, and Rev. J. W. Stone for assistant. My association with these dear brethren was of the most pleasant character. Brother Marlay was one of our ablest theologians, and when his soul became thoroughly engaged in his sermon, he preached with overwhelming power. Owing to the metaphysical bent of his mind, his ordinary sermons, and oftentimes the introductory part of his discourses, were regarded by common hearers as dry; but intelligent hearers always listened to his purely intellectual efforts and the least impassioned parts of his discourses with much profit. He was an excellent presiding elder, courteous and kind to his preachers, and firm in the discharge of official duty.

Brother Stone was pious, zealous, and faithful; an able divine, considering his years in the ministry. He commanded the confidence of the people, and did efficient service on the circuit. We had nineteen appointments, of which the following is a list: 1. Bainbridge; 2. Bourneville; 3. Twinn; 4.-Long's Hill; 5. Thomas's Hill; 6. John Haine's; 7. Martin Haines's on the "knobs;" 8. Salem; 9. Mt. Carmel; 10. Bethel; 11. Campbell's Meeting-house; 12. Sinking Springs; 13. Legg's; 14. Bristol's; 15. Cynthiana; 16. Edmonson's; 17. Valley Forge; 18. Loudon; 19. Nessel's.

We had a pleasant year and some measure of prosperity. We closed the year with a camp-meeting near Bainbridge; the attendance was large; the preaching attended with great power, the result of which was the conversion of souls and additions to the Church. William M. D. Ryan, then commencing his ministry as junior preacher on an adjoining circuit, was with us and exhorted with much power.

September 28, 1842, the Conference met at Hamilton and Rossville, Bishop Morris presiding. The following persons were admitted on trial: William J. Thurber, William I. Fee, David N. Smith, Jesse Botkin, James Hood, Charles Ferguson, Charles H. Warrington, Moses Smith, Abraham Cartlich, John W. Fowble, Levi Cunningham, Charles Koenecke, Thomas Coleman, Nathan T. Ayres, J. G. Blair, Archibald Fleming, Wesley Webster, John Guyer, Daniel D. Mather, Barton Lowe, Alexander Dinkins, William R. Litsinger—22. Out of this class I afterward had many valuable co-laborers in the most difficult field to which I was ever called. I shall have occasion to speak of them as I progress with my narrative.

Two of our able and honored standard-bearers had ascended during the past year, and their names are now recorded on the list of the beloved dead. They were Rev. William B. Christie and Rev. I. C. Hunter. Brother Christie was born in Wilmington, Ohio; educated at Augusta College, Kentucky; entered the Ohio Conference in 1825; rapidly rose to distinction in his Conference and the connection. During the later years of his ministry he had few superiors in pulpit power or ministerial influence. As I call up the recollections of the man and the grandeur of his life and labors, I hardly know how to pass him with so brief a notice. But he is well known to the Church, as but few contemporary Western Methodist ministers have failed to record the labors of our beloved Christie.

Brother Hunter was born in Bellefoute, Center county, Penn., August 30, 1798. He joined the Ohio Conference in 1819, and labored with unceasing ability and appreciation until he died, the 27th of June, 1842. Whether in charge of circuit, or station, or district, he was faithful and efficient, and his preaching was with demonstration of the Spirit and with power.

I was returned to Bainbridge circuit, with Rev. Alexander Meharry for my assistant. He came on to the work full of faith, and zeal, and power. Our souls united, and as we entered upon the year's work, expectation soon pervaded the whole circuit, and many began to prophesy that it would be a year of extraordinary revival influence. We arranged for a series of two-days' meetings, intending to protract them as providential indications should suggest. The first meeting proved such a success that the members of the society at which the next meeting was to be held set themselves to get ready, and as that progressed with power, the next society was busy getting ready, and thus the notes of preparation were heard all over the large circuit. The result was, we did not have to spend days in urging the membership to do their duty; already the way of the Lord was prepared. The Word took hold of the people with mighty power. Sinners were awakened, convictions were deep and pungent, and they were heard to cry aloud, "God be merciful to me a sinner!" As a result the conversions were clear and satisfactory. The flame spread so mightily that usually we found it necessary to protract one meeting up to the time of commencing the next. We would close our meeting late at night, and then move on to the next appointment to commence at 11 o'clock, A. M., next day. If the distance was not too great many of the members and young converts would follow us up, and so become more thoroughly established in experience and labor. It turned out to be not so much a series of meetings as one continuous meeting, marching grandly and triumphantly around the whole circuit. Our custom was to gather the slain of the Lord into the Church—Christ's hospital—every day. We had none of that squeamishness that some seem to feel in regard to inviting people to join the Methodist Episcopal Church. As we found the Church to be to us a good and happy home, so we conscientiously believed that those to whom we preached the Gospel would find it a good home. We told the people that the doors of the Methodist Episcopal Church, like the doors of Gospel grace, "stand open night and day," and we invited them to come in. At the close of this great campaign we summed up results, and found, to the glory of God, that *nine hundred and twenty-five* had closed in with the offer of mercy and placed their names on the muster-roll of Christ's army. We felt to praise the Lord and to say, "And let all the people praise HIM."

The attendance upon these meetings was so great that the Church accommodations were too strait, and increased accommodations became a necessity. The people were just in the proper state of mind to move forward in this work. In one neighborhood a call was made to consider the propriety of building a house of worship. The attendance was good; all saw the propriety of building at once. It was determined to build of hewed logs, as timber was abundant. They proceeded immediately to elect a suitable brother as chief manager. He divided his men into companies, appointing one company to fell the trees, another company to score and hew them, another to haul them to the building site, and another to get the flooring, doors, sash, etc., ready. All this was done ready for raising the first day. The second day the house was raised, roofed, floored, seated, and an altar and pulpit prepared, and at night it was lighted up, dedicated, and sinners gathered around its newly consecrated altar. Other neighborhoods hearing of this imitated the example. Thus they brought the tithes into the store-house and proved God therewith. The sisters, always ready to do their part—and, blessed be

God! in the Methodist family they are recognized as fellow-workers—did their full part in these Church enterprises as well as in the worship of the sanctuary. On these building occasions they came on the ground with all the appliances for cooking, and spread upon the extemporized tables hearty and inviting food for those doing the work; and they did all eat their meat with singleness of heart, giving glory to God. The people did not look with more of wonder upon the invincible host that marched with Sherman to the sea, than did the people of Bainbridge circuit look upon this conquering host marching under the command of the Lord Jesus. And, unlike the armies in carnal warfare, the army of the Lord left not desolation, or blackened walls or widows, or orphans along its path, but smiling faces and happy hearts, and redeemed and united families marked the pathway of the conquering host.

I will give a few incidents of these revivals, but it would require a volume to record them all. The first great revival broke out at Bourneville. We had there the walls of a church edifice which stood in an unfinished state, indicating that they had begun to build and were not able to finish. The first time that my colleague preached there, he told them that if they would go forward and finish their house, he believed God would convert one hundred souls, and that if they did not go forward the curse of God would rest upon them. Fear stimulated some and faith inspired others; they took counsel the next day and determined to go forward. The prediction of the preacher was more than fulfilled, for one hundred and eighty joined the Church at that place during the year. The work commenced breaking out the very next Sabbath, first among the children. Judge M'Cracken meeting brother Meharry said, "You are catching minnows." "Yes," said the preacher, "yes, we are catching minnows, and they are excellent bait." A few days afterward, when the work had made a break in the adult population, and the slain of the Lord were many, and among them a son and daughter of Judge M'Cracken, he met the preacher again and said, "You began with minnows, but you are catching fish now."

During this meeting the hotel-keeper of the village was seized suddenly with sickness, and sent for Dr. Hull to come and see him. The Doctor soon found that it was not bodily but spiritual disease that ailed him, and advised him to send for the preacher. He did so; brother Meharry slipped out of the prayer-meeting—which was at brother Howser's house—and went over to the hotel to see him, and as soon as he ascertained the nature of the case, sent back a request that the prayer-meeting should adjourn to the hotel. It was done, and soon chairs were arranged in the sick man's room for mourners, and he was exhorted to get out of bed and down on his knees, and cry to the great Physician who could cure soul and body. He thought he was too sick to get up, but the preacher took hold of him and helped him out, and once down upon his knees he commenced crying to God mightily for mercy. Some eight or ten others came forward for prayers, and at that meeting the converting power of God was present. Brother Snyder and his wife and the landlord were among the converted. There was to have been a dance at the hotel that night, but it was a meeting of a very different sort. A wild fellow who had come from some distance, and had not heard the news of the changed state of things, as he approached the hotel, heard the noise and supposed there was a fight. He dismounted and hurried in to see the fun. As he opened the door such a sight and such sounds as greeted him struck him with such alarm that he retreated, mounted his horse, and fled from the town as though Death was after him. At 9 o'clock, P. M., the company adjourned from the hotel to the church to commence the watch-night service. It was a powerful meeting; several were converted, and brothers Perill and Dill joined the Church. Before the close of the next week upward of ninety had come out on the Lord's side, and before the meeting finally closed one hundred and eight had joined, so literally and promptly had brother Meharry's prophecy been fulfilled. At this meeting brothers Thomson, and Dunlap, and Armstrong gave assistance in the pulpit and altar work.

Our first quarterly-meeting was at Loudon. The principal families in this neighborhood were Virginians, and of Quaker extraction. Brother Marlay, the presiding elder, and the venerable James Quinn were with us at this meeting. We protracted it, and some forty new recruits were gathered within eight days. Brother Enos Gore, one of the noblest of men, had for several years been connected with the Church as a probationer, but to this time had clung to his Quakerism so far as to decline baptism. He now saw it to be his duty to be baptized, and on Sabbath morning, in connection with family devotions, I baptized him and his household, consisting of the parents and two children. It was a beautiful and impressive sight.

The 25th of January we commenced at Mt. Carmel and continued seven days, when our previously announced plan required us to go to Bainbridge. At Mt. Carmel fifty-five joined, and the wave of influence was swelling rapidly, when we had to move on to attack the enemy at Bainbridge. We anticipated that at this latter point we should have our hardest battle. It was the citadel, and the enemy was organized and strongly fortified, but a noble band of workers came up from Bourneville to our help, and on Wednesday night the battle turned, and the ranks of the enemy were completely demoralized. We pushed the battle to the gate, and within sixteen days one hundred and fifty were gathered into the Church. Some were fearful of excitement, and one man who had made up his mind to serve the Lord waited until he thought he was perfectly calm and collected, and when the preacher announced a hymn, he arose and started the tune, and then walked up deliberately and joined. Another, while we were singing the stirring chorus,

"For I can no longer stay away,"

started from the back part of the house, and, as the great tears ran down his cheeks, made longer and longer strides as he neared the altar, and in the intensest condition of excitement, enlisted in the army. The first of these did not hold out six months, while the last, up to my latest intelligence of him, was still shouting on his way to glory. An immortal spirit convinced of its awful danger, or assured of its escape from ruin, ought to be excited, and no condition of intelligence, culture, or purity needs to be afraid of religious excitement, for it reaches to the very "angels of God."

February 21st we opened our batteries at Sinking Springs. The meeting continued thirteen days, and sixty-two were added to the Lord. The last one that joined at this meeting was William Manlove, and he made the five hundredth recruit since Conference. He proved to be a good soldier, and "stood fast in the Lord."

We had now been pushing the battle for more than three months almost without intermission. Our second quarterly-meeting was at hand, and it was to be at Bourneville, the place where we had commenced our series of meetings. Some thought that it was now time to rest, and others that the harvest was fully gathered. March 25th the quarterly-meeting commenced; Elder Marlay was with us in the spirit of the Master. The power of God rested on the congregation. Rich and poor, old and young, came thronging to the altar, crowded the altar, and for nine days the wailing of penitents and the shouting of converts were familiar sounds in the temple of the Lord. Upward of sixty joined, many of whom proved to be patterns of piety and way-marks to the kingdom of God. It was at this meeting that R. R. Seymour and his wife joined the Church. He was a wealthy farmer, living near Bainbridge, surrounded with every thing of this world that heart could wish. He was given to hospitality, and always delighted to entertain the ministers of the Gospel at his princely residence, but he had passed middle life neglecting the Savior, and it was feared that he would continue to neglect the most important interest. Great was the rejoicing when he came out on the Lord's side. He was decided and consistent, and immediately it was evident that his time, talents, home, and property were all dedicated to God. His tenants, hired men, business associates, and neighbors all saw the change, and many followed him to Jesus. The many happy seasons spent by myself and companion, religiously and socially, at the house of brother Seymour will never be forgotten.

Judge Morris received a new baptism during this meeting. Many will remember his feeling remarks in one of our speaking meetings. He narrated how he had endeavored to be an infidel, and the reluctance of rich men to yield to the convictions of the Spirit. Said he, "The rich are nearly always behind; last to get to church, last to seek the Lord; behind the poor in the measure of their liberality, in the support of the Gospel, and the erection of churches. I feel," said he, "like getting ahead and not remaining in the rear any longer." He was much blessed, and his experience and declaration of purpose were made a blessing to others. The converts of this meeting came out very clear and strong.

There was a young man of great worth and promise who attended that meeting, and was almost persuaded to become a

Christian. Indeed he confessed privately that his mind was made up, but that "just one thing was in the way of his starting now." He resisted the Spirit, launched out into grander speculations, and by and by financial disaster, dissipation, divorce demonstrated what a terrible thing it is to trifle with the strivings of the Spirit of God. Had he accepted then the offers of mercy, and united himself with the people of God, I have no doubt that to-day his home would have been one of the brightest, and his record one of the most honorable, for he was a man who would have been among the first in every good work had he given his heart to God. If he is still living I here record the prayer that he may yet be constrained to say, "I will arise and go to my Father."

April 6th, we planted the standard of the Lord at Cynthiana. Up to Saturday night, fifteen had enlisted. On Sabbath thirty-five came over on the Lord's side, and the meeting went on with great power. Wednesday I found myself so much exhausted that I suggested to brother Meharry whether it would not be well to rest a few days, but he thought it was best for us to retain our vantage-ground and push the enemy to the wall. We did so. The afternoon prayer-meeting was a time of power, and at night we had a grand victory. The crowd that gathered was composed of all sorts of hard cases. Brother Meharry preached from Joshua vii, 25, "Why hast thou troubled us?" The Lord helped him wonderfully. Some thirty sinners, among whom were old and hardened sinners, came out for the Lord that night. We closed up the next Sabbath night, having enlisted one hundred and twelve recruits during the meeting.

Our third quarterly-meeting was at Sinking Springs, and was a good time. We held several meetings during the Summer at different points, at all of which the Lord was present to heal.

The first of September I told my colleague that if he had faith he might go over to Bethel. He went, and after a few days' earnest labor the fire broke out, and victory after victory was achieved, until upward of sixty had come out on the Lord's side. One poor sinner, pierced by an arrow of truth, went home, and taking to his bed thought he was going to die. He sent for the preacher, who, when he came, ordered the man at once to get out of bed and kneel down if he wanted him to pray for him. He obeyed, and soon found the Lord.

September 8th, the fourth quarterly-meeting commenced at Bainbridge. As this was the last quarterly-meeting for the year, and as the revival fire had been burning all over the circuit and all through the year, the attendance was large. The quarterly conference was a very able and dignified body of men. We had five local preachers, each of whom had his peculiarities and excellencies—Lewis Holler, Frederick Curp, Archibald Lockard, Reese Wolf, and John Haines. Brother Wolf was a man widely known, eccentric, and loyal and faithful to the Church of his choice. We had occasion to mention him in the early part of this narrative as one of the pioneers in Western Virginia in an early day. Brother Haines was a man of great simplicity of character and purity of life. Blessed with a peculiarly tenacious memory, he applied it to the storing away the truth of God, and he had large portions of the Word written indelibly on the tables of his memory. He could repeat for hours without interruption. Among our exhorters were Alexander Jester, Isaac Kelly, Joel Wolf, John L. Smith, Stephen Miller, Joseph Ross, and George Nessel, some of whom were soon after this licensed to preach. Then in other offices, as members of the quarterly conference, such men as Taylor, Maulove, Gore, Guilliford, Nellis, Easton, Reed, Fleming, Smith, Heaston, Elliott, and a host of others.

My son, William Fletcher Stewart, had just reached home, having completed his course of study and graduated at Augusta College. He had been licensed as an exhorter some time before, and purposed giving himself to the work of the ministry. But neither he nor myself had any thought of his entering immediately upon that work. He was only eighteen years of age, and apparently nearly broken down in health. The presiding elder, however, thought that by deferring the matter he might be diverted from the ministry, and that horseback exercise was just what he needed to bring him out physically. I had great confidence in brother Marlay, and deferred to his judgment in the matter. My son was willing to leave his case in the hands of the Church, preferring to wait a year, or consenting to go at once, as the Church might say. Before organizing the conference, the presiding elder called a leaders' meeting, which recommended the young man to the quarterly conference for license. He then organized the conference, and William Fletcher was licensed and recommended to the Ohio Annual Conference for the traveling connection. This was to me an event of deep and grateful interest. My first and greatest desire in regard to my children had always been that they should be members of the family of God, and then I had felt that I could not only cheerfully give my sons to the Lord for the work of the ministry, but that I would rather have them in that work—if truly called of God to it and faithful—than to see them successful in any other avocation in life. I thought, in regard to this son, that if his days were to be but few on earth, if the Lord would make him instrumental in the gathering of some souls for Christ before he called him hence, I would feel that my labor and expense in giving him the opportunities of education would not be spent in vain.

The quarterly-meeting was a good one, and several more

joined the Church. After quarterly-meeting we had several two-days' meetings before Conference; one at brother Nessel's, conducted by brother Mcharry, assisted by my son. There he made his first attempt to preach—text Luke xii, 32. The meeting was successful and resulted in several conversions and additions to the Church. September 16th, we commenced a four-days' meeting at Mt. Carmel. It was a noisy meeting—a time of great rejoicing on the part of the Church, and some conversions. September 24th, our winding-up two-days' meeting at Bourneville. We recounted all the way in which God had led us, and were made very happy. We had held eighteen quarterly and protracted meetings, besides attending the regular work of a large four-weeks' circuit; had received on probation nine hundred and twenty-five, and should carry up to Conference a report of six hundred and forty-nine net gain for the year. Out of that large class of converts we were confident God would raise up some to preach the Gospel. My soul had become knit to my colleague, and I loved him as though he was my own son.

CHAPTER XXIV.

KANAWHA DISTRICT, VIRGINIA.

1843-46.

SEPTEMBER 23, 1843, the Conference met at Chillicothe. Bishop Soule presided. Little did we think as we looked upon his manly and venerable form, and listened to his words of counsel and exhortation, and received our appointments at his hands, that the time would ever come when we should fail to welcome him as our presiding officer. He had long had his episcopal residence at Lebanon, within the bounds of our Conference, and he was particularly endeared to us, but, alas! this was the last time that he was to preside over our Conference.

This session was a pleasant and profitable one. The brethren of Chillicothe, proud of their long-established character as loyal and enthusiastic Methodists, gave the Conference a hearty welcome and extended warm hospitality in their families to the preachers. Many of the preachers brought excellent reports of the success of the past year. I believe that my circuit reported the largest net gain of any one, and it was no small gratification to me to see Bainbridge circuit elevated to the position of third in the whole Conference as to numerical strength. The banner charge was old "WHITEOAK"—called Felicity the year that I traveled it. It had one thousand eight hundred and twenty-eight members. The second was Troy, one thousand seven hundred and three members; and then Bainbridge, one thousand six hundred and forty-seven members. During the year three preachers had withdrawn from the Methodist Episcopal Church and connected themselves with a small seceding body called "True Wesleyans;" namely, Richard Brandriff, Joshua Boucher, and Silas H. Chase. One faithful brother, Rev. Alfred Hance, had been transferred from the Church militant to the Church triumphant. From the time that he joined the Conference, in 1837, he had been a pattern of industry and fidelity in the ministry, and his labors had been crowned with abundant success. His memory on M'Arthurstown circuit, where he fell at his post, will long remain as ointment poured forth. A little while before he breathed his last, one said to him, "You are sinking fast." To which the triumphant saint replied, "I am rising! rising!"

We received a large class on probation, most of them vigorous young men, and some of them young men of more than ordinary education and culture. The following are the names: Andrew J. Lyda, William H. Sutherland, John W. Locke, Pearl P. Ingalls, Lorenzo D. M'Cabe, David H. Sargent, James F. Chalfant, Harrison Z. Adams, William F. Stewart, Alfred L. Westervelt, Charles H. Warren, Isaac N. Mark, Moses T. Bowman, Henry Lewis, Abraham Thompson, Barzillai N. Spahr, George S. Stephenson, Jacob Pierce, James J. Dolliver, William Rutledge, Ezra M. Boring, Peter F. Holtsinger, John W. Keeley, George Hanawalt, Peter Wilkins, Matthias Ruff, and John M. Hofer—27.

As I inquire after this class now, after the lapse of a quarter of a century, I find that they are greatly scattered; several of them are occupying leading positions in the Ohio and other Western Conferences, and several of them have accomplished their work and gone to their rest on high.

Very unexpectedly to me I was elevated to the very

honorable and responsible position of President of Brush College. I received the announcement with no little trepidation, and was very sure that, as all my predecessors had experienced, so I should have "my ups and downs" from the beginning to the close of the term. But before the close of my connection with the district, as my narrative will show, I had more serious ups and downs than the climbing of mountains and descending of valleys. The same influences that were to separate our beloved Soule from us were to make the Kanawha district a terrible battle-field. Could I have drawn aside the curtain so as to get a glimpse of what was before me, I should have shrunk back appalled.

The General Conference was to meet in the city of New York the first of May next, 1844, and we elected the following brethren as delegates to that body: Charles Elliott, J. M. Trimble, Z. Connell, W. H. Raper, J. B. Finley, E. W. Sehon, and Leonidas L. Hamline. The last one on the list was destined to be the marked man of the General Conference.

My first year on the district was far more pleasant than I had anticipated. I found that the labors and responsibilities of the presiding elder differed a good deal from those of the pastor, but that the same God who is rich in grace to all, was ready to hear me and assist me in my new relation, as he had heard and assisted me in relations I had hitherto sustained. I found under my charge ten large circuits spreading over as many large mountainous counties in Western Virginia. I found, too, the extremes and all the intermediate grades of society: the wealthy in their splendid palaces, surrounded by their obsequious servants, and faring sumptuously every day, and the hardly tamed mountaineer, making a precarious living by hunting and fishing. The district was so mountainous that it could only be traveled on foot or on horseback. But while the population differed so much in some things, they were alike in one thing, and that was in respect to preachers of the Gospel. In the wildest cabin and the stateliest mansion, whether professors or non-professors, the Methodist traveling preachers were welcome, on one condition, and that was, that they deal tenderly with the "peculiar institution." But the time was just at hand when Methodist preachers must say to that desolating flood, "Thus far shalt thou go, and no further," and then will this hospitality in many places turn to the most bitter and relentless persecution.

But I am anticipating, for, as I have already said, my first year on Kanawha district was one of peace and prosperity. I had a band of faithful preachers, and most of them were adapted to the work and efficient. I will mention their names in connection with the charges they served, and record the results of my acquaintance with them.

Charleston circuit embraced much of the wealth of the Kanawha Valley, where the most valuable salt-works were operated. William T. Hand and John W. Fowble were the preachers on this charge. Brother Hand was a very popular pulpit man. He had, in an eminent degree, the "copia verborum"—a fine imagination—great tact in the relation of anecdotes, and withal a fine personal appearance. He attracted much attention, and made a strong impression upon the charge that he served. Brother Fowble, though young in his ministry, indicated a strength of intellect, mental culture, and devotion to his work that gave much promise of his future. The prophecy is being fulfilled.

Point Pleasant circuit occupied the lower part of the valley and portions of the Ohio River bottoms, as well as adjacent mountain ranges. Thomas Gorsuch had charge of this work. Amiable, chaste, and graceful in all his intercourse with the people, and more than medium in his pulpit ministrations, he drew the people to him, and did them good. I always thought I did well for the charge to which I nominated Thomas Gorsuch. He has completed his work on earth, and now sings with the saints and angels.

Guyandotte circuit lay in Cabel, Logan, Kanawha, and Mason counties, embracing a portion of each, a very extended and mountainous region. Michael G. Perkhizer had charge of this circuit, assisted by James G. Dolliver. The preacher in charge was a workman who needed not to be ashamed—always faithful and devoted. The junior preacher had just appeared on our Conference roll, and proved to be a valuable worker, "full of faith and the Holy Ghost." God gave him a tongue of fire, and blessed him very much.

Logan Court-house circuit embraced Logan and part of Fayette and Kanawha counties. George G. West, who had charge of this rugged work, was a meek, quiet, studious, holy man. He preached faithfully and well, worked diligently and wisely. Those who knew him best, prized him most, and the circuit favored with his labors one year, would hardly fail to desire his continuance with them.

Coal River circuit lay on the waters of Coal River, running through some of the counties already mentioned. Charles Ferguson had charge of this work. He was a many-sided man, and gifted in every direction. Whether in song or prayer, or exhortation or preaching, he was a power. Never letting down the dignity of the minister, he remembered that he was the herald of a Gospel which should be preached to every creature, and he addressed himself to his work, publicly and privately, with abundant success.

Fayette Court-house circuit lay mostly in Fayette county, and principally on the waters of Loop Creek. Isaac N. Whitnell had charge of this work. As a theologian and sermonizer, he compared favorably with many who far outstripped him in efficiency and success. He remained in the regular ministry only a few years, when, perhaps convinced that he had better adaptation for some other department of labor, he retired from the regular work. It seemed a pity that his excellent talent could not be made fully available in the ministry.

Summerville circuit embraced Nicholas county. Jonathan F. Conrey had charge of this work. Having enjoyed association with him as my assistant on Georgetown circuit a few years prior to this, and holding him in high esteem as I did, it was very pleasant to me to have him in my district. The appointment to him was like "a clap of thunder from a cloudless sky." He had been stationed in the city of Zanesville the year before, and was much disgusted at first with the idea of entering "Brush College," but he went to his work as a loyal Methodist preacher should, made full proof of his ministry, did a noble work for God and the Church among the mountains, and from their loftiest crags and their deepest valleys often sounded the high praises of God. Though he has well and successfully sustained himself in the prominent positions of his Conference since then, I doubt not he looks back to that as one of his happiest and most successful years.

Suttonville circuit lay on the waters of Elk River. Addison Hite had charge of this circuit. He was a preacher whose consistent piety commanded the confidence of the people, and made him useful in the work. He, after some years, retired to the local ranks.

Ripley circuit lay in Jackson county. James W. Southard was the preacher in charge of this work. He was seized with the unfortunate idea that he was not appreciated by his brethren according to his merits, and so commenced casting about for some new home, where he might have a better chance. After another year in our Conference, he withdrew and united with the Protestant Methodists.

Between these men and myself existed the most pleasant relations. They treated me as a father in the Gospel. They were on my heart day and night, and I had much comfort in pleading for them at the throne of grace. Having but ten charges, I was able to attend all of the quarterly-meetings in person. Preachers and people looked forward to these occasions with fasting, and prayer, and expectation. Many of them made long mountain journeys, to get to the quarterly-meetings, and God blessed us all together. Mountain cabin accommodations and fare were sometimes wild, and amusing scenes sometimes transpired, but beneath the coarsest garments often beat the truest and noblest hearts, and around those blazing hickory fires in the wide-mouthed fire-places, I have listened to the hunter's thrilling story of adventure, and the Christian's stirring narrative of Christian experience, and felt as happy as when enjoying the hospitality of the salt princes in the valley.

Amusing stories were told of some of my predecessors on the district. It was said that when a certain brother was appointed to the district, some brother, with feigned seriousness, had suggested to him that when he reached the mountain regions they would feed him on wild-cats. He was a man of great purity and simplicity of character, and not being accustomed to indulge in a joke, he took the matter in earnest, and made up his mind that he would keep a sharp look-out in regard to the meat that he should eat. During the year, as he was in a wild portion of the district, one day he called at a certain brother's house, and as he passed through the yard from the gateway, he espied the paws of an animal where they had been chopped off and lay by the side of a stump. He at once made a note of that in his memory. By and by dinner came, and after he was seated at the table the reverend host said:

"Brother ———, will you take a piece of the meat?"

"Thank you, brother," replied his guest, "I don't eat wild-cats myself."

"O, no," rejoined the astonished mountaineer, "neither do we; this is not wild-cat."

"You can't fool me, brother. I saw the feet lying by the stump as I came through the yard."

The incident was ludicrous enough, but it was all in sincerity and good humor, if the story is to be regarded as authentic.

On the first of May, 1844, the General Conference assembled at New York city. It proved to be a memorable session. The fact coming to the knowledge of members of the Conference that Bishop Andrew had become connected with slavery, that question which had agitated the Church so long came up in a new and exceedingly embarrassing form. Bishop Andrew personally was much beloved, but the conscientious members, especially from the free States, thought that it would be disastrous to the Church if this matter was passed over. The result was, after long and earnest discussion, the passage of a resolution offered by members of our Conference to the end that the Bishop should cease the exercise of the functions of his office until he was released from slavery. The Southern preachers took fire at that and demanded a plan for the separation of the Church. A conditional plan was offered and agreed to. The Bishop declined a proposition of some friends to raise the money to purchase and manumit his slaves. Intense excitement prevailed, and at the adjournment serious apprehensions pervaded the entire denomination. The Southern delegates went home, many of them to stir up the people and sow the seeds of secession.

September 4, 1844, the Conference met at Marietta. Bishop Waugh presided. Bishop Soule was also present part of the time, but his evident want of sympathy with the action of the majority in the late General Conference, and the decided position of the Ohio Conference greatly impaired the confidence that had hitherto been reposed in him. At an early period in the session the venerable Jacob Young offered a preamble and resolutions indorsing the course pursued at the General Conference by the majority of our delegation. As Edmund W. Schon had sympathized and acted with the South, he took alarm at this movement. The venerable William Burke espoused the cause of the South and became greatly excited. By motion of J. F. Wright, the resolutions were referred to a committee of nine to consider and report. In due time the committee reported in favor of the resolutions, and they passed triumphantly.

The reports from the preachers indicated that this year had not been one of as great prosperity as the preceding. At Chillicothe we had reported an aggregate increase of six thousand seven hundred and eighty-six, while this year we reported a decrease of two thousand five hundred and fifty-five.

One of our valuable young men, Rev. J. W. Kanaga, had died during the year. He was licensed to preach in 1840; received on probation in the Ohio Conference in 1841; was received into full connection at Chillicothe in 1843, and appointed to Clarkesville circuit, where he finished his work soon after his second quarterly-meeting. At that meeting he preached his last sermon from 2 Timothy iv, 6-8: "For I am now ready to be offered, and the time of my departure is at hand," etc. He preached as though he had a premonition that it would indeed be his last sermon, and as though his triumphant spirit already caught sight of the glittering crown. The fever had already commenced its work. It soon assumed a malignant type, and baffled the skill of the physicians. He was rational to the last, and gave abundant evidence of the sufficiency of grace to support in death.

The following persons were received on trial: Elias H. Sabin, Dewitt C. Johnson, David Whitmer, Richard Pitzer, William W. M'Comas, Valentine Beamer, Isaac Dillon, Christian Wittenbach, John Mann, John Hopper, and Charles Shelper.

Upon the whole this was a very interesting Conference. The preachers who had not visited Marietta before, heard with interest the legends of the old "Ohio Company," which had established its head-quarters at this point in the early years. Remains of the old stockade and landmarks of the earliest pioneer times were still visible.

I here took my first lessons in the mysteries and delicate responsibilities of the Bishop's cabinet. I found that an inside view differs largely from an outside view, but my experience during this Conference confirmed me in the opinion I had entertained for years, that the Bishop and his counselors, in studying the necessities of the whole work, endeavored sincerely and earnestly to secure such an adjustment of the laborers as would secure the greatest efficiency and success. It is utterly impossible that every charge can secure their preference in regard to their preacher, for here are several charges preferring the same man. It is equally impossible that every preacher can have his preference as to his field, for here are several preachers desiring the same field. Then there are good men who are really superannuated, either mentally or physically, but do not realize it; others who possibly think of themselves a little more highly than they ought to think; others who are "constitutionally tired," and do not perform the amount of pastoral labor and pulpit preparation necessary to endear them to the people or secure success. And then there are others who have marked eccentricities, and men who ride hobbies, and men whose time is partly engaged in purely literary or other secular matters. There are preachers who desire especial accommodations on account of family matters, pertaining to health, or education of children, or support. And so I might go on to enumerate many more matters, all of which have to be taken into the account in the Bishop's cabinet. It is indeed a responsible work, and requires sympathy, and courage, and judgment, and faith, and divine illumination. Let those who have faith in God pray that the Spirit may always direct in the selection of Bishops and presiding elders, and influence their minds so that they may successfully meet their responsibilities.

I took back with me to the Kanawha district, in the main, the same band of faithful men who had labored with me the previous year. I parted company, however, with a few whom I loved dearly, and welcomed others who proved to be faithful workers. I had this year, as my assistants, as follows:

Charleston Circuit—Thomas Gorsuch and William H. Sutherland. Brother Sutherland was one of my new men. He was talented, very studious, and inclined to cultivate rigid system in the division of his time and labor. I prophesied a bright future for him, and have not been disappointed in my expectations.

Parkersburg—Arza Brown. He was pure gold, a man of ripe Christian experience, and an able advocate of the doctrine of Christian perfection. Feeble in health, but abundant in labors, he was to me a valuable counselor and efficient co-worker. His excellent companion, too, was full of holy fire and zeal in the cause of the Master, ready for every good word and work. After years of separation, I have had the privilege of meeting them, in 1868, in their pleasant home, in Chicago. But the missionary fire still burned in their hearts, and they soon after sought work among the freedmen, in Louisiana, instructing, exhorting, and preaching.

Little Kanawha—Charles Ferguson and D. D. Mather. This was brother Mather's first year with me. He was endowed with large intellectual capacity, and was rapidly developing into an able preacher of the Gospel. He has long since taken a prominent position in the ministry.

Ripley—Samuel Black and Thomas K. Coleman. Brother Coleman was a young man of sprightly intellect, fine imagination, and tenacious memory, and made his pulpit efforts very attractive. He was faithful to his trust, and did not sympathize with the preacher in charge, who this year espoused the cause of the seceders, and did all he could to hand the circuit over to the Church South.

Point Pleasant—John F. Longman and William W. M'Comas. Brother Longman was an Englishman, of good preaching ability. Had he felt fully the responsibility of the Christian ministry, and met his engagements punctually, with the ability he possessed he could have done a noble work. I had licensed brother M'Comas to preach, and carried his recommendation to the Ohio Conference, thinking that he would prove to be a valuable accession to our traveling ministry. He had extraordinary elements of power and usefulness, but he became tinctured with the leaven of secession, and turned his hand against his ecclesiastical mother with a fierceness and venom which was terrible.

Guyandotte—William T. Hand.

Wayne Court-house—James J. Dolliver.

Logan Court-house—George G. West.

Coal River—Jesse Botkin. He was a man of sterling worth, not so successful in gathering as some, but what he gathered into the fold he was apt to retain for the Master. He stood up for the Church against all opposers, at whatever cost, feeling that it could not cost too dear.

Summerville—Archibald Fleming. He was a man whom any charge might deem itself fortunate to have as its pastor.

Elk River—Isaac Whitnell.

Suttonville was left to be supplied. I employed brother Chambers, a local preacher.

This year the gathering storm began to burst upon us in its fury. To me it was indeed a fiery trial. During my first year on the district, every face had been the face of a friend, and every voice the voice of friendship. Though the fare was sometimes rough, and the labor always hard, yet I had been happy in the work. But this year there was a dividing. A few leading and designing men had raised the cry of "Abolitionism," and foreign "interference with the institutions of Virginia." Countenances that had always smiled upon me now turned from me, or met me with the blackness of the thunder-cloud. Voices that had addressed me with respect and affection now railed out in accents of anger, or, behind my back, endeavored to poison others against me; and homes where I had been welcomed and entertained as an angel of God would now have loathed my presence. Nor were these shafts leveled at me alone. All of my assistants who were true to their ordination vows, and all of the members who were true to the Discipline of the Methodist Episcopal Church—and they constituted the great majority—were sharers in the proscription and opposition. The most of my preachers were not only true as steel, but possessed the qualifications needful for such an emergency. In the midst of misrepresentation, and slander, and threats of personal violence, the faithful itinerant said, "None of these things move me; neither count I my life dear to me, so that I may finish my course with joy."

September 3, 1845, the Conference met at Cincinnati.

Bishop L. L. Hamline presided. Bishop Soule visited us again, and caused us a good deal of trouble. We were justly proud of Bishop Hamline, not only on account of his eminent scholarship, and eloquence, and piety, but because he had grown up religiously within our bounds, and was recognized as an Ohio Conference man. Probably he was never placed in circumstances more embarrassing than on the morning when Bishop Soule entered the Conference-room, and placed himself in position to be invited to occupy the chair. Could he ignore the venerable Bishop? Could he summon courage to invite him to the chair against the wishes of almost the whole body of preachers? He did invite Bishop Soule to the chair. Immediately upon Bishop Soule's taking the chair, a scene of confusion transpired; the Conference refused to do any business under his presidency, and he as resolutely willed that the business should go forward. When he found it utterly impossible to control the Conference, he called brother James Quinn to the chair, but still the tumult increased. Now Hamline stepped upon the platform, resumed the reins, and, with the hand of a master, restored at once the order of the Conference.

Received on trial at this Conference: Henry E. Dreyer, Leonard Mulfinger, Christopher Keller, Moses M'Lane, John Myers, Paul Brodbeck, Ernst H. Pelens, John J. Hibner, Christopher Hoevner, James B. Morrison—10—a small class, and several of them for German missionaries.

It was a time of peculiar tenderness and solemnity when a tribute of respect was paid to those who had died during the year. Three honored and venerable men had been called home—men who had labored long and well—men whose praise was in all the Churches, and who had turned many to righteousness. They were John Collins, Greenbury R. Jones, and H. S. Farnandis.

In a previous part of this narrative we have spoken of

brother Collins as a man of God and a preacher of the Gospel. In no part of the Conference was he more highly prized than in Cincinnati, where our Conference was now holding its session. He had organized the first class in the city, and laid there the foundation of Methodism. He was born in New Jersey in 1769; came to Ohio in 1804; entered the traveling connection in 1807; and died in the city of Maysville, August 21, 1845. "His setting sun was without a cloud. His last words were, 'Happy! happy! happy!' and all was still."

Brother Jones was a Pennsylvanian. He was admitted on trial in the Ohio Conference in 1818; superannuated in 1832; was made effective again in 1839. He was a superior executive officer and an efficient worker, made full proof of his ministry, and died at Marietta, September 20, 1844. His last days were days of triumphant experience.

Brother Farnandis was a Virginian. He was born in Loudon county, December 1, 1793. He entered the traveling connection in 1819. Though not remarkable for the shining qualities of the orator, he possessed such a combination of gifts and graces as seemed to make him a favorite with God and men. He led a great many souls to Christ, and in his crown of righteousness will be found many stars, and stars of the first magnitude. During his last illness he was much blessed of God, and sent assurances to his brethren of the Conference of his joyful hope of immortality. He fell asleep in Jesus on the 17th of May, 1845, in his own house, in Rushville, Ohio, surrounded by loving family and friends.

My three years on the Kanawha district constituted perhaps the most responsible as well as trying period of my whole ministry. As soon as I had taken my position, after the secession, the Southern press began to misrepresent me, and its whole power was used to crush me. Insinuation, innuendo, and downright falsehood were used and circulated industriously by hot-blooded agitators and mischief-makers, but I put my trust in God, and endeavored conscientiously to do my duty. Since I commenced writing this chapter, I have thoroughly reviewed the whole controversy, and I am satisfied that I was not only true to the Church, but consistent with myself during the whole of my administration. The Methodist Episcopal Church at that time occupied conservative ground on the subject of slavery, denouncing the principle as sinful, the system of American slavery as the "sum of all villainies," but allowing that the legal relation of master and slave did not necessarily, under all circumstances, involve sin. She prohibited, unequivocally, the traffic in slaves; required her ministers who had become involved in the relation to emancipate their slaves whenever the laws of the State would allow the emancipated slaves to enjoy their liberty. The spirit of slavery, however, true to itself, had for some time been steadily making aggressions, until quite extensively through the South the wholesome regulations of the Church were practically ignored. A traveling preacher in the Baltimore Conference set the Church at defiance. He was tried by his own Conference and found guilty. He appealed to the ensuing General Conference, and the decision of the Annual Conference was sustained. Bishop Andrew became the owner of slaves by marriage, and the facts coming before the General Conference of 1844, which sat in the city of New York, the Conference required that he should manumit his slaves or desist from the exercise of his episcopal office. It was certain that a slaveholding Bishop could not be acceptable as a presiding officer in the free States. Brethren anxious for a peaceful solution of this difficulty, proffered to put into the hands of the Bishop the value of the servants, so that his wife's estate should not be injured. He, however, acting under the advice of the magnates of the South, declined all such pacific overtures, and so compelled a direct issue. The Conference met the issue promptly. The Southern delegates consulted and handed in a "*protest.*" They expressed the conviction that a rupture of the Church would be inevitable if the majority did not recede, and demanded a plan by which the separation, if found inevitable, might be consummated peacefully. The result of a protracted and very earnest discussion was the adoption of the famous "plan of separation." It was granted on the part of the majority, as an "olive branch," and with the belief that the Southern delegates returning to their people and laying the matter honestly before them, would find the majority of them true to the Church and averse to separation. These delegates, however, determined upon separation before they left the city, and went home, not to consult with the people and try to allay strife and save the unity of the Church, but to prepare the people to submit, unresistingly, to the disintegration of the Church. Up to the time, however, of the final action of the Louisville Convention, many of us believed that in case a Southern Church was organized, it would maintain the old landmarks of Methodism, and carry out the spirit and letter of the plan of separation.

It was claimed that the radical views of agitators in the North had created a feeling in the South that greatly embarrassed our work in that section, and that the antislavery rules and spirit of the Church could be much more efficiently enforced if the cry of Northern interference could be arrested. There was plausibility in this position. We felt its force in the Kanawha district. Had the delegates gone home and represented the action of the General Conference in the true spirit by which it was actuated, my belief is that it would have allayed in great measure what discontent then existed. Or if, upon a calm and honest interchange of views, it had been decided to organize a separate Church, with the avowed purpose of maintaining sacredly the old landmarks of Methodism, the separation might have been consummated in accordance with the provisions of the plan without serious friction. I was invited to attend the Louisville Convention, but my duties were such as to make it impracticable for me to do so. I addressed the Convention, by letter, through Bishop Soule, expressing my convictions touching the interests of the Kanawha district. I then thought that should a separate Church be organized in good faith, in accordance with the plan, it would be best that all the territory within the slave States should be embraced in that Church.

Immediately after the organization of the new Church, however, its animus indicated such a hostility to genuine antislavery Methodism, and such a determination to swallow up the people in the new organization, without regard either to their wishes or the plan of separation, that I found I could not in conscience either be a party to any such procedure, or allow such procedure within the bounds of the Kanawha district. I laid the question before the quarterly conferences, and, with scarcely a dissenting vote, they all decided to remain in the Methodist Episcopal Church. This greatly exasperated those in the interest of slavery, and thenceforth a most persistent effort was made to get me out of the way, or destroy my influence among the people. One instance of the length to which those who became my enemies would go to injure me, will be all that I will place upon the record.

In Parkersburg a minority, in flagrant violation of the plan of separation, not only received a preacher from the Church South, but took possession of the church edifice. Rather than resort to law or violence, our brethren went to work and erected, with great liberality and dispatch, a new church. Efforts were made to intimidate me from attending my quarterly-meeting at that place, and a plan was concocted to involve me in difficulty should I come. G. Neal and H. Phelps were the most prominent actors in the matter.

On Sabbath, as I was passing along the street, Mr. Phelps called to me, and then approaching me with a smile on his face, said, "How do you do, brother Stewart?" Having received a very insolent letter from him some time previously, and well knowing the man, I conversed with him civilly, but was careful to be on my guard. He invited me to visit him before I should leave the town. I answered perhaps I might. He urged me to do so, and I replied that if I did not leave town that day perhaps I would call next day. We then parted, and I called the attention of brother Jennings, who was with me, to the guarded manner in which I had replied to the invitation.

I had expected to leave on Monday, but learning on the morning of that day that Phelps had what purported to be a copy of the letter that I addressed to the Louisville Convention, and that he was using it to my injury, and learning that several of the Southern preachers had copies of that letter which they read to their congregations, and commented on at great length to my prejudice, I determined to make an effort to see the copy, that I might satisfy myself whether it was genuine or counterfeit. Monday evening, taking brother Wolf with me, I sought an interview with Mr. Phelps, and asked for a copy of the letter he was said to have in his possession. He said he had it, but refused to give me a copy of it. I then expressed my wish that he would publish it. He said that he had intended to do so, but had ascertained that the cost would be more than he was willing to pay. I proposed that if he would give it to me I would publish it. He declined that proposition, whereupon brother Wolf and myself bade him good-by and terminated the interview.

Next morning he sent me word that he would meet me at any place that I would appoint for another interview. My friends were divided in their counsel as to the proper course to pursue, but I decided to see him, and so taking an excellent member of our Church, brother Maddux, with me, I proceeded to Mr. Phelps's office. I told him that I had not come for controversy, but simply to ask for, and, if possible, obtain a copy of the letter said to be written by me which he claimed to have in his possession. After some conversation he absolutely refused to let me have it. I asked him if any other person had a copy. He informed me Samuel Black had a certified copy. "Can I get a copy from him?" I inquired. He answered emphatically, "No." As I was about to retire he stated that I had authorized him to publish it the night before at my expense. I told him to give it to me and it should be published at my expense. Of course I could not consent to any other arrangement, and prohibited the publication of any thing at my expense, unless it went through my hands to the printer.

Leaving Parkersburg, I proceeded by the way of my father's to Ravenswood, where my next quarterly-meeting was to be held. I arrived on Saturday, and the meeting commenced at eleven o'clock, A. M. The services, morning, afternoon, and night, gave promise of an excellent meeting.

Sabbath morning early Messrs. Neal and Phelps, of Parkersburg, arrived by steamer. The former sought an interview with me, and manifested great friendship. He complained that I had not visited him while in Parkersburg. I told him frankly that I did not feel safe to do so. The quarterly-meeting was held at a private house, and I learned at the close of the love-feast that application had been made for liberty to address the congregation on an important matter of controversy between the said Phelps and the presiding elder. The proprietor of the house informed them that he had given the use of his house to me for the quarterly-meeting. They then requested him to ask my consent. I told him that I had no controversy with Mr. Phelps, and if I had, this was neither the place nor the day for such business.

We had a time of refreshing during the love-feast. At its close I retired to the woods, to put my case into the hands of God. After an intermission of fifteen or twenty minutes I commenced the public service. The Lord was with me indeed, and the Word was clothed with power. My text was, "The Lord God is a sun and a shield," etc., and I truly felt that while his broad shield was over me I could say, "I will not fear what man can do unto me." I announced a sacramental service for four o'clock, and preaching at candle-lighting.

As soon as I pronounced the benediction, Phelps arose and stated that there existed a difficulty between himself and John Stewart, presiding elder of the Kanawha district, involving the important case of veracity. He had procured leave of Mr. Fetschur to settle the difficulty at his house, and that the presiding elder and congregation were requested to attend there for that purpose at two o'clock, P. M.

As the people were assembling in accordance with that appointment, a steamer touched the wharf, and brothers Wolf and Diltz, of Parkersburg, stepped ashore. I now saw that God proposed to vindicate my cause more promptly than I had expected. These good brethren, having learned providentially that Neal and Phelps had embarked at midnight for Ravenswood, inferred at once that they had some malicious intent, and followed them by the next boat. Their arrival and presence in the congregation gathered by my enemies was exceedingly opportune for me. As I did not attend the meeting, of course I state what occurred on the authority of my friends who were present.

Neal and Phelps both addressed the congregation, the latter protracting his remarks at great length, apparently for the purpose of defeating the sacramental service of the afternoon. He read and commented on the copy of a letter which he had refused to give me. He also read two affidavits, purporting to be from persons who had heard our previous conversation in regard to the publication of the said letter at my expense. One of them stated that I had consented that Phelps might publish and I would pay the cost. The other understood that I consented to publish it, if given to me, at my own expense.

Brothers Wolf and Diltz then reported themselves to the congregation; announced that they had personal knowledge of the fact; had just arrived from Parkersburg, and, if they could be permitted to do so, would state the facts in the case. My accusers would not allow them to speak. The people now began to open their eyes.

Rev. D. G. Morrell, who was also a lawyer and commanded great respect, asked the attention of the congregation for one minute only. It was granted. He stated that they had been listening for hours to hear something that would fix a stain upon the moral character of their presiding elder. He has been charged with falsehood, and in support of the charge two affidavits, taken in his absence and without his knowledge, have been read. They are ex-parte evidence which would be thrown out of any court. Here are two men whose testimony would be competent evidence, who claim to know the facts and wish to state them, but they are not permitted to do so. The claim that the presiding elder would allow the publication of the letter without seeing it, at his expense, is unreasonable, and the accusers have utterly failed. He expressed the opinion that the presiding elder had lost nothing in the confidence of the people by the prosecution.

It broke down so utterly as to appear almost a farce. My accusers took their departure by the first boat, greatly chagrined, and my friends returned with them, happy that they had been able to foil a malicious purpose. I might have enlightened the people touching the moral character of Mr. Phelps and the experiences the Church had had with him, but I could well afford to spare him under the circumstances.

Having written to Bishop Soule during the session of the Louisville Convention the famous letter which afterward, in its various editions, became a sort of text-book for Southern border preachers, and having made repeated unsuccessful endeavors to get a copy of the said letter, I wrote to Bishop Soule again, April 28, 1846, taking care this time to preserve a copy of my letter. In it I gave him a detailed and faithful exhibit of the state of facts in the bounds of the Kanawha district. The following extracts from that letter may be of interest to the reader:

"I saw, after a careful examination of the plan of the General Conference and the action of the Louisville Convention, that the line separating the two Churches was fixed, and could be altered only by a vote of a majority in a *society, station,* or *Conference* on the border of the two Conferences; and that if a majority of any society, station, or Conference on the border voted to belong to the Church on the other side of the line, then the line was changed so as to conform to that vote. It then became a permanent line, and each Church was bound by it. Interior charges were, therefore, to remain in the unmolested care of the Church within whose bounds they were located. I have no disposition to discuss the merits of the plan itself, but I assume that the Bishops of both Churches intend to conform to it. I do not believe that the Bishops of either Church will knowingly send men over the lines thus established. Now I wish to communicate to you the facts touching the Kanawha district:

"We have thirteen circuits and one station, though the station is now attached to the Little Kanawha circuit. We have six circuits that border on the Ohio River, and four that border on the Southern Church. These latter are WAYNE, LOGAN, COAL RIVER, and FAYETTE. In regard to these I wish to give you particular information.

"WAYNE circuit has from six to seven hundred members, not more than one hundred of whom have signified a wish to belong to the Church South. It has six societies that border on the Kentucky Conference. They are as follows: 1. *Hatton's*, three miles from the mouth of Sandy River. It has twenty-seven members, twenty of whom adhere to the Methodist Episcopal Church. 2. *Round Bottom*, twelve miles from Hatton's and fifteen from the mouth of Sandy. It is a large society, and all the members adhere to the Methodist Episcopal Church. 3. *Perry's*, three miles from Round Bottom, and eighteen from the mouth of Sandy. It is a large society and *all* remain. 4. *Mill Creek*, nine miles from Perry's and twenty-seven from the mouth of Sandy. The society numbers forty-eight, and thirty-eight of them remain with the Methodist Episcopal Church. The fifth society is at the *Falls of Tugg;* a large society, and all but one remain in the Methodist Episcopal Church, and that one desires license to preach. The Falls of Tugg are eight miles from Mill Creek, and thirty-five miles from the mouth of Sandy. The sixth society is at *Copley's*, ten miles from the mouth of Tugg, and forty-five from the mouth of Sandy. That is a large society, and all remain in the Methodist Episcopal Church.

"Next in order is LOGAN circuit. It stretches along the

line about forty miles. On that circuit, every society has resolved to remain in the Methodist Episcopal Church. At their last quarterly-meeting last year, the conference—say thirty in number—voted to remain, and I am informed that only three persons in the whole circuit would prefer to belong to the new Church organization.

"The next on the border is COAL RIVER circuit. It stretches along the line say thirty miles. The quarterly conference on this charge also passed a unanimous vote to remain where they they are. Not an individual on the charge desires to adhere South.

"The next charge is FAYETTE circuit. Brother Morrison, the preacher, has informed me that not more than ten in the whole circuit had expressed a wish to go South.

"I have taken great pains to ascertain the facts, and to the best of my knowledge the foregoing are the facts in the case. Now to the point to which I desire especially to call your attention.

"Notwithstanding the facts above stated, a Southern preacher has crossed these circuits, penetrated the interior of the district, and formed a circuit spreading across Wayne, Guyandotte, and Point Pleasant circuits. He has three or four appointments in the bounds of Wayne, six or seven in the bounds of Guyandotte, and three in the bounds of Point Pleasant. At some of these appointments he has majorities, and at some of them minorities. At seven of them the preachers of both Churches preach. The presiding elder of the Maysville district, Kentucky Conference, Church South, has held two quarterly-meetings for that new circuit so constituted. I have believed that this course has been pursued either without the authority of the Bishops of the Church South, or that they have authorized the formation of the circuit without a knowledge of the facts in the case. I have believed, too, that Rev. Mr. Harrison, the presiding elder, and Rev. Mr. M'Gee, the circuit preacher, have been deceived, or they would not have crossed the line in such palpable violation of the law in the case. I could have penetrated the Kentucky Conference if I had deemed it right to do so. One circuit, by a unanimous vote of its quarterly conference, decided to remain in the Methodist Episcopal Church, but I have steadily declined acting otherwise than in strict conformity to the plan of separation. I will give you briefly the state of facts on the several charges on this district at the present time.

"PARKERSBURG, of two hundred and one members, returned last year one hundred and eighteen; are under the care of brother Dillon. On the LITTLE KANAWHA circuit, at my last quarterly-meeting, not more than one hundred had determined to connect themselves with the Church South. That is less than one-fifth of the membership. On RAVENSWOOD no action has been taken this year. Perhaps one-fourth might prefer to go. On RIPLEY Samuel Black has been preparing the people, for nearly two years, to go South, and I am told that he has gone over with as many members as he could induce to go with him. It is a rough and broken circuit, but it lies in the center of the district, so that it would be very inconvenient for us to lose it, or for you to serve it. Perhaps three-fourths of its members would now prefer to go South. On POINT PLEASANT circuit perhaps one-fifth prefer to go. On GUYANDOTTE circuit six hundred and forty-five were returned. Of them sixty-six were colored people. Apart from them, brother Smith says, three hundred and fifty have signed resolutions to remain where they are. I have already spoken of WAYNE; perhaps one-seventh on LOGAN; COAL RIVER, not one in two hundred; on FAYETTE, not one-sixth; on SOMERVILLE, perhaps one-third; on SUTTON, perhaps one-third; on ELK RIVER, none; on CHARLESTON circuit, not to exceed one-fourth. I believe that these estimates will be found very near correct.

"I am aware that great effort has been made to mislead you in regard to the state of facts in this district. The two Spurlocks and the two M'Comases, all men of talent and influence, are working hard for the South. I have been much misrepresented, but I think I have been consistent with myself and the Church from the beginning.

"With my best wishes for your personal welfare, yours most respectfully," etc.

During this controversy the emissaries of the Church South were continually harping on the fact that the preachers of the Methodist Episcopal Church, supplying the Kanawha district, were from Ohio, and not in sympathy with the people of Virginia. The conviction gradually fixed itself upon my mind, that the interests of the Methodist Episcopal Church would be best promoted by the organization of a Western Virginia Conference. Finding that my preachers, and the people with whom I consulted, agreed in this opinion, I began to shape matters for the securing of that end. In pursuance of this plan, I opened a correspondence with the presiding elder of the Rockingham district of the Baltimore Conference, and advocated the measure in the columns of the Western Christian Advocate. The proposition met with favor, and I had the pleasure, at the next General Conference, of assisting to make it the law of the Church. The results have been such as I anticipated. The Church has not only maintained her ground, but has grown and prospered, and, when the spirit of secession developed itself against the flag of the Union, the Methodist Episcopal Church, in the bounds of the Western Virginia Conference, was sound to the core and true to the country. Their blood has fertilized their native mountains, but some of them still live to recount the conflicts, and rejoice in the victories they achieved over rebels and secessionists, both in Church and State. How it would gladden my heart could I once more grasp the friendly hands of those brave men and women! Be faithful, my fellow-soldiers, and we shall soon greet each other where "the wicked cease from troubling, and the weary are at rest." Let us not cherish in our hearts any enmity against those who, in their infatuation, ill-treated us. They sowed the wind, and they have reaped the whirlwind. Let us pray that they may fly from the wrath to come, and find pardon and salvation in the merits of Him who has taught us to say, "Forgive us our trespasses as we also forgive them who trespass against us."

CHAPTER XXV.

PORTSMOUTH DISTRICT, OHIO.

1846-50.

THE Ohio Conference met at Piqua, September 2, 1846, Bishop Morris presiding. Received on trial: John Phetzing, Stephen M. Merrill, Oliver E. Peebles, Michael Sheets, Jacob Holmes, Joseph H. Creighton, Jacob Bonham, Charles H. Lawton, W. W. Cherington, David A. M'Ginnis, Richard L. Brooks, Charles Bauer, Charles Helwig, Frederick Heller, George M. Bush, Lewis Nippert, B. F. Deemer, Adam Cline, Conrad Gahn, John M. Hartman, Jacob Rothweiler, E. H. Peters, Thomas D. Crow, Charles D. Meredith, Thomas M. Gossard, Addison Nichols, Alexander Nelson, William Porter, Allen W. Tibbits, Truman S. Cowden, Sanford Haines, Banner Mark, William Wilson, William J. Quarry, Francis Guthrie, Lewis A. Atkinson—36. This was a large class, and contained many valuable names. Some of them now occupy leading positions in the Church, and give promise of continued usefulness.

The names of the following persons were recorded as having finished their work and gone to receive their crown: John Ferree, Jacob Delay, Benjamin Cooper, and William R. Anderson.

Of Rev. John Ferree, the first on the list, I have already spoken in former parts of this narrative. We had been associated at different times, both in the pastorate and the eldership. I had known him intimately, prized him highly, and loved him dearly. Though some may have excelled him in shining qualities, speaking after the manner of men, very few excelled him in solid worth; and perhaps few will have a brighter crown than he. He was born November 22, 1792, in Lancaster county, Penn., and died in Jackson county, Ohio, October 4, 1845.

Jacob Delay was born in Pennsylvania, December 17, 1781, and died at his residence in Jackson, Ohio, October 18, 1845. While he was young his parents settled in Pickaway county, Ohio, where he experienced religion under the preaching of the Rev. James Quinn. He was licensed as a local preacher, in which relation he served the Church faithfully for many years. In 1824 he was received as a probationer in the Ohio Conference, of which he continued a member, either on the effective or supernumerary list, until at last he fell at his post and was called home. His last days were peaceful and at times triumphant. In death he left this testimony: "The religion which I have preached to others for more than forty years supports me in this trying hour."

Benjamin Cooper was born in Perry county, Ohio, June 3, 1802, and died in Hancock county, Ind., May 13, 1846. He was a bright example of early piety, and was admitted as a probationer in the Ohio Conference in 1827. In 1836, his health having failed, he was superannuated. He then moved to Indiana, where he spent the residue of his days. His ministry was useful, his whole life an example, and his death a sublime illustration of the sufficiency of the grace of God.

William R. Anderson was born June 21, 1810, in Ross county, Ohio, and died February 25, 1846. When a lad but fourteen years of age he gave his heart to God, and joined the Church at a camp-meeting held on Deer Creek circuit. In 1836 he joined the Conference. In 1837 he was my assistant on Athens circuit. He was a young man of more than ordinary promise, and labored acceptably and usefully to the close of his ministry. When death came he was ready. Instead of needing to make preparation for another world, he spent his dying breath in urging upon those who were neglecting the Savior to improve their present opportunity, and seek the Lord.

The secession of the Conferences in the slave-holding States was the leading topic of conversation among the preachers at Conference, and there remained among us a few brethren who had had sympathy with them. The preachers who officiated in the pulpit during the session had liberty, and administered the Word with power. Among the young men of the Conference, brothers R. S. Foster, J. Miley, Moses Smith, John Dillon, J. S. Inskip, and Joseph T. Lewis preached much to the profit of the people. Bishop Morris urged me to consent to return to the Kanawha district, but finally yielded to my solicitation and requested me to nominate my successor. I nominated David Reed, and he was appointed, and proved to be a wise selection for that work. I was appointed to the Portsmouth district. The district embraced the following appointments and preachers:

Portsmouth—David Whitcomb. This station, located on the Ohio River at the mouth of the Scioto, was the principal charge, and the preacher was the strong man of the district. He had clear perception, ready utterance, intimate acquaintance with the Scriptures and with systematic theology, was a close and strong reasoner, and had a rare power of making error look ridiculous and loathsome, and of clothing truth and righteousness with beauty and grace.

Gallipolis—Charles C. Lybrand. Gentlemanly in appearance, dignified in deportment, and respectable in pulpit ability, he always commanded the respect of the Church and people. He had adopted the opinion that one year was long enough for him to remain in a charge, and usually he packed his goods before Conference, ready to be shipped as soon as he should receive his appointment.

Piketon—David Smith and Truman S. Cowden. As brother Smith was associated with my work in Virginia, I have spoken of him in that connection. Brother Cowden was just commencing his itinerant life, and gave good promise of becoming a valuable worker, which prophecy has been abundantly fulfilled.

Waverley—Joseph Barringer, Addison Hite. Brother Barringer was one of our best critics, and excelled in the exposure of doctrinal errors. He was skillful and able in the management of controversy, and diligent and efficient as a pastor. I have spoken of brother Hite in connection with the Kanawha work.

Richmond—Clinton W. Sears. He was a man of undoubted piety, great industry, and superior pulpit ability. This was a year to him of much trial. He felt that he was not in the right place, and so failed to realize his usual success.

French Grant—William R. Litsinger, Lewis A. Atkinson. Brother Litsinger was a man of superior natural ability, which compensated in great part for his lack of educational advantages. He made a fine impression among the people, and had his stability been equal to his other endowments, he would have been of permanent value to the Church. The junior preacher, just beginning his work, was well received, and until his declining health in after years required him to superannuate, brother Atkinson was a worthy and beloved pastor.

Burlington—William T. Hand, W. W. Cherington. Of the preacher in charge I have spoken heretofore. Brother Cherington was a laborious, faithful, and useful preacher, and looked well after the interests of the charges which were intrusted to his care.

Patriot—Alfred L. Westervelt. He was deeply pious and devoted to the work, and was made a great blessing to his charge.

Gallia—Samuel Maddux, Andrew J. Lyda. I have spoken of brother Maddux heretofore. Brother Lyda was a Virginian; educated himself at Augusta College by the avails of his own industry. He possessed those substantial qualities, industry, devotion to purpose, and indomitable perseverance, which give surer promise of ultimate success than the rarest talent and genius without them. He was beloved by the people on Gallia circuit, and has gone on in the even tenor of his useful way until he now stands among the most prominent members of the Western Virginia Conference, of which he is now a member.

Jackson—Charles Ferguson, M. Sheets. These brethren were blessed with a most extensive and glorious work of revival on this charge this year. Of the preacher in charge—a princely man—I have spoken heretofore. The junior preacher was an active pastor, diligent and successful in circulating religious literature among the people, preached good sermons, and did good work.

Rockville—Samuel Brown. He, too, had been among my Kanawha preachers. On this charge he felt at home, and earnestly addressed himself to the work.

My first year's experience on the district was altogether pleasant. The territory was somewhat broken and the roads bad. It being an iron region, the heavy teams carting ore, and coal, and iron, and provisions, cut up the roads badly, but it was a great improvement over the Kanawha mountain rides. The population in the iron region was fluctuating, its ebb and flow being controlled by the prosperity or depression of the iron interest. The preachers and people treated me with marked kindness, and it was a happy year. At the quarterly-meetings of those brethren who had fought by my side on the other side of the river, we enjoyed a rare feast in calling up the memories and recounting the stirring scenes of that warfare.

As my companion spent a portion of this year traveling with my son, who was at that time out of health, I spent much of my time among the people on the work. We boarded part of the year at Gallipolis and part of the year at Richmondale.

The Conference met at Columbus, Ohio, September 1, 1847, Bishop Janes presiding.

The following persons were admitted on trial: J. H. Seddelmeyer, Frederick Schimmelpfennig, Henry Henke, Valentine Ballduff, George F. Jahnke, Adolph Koelter, John Strauch, Charles Schelper, Nicholas Nuhfer, Benjamin St. James Fry, Moses G. Bennett, Samuel D. Clayton, James A. Taylor, James Mitchell, J. R. Prose, A. Head, H. S. Sellman, T. J. M'Mahon, J. B. Hill, W. B. Jackson—21—a class largely composed of Germans to supply that rapidly growing and very promising department of our work.

Rev. Thomas E. Bond, editor of the Advocate and Journal, was a visitor at this session, and added to its interest by his genial spirit in the social circle and his able ministrations in the pulpit. He preached a sermon of great clearness and strength on the "new birth." The election of delegates for the ensuing General Conference elicited considerable interest, and the following persons were chosen: James B. Finley, C. Elliott, Jacob Young, G. W. Walker, J. S. Tomlinson, William Nast, William Herr, J. M. Trimble, J. F. Wright, John Stewart. I had not anticipated being elected, but in view of my intimate acquaintance with the necessities of the border work, I was gratified that I should have the opportunity to represent it.

The boundaries of my district were slightly changed by the transfer of Waverly circuit from it to the Chillicothe district, and the addition of M'Arthurstown circuit from the Marietta district. The district was manned this year as follows:

Portsmouth, David Whitcomb; Gallipolis, William T. Hand; Piketon, D. Smith, L. A. Atkinson; Richmond, Joseph Barringer; French Grant, William R. Litsinger, T. J. M'Mahon; Burlington, Alfred L. Westervelt; Patriot, Levi W. Munsell; Gallia, Orville C. Shelton, Michael Sheets; Jackson, Charles Ferguson, W. W. Cherington; Rockville, Samuel Brown; M'Arthurstown, William T. Metcalf, Richard Pitzer.

In the new men brought into my district I found some valuable workers. The last one on my list, especially, greatly endeared himself to me by his untiring industry and unflagging devotion to the work. In the Spring I took Mrs. Stewart to Athens county, to visit at my father's and among our family connections, while I should attend the session of the General Conference at Pittsburg. Taking a steamer at the mouth of Hocking, I was gratified to find on board Rev. Joseph S. Tomlinson, D. D., and Rev. J. F. Wright, D. D., of our delegation. They were both able men and genial companions, and made the journey a very pleasant one. Saturday night found us at Beaver, and being unwilling to give our example in favor of Sabbath travel, we landed and spent the Sabbath in the village, and preached the Gospel to the people. Taking boat again on Monday we arrived at Pittsburg, and were soon assigned to comfortable quarters. I had the pleasure of rooming with my early and esteemed friend, Rev. E. H. Pilcher. The Conference being organized and the committees raised, I found myself on the committee to examine the Conference journals, which afforded me ample work.

The great secession occupied much of the time of the Conference, and at times the discussion was impassioned and eloquent. A delegation from the Methodist Episcopal Church South was in attendance, but was not recognized, the Conference feeling that the indorsement of slavery by that Church, as well as their flagrant violation of the "plan of separation," made it impossible for us to fraternize with them without giving indorsement to iniquity. Bishop Soule sat in the gallery much of the time, and during some portions of the discussion, especially while Dr. Curry was addressing the Conference, heard strictures upon his course that must have produced a profound impression on his mind in regard to his responsibility. Dr. Dixon, President of the Wesleyan Conference of Great Britain, was with us, and added much to the interest of the session. In dignity and gracefulness of personal presence, and in strength, wisdom, and eloquence of pulpit ministrations, he had few equals. When after his return to England he published his notes of the visit to us, we were much surprised and disappointed to find that his sympathies were evidently somewhat with the pro-slavery branch of the Church. This, from our English brethren who could hardly fraternize with us heretofore on account of our connection with slavery, we could hardly understand.

Returning to my district I found the preachers generally faithfully at their work, and the rest of the year was soon passed in the labors of my large and interesting field. We boarded this year in the family of brother Barringer, on the Richmond circuit, and enjoyed there the society of excellent Christians and good neighbors, such as the Joneses and Drummonds, Davises, Ridenours, Gundys, Dawsons, Watsons, and Claypoles, from whom we received very frequent proofs of their kind regard.

The Conference met at Newark, Licking county, O., September 27, 1848, Bishop Hamline presiding. The following persons were received on trial: Benjamin P. Wheat, John W. Ross, Gilbert C. Townley, James F. Given, Joseph H. Creighton, Conrad Bier, John H. Westervelt, John Ficken, Levi Heiss, Ferdinand A. Sander, Enoch West, John Haight, Michael Kauffman, Samuel Middleton, Andrew B. See, William H. Black, Samuel M. Bright, James T. Bail, John W. Ferree, Joseph C. Harding, Isaac B. Fish, David A. Dryden, Hiram W. Curry, Smith Hill, Jacob Adams, Neriah Redfern, Joseph Blackburn, Timothy Wones, Lafayette Van Cleve—29—a large and good class.

The following brethren had died during the past year, and their memoirs were placed on the record at this Conference: James Quinn and William Parish.

Brother Quinn was one of the pioneers of the Western Church, and one of the patriarchs of our ministry, having entered the ministry before the beginning of the present century, and having commenced his labors in the Western Conference in 1804. He was of Irish descent, born in Washington county, Penn., in 1775, and died at his residence, near Hillsboro, O., December 1, 1847. In childhood his educational advantages were small, but such was his thirst for knowledge that he formed habits of reading and study which resulted in the accumulation of a rich store of knowledge. The class of appointments which he filled during his connection with the work in Ohio is evidence of his high standing among his brethren. He was presiding elder twelve years, was stationed in cities six years, and was eight times sent to the General Conference. He was an able theologian and an admirable preacher. During his last illness he delighted in meditating upon the exceeding great and precious promises, and frequently quoted this passage from the Psalmist: "My flesh and my heart faileth, but God is the strength of my heart, and my portion forever."

Brother Parish was born near Lexington, Ky. He was admitted to the Ohio Conference in 1837, and died at Huntsville, Butler county, Ohio, October 17, 1847. He was a man of warm sympathies and high sense of honor, and preached the Gospel with zeal, ability, and success. His last sickness was protracted and severe, but his confidence in God was unshaken, and his mind was kept in peace. About an hour before his departure, he testified, with great confidence, that the Gospel which he preached to others supported him in the near approach of death.

On reaching the seat of Conference, I was surprised to find the Bishop and all of his counsel, except myself, in session, and the work of stationing, except my own district, well-nigh completed. Bishop Hamline explained to me, that for the purpose of economizing time, he had sent notices to the presiding elders to meet him a few days before the session of the Conference. The notice had failed to reach me, but, as they had dealt fairly with me in my absence, neither my district nor my preachers had suffered any. My work was supplied this year as follows: Portsmouth, P. P. Ingalls; Gallipolis, William T. Hand; Piketon, L. A. Atkinson and S. Parker; Richmond, Samuel Brown; Waverly, D. Smith and J. T. Bail; French Grant, James T. Halliday and M. Sheets; Burlington, A. L. Westervelt and J. W. Ferree; Patriot, W. W. Cherington; Gallia, O. C. Shelton and B. St. James Fry; Jackson, Levi Munsell and Jacob Adams; Maysville, J. F. Chalfant and C. G. Meredith.

The boundaries of the district were this year greatly enlarged by adding to it the Kentucky work. This year the cholera prevailed extensively, and especially along the Ohio River there was great mortality, and, as my district lay along that river all the way from Maysville, Ky., to Gallipolis, I was much exposed and frequently threatened with the premonitory symptoms. I had a very dangerous attack during one of my visits at Portsmouth, and probably, but for the skillful and unremitting care of Dr. W. H. M'Dowell, I should not have survived it. So great were the probabilities that I would be carried off with the disease, that for some months I made my arrangements each day and night, so that if I should be cut down in an hour, my preparation, in regard to things both temporal and spiritual, might be complete. I looked death squarely in the face, and rejoiced to know that if the earthly tabernacle should fall, I had a building of God on high.

Several of the preachers in my district this year were now associated with me for the first time, but among them I found workers of great value and promise. P. P. Ingalls, though much younger than his predecessor, filled the charge at Portsmouth with great success. He had a clear intellect, a sweet spirit, a winning manner, an eloquent tongue, and good executive ability, and rapidly took position in the hearts of the people. To me he was like a very affectionate son in the Gospel, and both myself and companion are under lasting obligations to him and his excellent companion for manifold attentions. Brother Parker this year did more work and better than he had done for years before, and made himself of value to the charge. Brother Halliday fully sustained the recommendation that his former presiding elder had given him, and proved to be an efficient Methodist preacher. Brother Bail was a young man on trial. My experience with him this year was such as to produce the expectation that his itinerant course would be a success. Brother Ferree was a noble scion of a noble stock. He was lovely and beloved, but his race, though a bright one, was destined to be brief. Brother Fry was a young man, of great activity, both of body and mind. It was evident that he would make an able preacher, and a leading business man in matters pertaining to the interests of the Church.

Brother Adams was a noble specimen of a Christian gentleman. A slight monotony in his style of delivery detracted somewhat from his pulpit popularity, but, bating that, he was loved and prized by all who were about him.

Brothers Chalfant and Meredith, on the Maysville charge, were both valuable men, and popular with the people. The preacher in charge was a remarkably ready and forcible preacher, and often rose to an elevated style of eloquence. My visits to the Kentucky work, though a great addition to my labors, were very pleasant. Having endured much persecution, the membership on that charge were generally bound to each other and to the Church of their choice with an ardent affection. They came long distances to attend the quarterly-meeting, and greatly prized these special means of grace. On such occasions we had a genuine exhibition of Kentucky Methodist hospitality. The residences of such as John Armstrong and M. A. Hutchins, at Maysville, and the Bullocks, at Stewart's Chapel and Orangeville, and Uncle Jesse Hambrick, at Canaan, were open to their utmost capacity. A bitter and proscriptive spirit had vented itself toward many of our people, and they were reminded of earlier days, when the disciples took joyfully the spoiling of their goods, and rejoiced that they were counted worthy to suffer shame for Christ's sake.

One of my assistants, an earnest and holy man, Rev. A. L. Westervelt, this year fell at his post, and ascended to heaven, but, as I have adopted the plan of giving obituary notices in connection with the Conference at which the announcement of the death was made, I will notice this good brother further in that connection. The year, on the whole, had been one of prosperity.

The Conference met at Dayton, Ohio, August 19, 1849, Bishop Waugh presiding. The following brethren were admitted on trial: Thomas Lee, Isaac J. Beall, Benjamin

Glasscock, William Cheever, Edward P. Hall, George W. Brush, Asa S. M'Coy, George H. Reed, John M. Leavitt, Samuel C. Riker, Edward C. Merrick, William G. Smith, William B. Zink, Alanson Fleming, Stephen C. Frampton, James H. Hopkins, John Ellis, William Fitzgerald, William M. Smith, Dewitt C. Howard, Oliver M. Spencer, William L. Hypes, Thomas J. N. Simmons, John F. Loyd, Isaac Neff, James Peregrine, Isaac D. Day, Christian Vogel, Benevil Browmiller, William Geyer, Peter Snyder, William Dressler, Charles Dierking, Frederick Heidmeyer, Conrad Muth, Frederick Decker, Philip Doerr, William Flocken—38—a large class, containing much valuable material.

The following brethren had been transferred from the Church militant to the Church triumphant during the past year: Benjamin Lakin, Nathan Emery, Asa B. Stroud, Martin Wolf, Alexander Morrow, Alfred L. Westervelt—6—the largest number that had ever been recorded upon our minutes as having died during one Conference year.

Benjamin Lakin was one of the fathers in our Israel. He was a native of Maryland, but settled in Kentucky when quite young. He commenced his career as a traveling preacher in 1794, and closed his labors early in February, 1849. During a considerable portion of that protracted ministry his name stood on the superannuated list, but all of the strength given him was freely dedicated to God. In his early days in the ministry he preached with great power and success, and during his whole life occupied a high position as a Christian and a preacher of the Gospel. Though in the eighty-second year of his age, and the fifty-fourth of his ministry, when his last sickness arrested him he had several appointments outstanding. He remarked to a friend concerning one of them, "If I live I will fill it, and if I die it will have to fall through." His work was done, and he went up to receive his reward.

Nathan Emery was another of the fathers in Israel. He was born August 5, 1780, in Cumberland county, Maine; commenced traveling in 1799, and went up to take his crown May 27, 1849. The largest portion of his active ministry was spent in New England, but from the year 1821 to the time of his death he resided in Ohio, and part of that time traveled as a member of the Ohio Conference. Sweet and amiable in spirit, practical and earnest in labors, he was popular and useful. He had often feared, or rather dreaded, the last conflict with the king of terrors. When convinced that death was near at hand, he besought the Lord for dying grace. His prayer was answered, and the grace abundantly bestowed. Visions of glory passed before his enraptured soul, and gazing upward, with his last expiring breath, he exclaimed, "Up! up! up!" and he mounted the chariot of God.

Asa B. Stroud was born April 11, 1807. He was admitted to probation in the Ohio Conference in 1830, and spent the first years of his ministry on some of the rugged circuits of the Kanawha district. He afterward filled various appointments in Ohio, and filled them well. During his last year the cholera prevailed about him, but like a brave and faithful shepherd he cared for the flock, never for a moment shrinking from the post of duty. During his last illness he often said, "Good is the will of the Lord concerning me," and September 23, 1849, he sweetly fell asleep in Jesus.

Martin Wolf fell at his post in the midst of a gracious revival of religion on his charge. He had in the beginning of his Christian life made sacrifices for the cause of God and Methodism, his parents having given him the alternative of abandoning home or Methodism. He gave up all for Christ, and thenceforth became an earnest Christian. In 1836 he was admitted on probation in the Ohio

Conference, and after an industrious and successful ministry was suddenly cut down with cholera, July 10, 1849.

Alexander Morrow was born in Northumberland county, Pennsylvania, March 21, 1800; removed to Ohio in 1818, and settled in Ross county. He afterward removed to Crawford county, and in 1827, under the labors of Rev. Arza Brown, he was led to the Savior. In 1833 he joined the traveling connection, and continued to labor faithfully and successfully until February 27, 1849, when he was suddenly seized with sickness during his quarterly-meeting at Georgetown, Ohio. The meeting had been protracted, and the Church was all aglow with the revival fire. He suffered six days, and then entered into rest. About two hours before his death he said, "It is getting dark," and then realizing that it was the shadows of death, he added, "I shall walk through the valley and shadow of death and fear no evil." After the power of speech had failed him he raised his hands and clapped them in holy triumph, and thus he passed away to his rest in heaven.

Alfred L. Westervelt died of cholera, July 31, 1849, in the 29th year of his age. His attack was violent, and the terrible disease rapidly accomplished its work. At ten o'clock, A. M., he was well; at twelve, M., he felt unwell; at three, P. M., he was in a collapse state, and at eight and a half, P. M., he calmly fell asleep in Jesus. He was a humble, holy, and useful minister of the Gospel; met death without fear, counseled his companion in regard to her future course, and having taught his people, by precept and example, how to live, he now taught them how to die. I preached his funeral discourse to a deeply sympathizing and bereaved people, and we laid his remains away in sure and blessed hope of immortality.

At this session of the Conference began the agitation of the "pew question" among us. Rev. George W. Walker, presiding elder of Dayton district, and Rev. J. S. Inskip, the stationed preacher in the first charge, Dayton, had come in conflict on this question. As yet there was not a pewed house in the Ohio Conference, and the preachers and people generally were much averse to the introduction of such. In all of our churches the old practice of the men and women sitting apart prevailed, and to the majority of our people the proposition to deviate in any instance from this practice was fraught with peril to the Church. After the matter was canvassed, brother Inskip promised the Conference that he would cease to agitate the question, and if he should thereafter feel it to be his duty to agitate it he would retire from his Conference connection.

I was returned to Portsmouth district, with the following corps of assistants: Portsmouth, P. P. Ingalls; Gallipolis, Samuel Bateman; Gallipolis circuit, James H. Hopkins, James A. Taylor; Gallia, L. W. Munsell; Piketon, S. Parker, J. W. Ferree; Richmond, Samuel Maddux; Ironton, James T. Halliday, Isaac Neff; Wheelersburg, W. T. Hand, Dewitt C. Howard; Burlington, J. H. M'Cutchen, J. Adams; Patriot, W. W. Cherington; M'Arthurstown, C. H. Warren, Asa M'Coy; Jackson, O. C. Shelton, L. A. Atkinson.

Several of the charges had been divided, so that much of the same territory appeared on the minutes under new names. The new pastors brought into my district proved to be good men and true. Brother Bateman this year had his first experience as a stationed preacher. He possessed unusual social power, and both in the pulpit and pastoral work succeeded. He was a choice man. Brothers Hopkins and Taylor succeeded well. The junior preacher had just commenced his itinerant life, and the preacher in charge had brought from the local ranks, where he had long served the Church, both experience and ability. He was an excellent circuit man. Brother Neff, a young man just received on trial, was exceedingly modest and unassuming. He failed in his pulpit efforts again and again until the people consented that he should retire from the circuit. He still felt, however, that he was called to the work, and that God had work for him to do. He went home and gave himself to prayer and study, came back to the next Conference, received an appointment, went to it, and succeeded. Thenceforward his itinerant life was successful. Brother Howard was a young man of excellent natural ability and prepossessing manners. He succeeded well this year; afterward married Miss Rankin, of a leading Methodist family, at Newark, Ohio, and connected himself with the Rock River Conference, where he labored with acceptability and usefulness until the breaking out of the war. His supposed want of sympathy with the administration rendered him unacceptable, and he finally joined the Episcopal Church and entered its ministry. The last that I knew of him he was earnestly engaged in the ministry of that Church, and doing good work. Brother Warren was diligent as a pastor and successful as a preacher. He had a passion for the natural sciences, and had acquired very respectable cabinets in geology, mineralogy, botany, and zoölogy. He had a good head and a very large and warm heart. Brother M'Coy was a young man of much promise, and has since transferred to the Missouri Conference, where he has made his mark as a workman that needeth not to be ashamed.

I had been exceedingly happy in my association with my preachers, and this year it seemed to me that I had about the cream of the Ohio Conference.

As my son was this year traveling as agent for the Ohio Wesleyan University, I took occasion of his canvass of my district to make a visit to the West. He held one round of quarterly-meetings for me, while my companion and myself visited our friends in Iowa. Taking our horse and buggy to Cincinnati, we embarked on board the steamer "Rainbow" for St. Louis. Thence we went by land through Illinois, visiting my brother-in-law, William Gamble, and other friends; then crossed into Iowa, at Fort Madison, and visited my brothers, William and Alexander Stewart, in Lee county, and my sister Sally, at Marshall, in Henry county, and a goodly number of old Ohio friends who had emigrated to the West. At Burlington I enjoyed a visit with Rev. I. I. Stewart, the pastor of the Church in that place, an old and valued friend of mine. We had expected our son, J. W. Stewart, at Burlington, but after remaining as long as we could, we left for home, and he, having been detained for want of a steamer, arrived a few hours after we had started for home. We returned by carriage through Springfield, Illinois, Terre Haute and Indianapolis, Indiana, and Cincinnati, Ohio. It had been to us a pleasant vacation from the district work, and we returned to devote our renewed energies as best we could in getting the district in the best possible order for the closing up of our constitutional term on it.

The four years on this district had been full of rich experience and profitable fellowships. Were I to place on the record the names of all those who were endeared to me on the several charges, I should swell this volume beyond reasonable bounds. The eastern portion of the district had belonged to "Letart Falls" circuit, which I traveled in 1816, and a few survived with whom I could recount the scenes of those early days. Methodism had taken firm hold of the soil; had grown into a strong and vigorous tree, and multitudes were now enjoying the refreshment of its shade.

CHAPTER XXVI.

DEER CREEK CIRCUIT, OHIO.

1850-52.

THE Conference met at Chillicothe, Ohio, September 18, 1850, Bishops Morris and Janes presiding. The following persons were received on probation: George Reiter, Gottlieb Nachtreib, Hughes Rehm, Peter B. Baker, Henry Lukemyer, Henry T. M'Gill, Thomas M. Thralls, Thomas Collett, John F. Marlay, Joseph C. Reed, John W. Cassatt, Amos Wilson, John C. Maddy, John J. Thompson, Silas Bennett, Thomas L. Lloyd, George W. Harris, Samuel T. Creighton, William Morris, Joseph Tiffany, Alfred Beall, James M. Cavin—22—a good class, in some of whom I felt a special interest, having introduced them into the ministry.

Brothers Warrington and Williams had crossed the river of death during the past year, but they crossed at the "Christian's ford." Rev. C. B. Warrington was born in Manchester, England, March 13, 1814; admitted to probation in the Ohio Conference in 1842, and died, after a brief but painful illness, February, 1850. Brother Warrington was an evangelist, and many led to the Savior by him will doubtless rise up to claim him as their spiritual father at the coming of the Lord Jesus. He was a man of cultivated mind, sweet spirit, great tenderness of heart, and a burning zeal for God.

Rev. Oliver P. Williams was born April 13, 1814, and in 1838 went from the practice of medicine to the work of a Methodist traveling preacher. He was a solid, unassuming, faithful man, whose light was shining as well from his daily walk as from the pulpit from which he preached the Word. While on Venice circuit he was attacked with inflammation of the brain, from the effects of which he did not recover until the great Head of the Church called him to his home above.

At this Conference we again had the question of "pewed sittings" up in a new and exciting form. As stated in a former chapter, Rev. John S. Inskip had promised to desist from agitating the question among the people of his charge, or retire from the Conference. He now came to the Conference charged with having failed to keep good his promise. Dr. Tomlinson and James B. Finley espoused his cause, and Jacob Young and Granville Moody prosecuted him. The verdict of the Conference was a censure. Brother Inskip, however, appealed his case to the General Conference.

I was appointed to Deer Creek circuit with Rev. David Sargent for my colleague, and Rev. James M. Jamison for my presiding elder. I was much pleased with both of them. The presiding elder was a very instructive preacher, and looked carefully after the interests of the Church in his district. Brother Sargent was a good preacher, and attended faithfully to his work.

My appointment to this charge was grateful to my feelings on many accounts. The state of my wife's health made it important that I should be at home more than I had been for some years past. Here I found not only what we called light work, but we anticipated the revival of friendships and associations of long standing. Two of our most pleasant years in the itinerancy had been spent on this circuit nearly a quarter of a century before.

We moved into the parsonage at Clarksburg, and soon

found that we had not reckoned too strongly on the pleasures of our new home. Very many, indeed, of those who were the pillars of the Church when we first traveled the circuit had passed away, but they had left a name behind them, and their children and grandchildren rallied about us and gave us cordial welcome, and renewed such attentions as we had been accustomed to receive from their parents.

I found the circuit much smaller in its boundaries than when I first traveled it. Its present list of appointments were, 1. Dry Run; 2. Asbury; 3. Locust Grove; 4. New Holland; 5. Hayes; 6. Williamsport; 7. Mount Pleasant; 8. Littleton's; 9. Hubbard's; 10. Cedar Grove; 11. Hoskins's Chapel; 12. Spring Bank; 13. Union Chapel; 14. Brown's Chapel; 15. Mount Zion; 16. Clarksburg. The distance between the appointments being short, and none of them being very far away from home, I was able to spend more of my time with my family than ever before. And this was providential, for my dear companion was sorely afflicted these years, so that much of the time we regarded her life to be in extreme peril.

The Conference met at Springfield, Ohio, September 17, 1851, Bishop Morris presiding. The following were received on trial: William Kaetter, Gottlieb Wahl, William Engel, Jacob Krehbiel, Charles Elder, John H. Damm, Gustaff Ricker, Henry Wilky, Augustus Verhoeff, Wesley Dennett, Benjamin F. Morris, Samuel B. Sheeks, Jesse M'D. Robinson, William Q. Shannon, Henry F. Green, William Grange, James Kendall, David Mann, Isaiah A. Bradrick, David C. Benjamin, Robert C. Fulton—21.

The following brethren were recorded as having died during the past year: James A. Taylor, Joseph T. Lewis, and Philip A. Mutchner.

Brother Taylor was received on trial in the Conference

in 1847, and performed efficient service from that time until his labors closed on the Jackson circuit, August 10, 1851. He was several years under my charge, and I regarded him as a young man of much promise and worth. He had a sprightly intellect, and his ministry was of a stirring and awakening character. He sent from his dying couch assurances to his brethren of the Conference that he had victory over death, and requested them to meet him in the paradise of God.

Brother Lewis was born in the city of Cincinnati, April 8, 1824. He was received into the Ohio Conference on probation in 1843, when in his nineteenth year of age, and immediately entered upon a brilliant and remarkably successful ministry. He was transferred the next year to the Rock River Conference, and the next year to Iowa. After serving several of the leading Churches in Iowa, he was transferred back to the Ohio Conference, where he continued to labor until laid aside by disease. He spent several years traveling, in the hope of regaining his health, for he had an ardent desire to live and labor for God. He died in the city of Philadelphia, November 3, 1850, full of peace and hope. He said to a brother who visited him near the close of life: "I would, were it God's will, desire to return home that I might die among my brethren, and my ashes rest beside kindred friends till the coming of Jesus," and then in calm submission added, "but I would not make a change if I could."

Brother Mutchner was born in Butler county, Ohio, January 10, 1817, and died in Darke county, Ohio, October 2, 1850. He was admitted on trial in the Ohio Conference in 1841. He was studious in preparation for the pulpit, and faithful in the declaration of the Word of God. He was deeply devoted to the work to which he was called, and enjoyed in a high degree the consolations of religion. As he drew near the grave he assured his companions that he was going home, and then peacefully closed his eyes in death.

According to mutual expectation and desire, I was returned to Deer Creek circuit, with Rev. Samuel Middleton as my colleague. He proved to be a zealous and useful minister, and commanded the confidence and respect of the people. My associations with the excellent people of this charge during these two years were mutually pleasant and profitable, and we regretted the closing of our constitutional term. During my first term on the circuit, as recorded in the early part of this narrative, my companion had been sick nigh unto death, and God had raised her up in answer to prayer, and during my present term she had again been sweeping along close by the borders of the grave; and I now felt that if it must be so that I must be bereaved of my dear companion, there was no place on earth where I would rather that her grave should be than by the side of the dear Christian friends who had fallen asleep on Deer Creek circuit.

Our Conference was represented in the General Conference which met at Boston the first of May, 1852, by brothers William Nast, J. M. Trimble, J. Young, C. Elliott, G. W. Walker, G. Moody, J. F. Wright, U. Heath, Z. Connell, C. Brooks, A. M. Lorrain, M. Marlay, and R. O. Spencer.

CHAPTER XXVII.

LONDON CIRCUIT, OHIO.

1852-54.

THE Ohio Conference met at Zanesville, Ohio, September 1, 1852, Bishop Janes presiding, assisted by Bishop Simpson. The following preachers were received on trial: Lovett Taft, Cyrus Felton, Joseph D. Crum, Robert J. Black, Albert G. Byers, W. A. Prettyman, Henry H. Ferris, Theodore D. Martindale, William S. Benner, William Catlin, E. H. Dixon, Elijah Fate, Joseph Cartlich—13.

At this Conference we recorded the names of two brethren who had died during the past year, both of whom were very dear to me; namely, Samuel Maddux and Ebenezer B. Chase. The former had labored by my side and under my direction faithfully and successfully amid the hardships of border warfare, and the other had been my colleague on the Felicity (Whiteoak) circuit. I have spoken of these dear brethren in the appropriate place in my narrative. They died in the faith and comfort of the Gospel. Brother Maddux was born in Ross county, Ohio, May 2, 1818, and died in Logan, November 19, 1851.

I was appointed to London circuit with Rev. J. S. Brown, an able, talented, and zealous minister, for my colleague. Though I had but a short distance to move, yet such was the health of my companion that it was extremely doubtful whether she could survive it. She however encouraged making the effort, and, by the blessing of God, suffered less than we feared. We received a cordial welcome, and were soon located in the parsonage at London.

The circuit had the following list of appointments: 1. London; 2. Wesley Chapel; 3. Bethel; 4. Concord; 5. Brush School-house; 6. Midway; 7. Ray's School-house; 8. Maple Grove; 9. California; 10. King's School-house; 11. Murphy's School-house; 12. Mt. Sterling; 13. Greenland; 14. Berry's School-house; 15. Yankeetown; 16. Cook's School-house; 17. Waterloo.

Though as this list indicates it extended from California to Greenland, and embraced London and Waterloo, yet it was not in fact a very large circuit. It was a mere garden-spot in comparison with many that I had traveled. As, however, the health of my companion made it important for me to be at home at night, my traveling, especially my night traveling, was pretty heavy. I had always been accustomed to make promptness at my appointments, the leading of the classes, and visiting the people at their homes a matter of conscience; and while I doubt not the people, who sympathized with us so sincerely and generously, would have excused me if I had neglected much of this labor, yet it had so become the habit of my life and joy of my labor, that I cast myself upon God for help and went forward.

We were blessed with an excellent revival of religion, and the year was one of prosperity. The circuit had a large and most excellent membership, who endeared themselves to us very greatly by their generous sympathy and constant attentions. Many, also, who were not members of the Church, vied with the membership in acts of kindness.

The Ohio Conference held its forty-second session in Lancaster, Ohio, commencing September 7, 1853, Bishop Morris presiding. The following persons were admitted on trial: William Z. Ross, Thomas G. Ross, William H. M'Clintock, Benjamin F. M'Elfresh, Marcus L. King, Thomas H. Hall, John T. Miller, Lemuel F. Drake, Thomas H. Phillips, Samuel Rankin, Edmund Mabee, H. G. G. Fink, Henry Gertner, Joseph Williams, David H. Cherington, Daniel Tracy, William Trone, John C. Gregg, Robert D. Anderson, Russel B. Bennett, William S. Taylor, Samuel Tippett—22.

During the past year the Rev. Samuel Hamilton and Rev. Henry Smith Hill had died, and their memoirs were now spread upon the journals.

I have had occasion to refer frequently to brother Hamilton in the preceding pages of my narrative. He was one of the able and influential members of the Conference. He was born in Monongahela county, Virginia, December 17, 1791; joined the traveling connection in 1815; and peacefully fell asleep in the arms of Christ May 4, 1853.

Brother Hill was born in Ross county, Ohio, December 12, 1820. In 1848 he was admitted on trial in the Ohio Conference. He labored faithfully and successfully until August 5, 1852, when he was summoned from labor and suffering to reward and rest. He was much beloved by the people to whom he ministered the Word of life, and will long be remembered as a faithful minister.

We were addressed at this session of the Conference by the Rev. Henry Slicer, agent for the Metropolitan Church at Washington City. That enterprise, after various advances and reverses, has finally—1869—succeeded, and the representative church edifice is now completed and dedicated.

Monday morning, at ten o'clock, the regular order of business was laid aside to hear the semi-centennial sermon of the Rev. Jacob Young. His text was Psalm lxxxvii, 2: "The Lord loveth the gates of Zion more than all the dwellings of Jacob." He stood before us the veteran warrior, worn and trembling, and almost blind, but full of the memories of the battles and victories of half a century, and still full of love and zeal, and faith and power. O how our hearts thrilled as we looked upon him and listened to his words!

Much to our satisfaction I was returned to London circuit, and again favored with an excellent colleague, Rev. Joseph Crum. We addressed ourselves to the work in right good earnest, and soon the revival fires began to break out and spread from appointment to appointment, until the whole circuit felt its influence. The most extensive work was at Wesley Chapel, Mt. Sterling, and Greenland. At these points the Lord was with us in power, and many were converted, and valuable additions made to the membership.

Washington Witherow, a man of high standing and extensive influence, was among the converts at Wesley Chapel. After the arrow of conviction penetrated his heart he wandered about some days, trying to throw off these feelings. One night, however, when the power of God descended upon the congregation, and many were at the mourners' bench, he reached a decision in the matter, and came forward and cried aloud to God for mercy. Many were comforted, but he was still comfortless when the meeting closed. I accepted the invitation of sister Witherow to go home with them, hoping to assist them in establishing at once the family altar. He kindled a fire in the open fire-place, and as the flames began to extend up among the wood I saw a tobacco-pipe among the wood, and called his attention to it, but he made no answer. After a few moments, hesitation, his wife remarked that probably he regarded the pipe as one of his idols. Though this was a small circumstance in itself, yet it indicated the spirit of the man, and was prophetic of not only decision, but of determination to serve God from principle, at whatever sacrifice of present gratification of the desires of the flesh. I was curious afterward to know whether his abandonment of the pipe was permanent, and was gratified to learn that it was. There is more heroism in abandoning tobacco, we are told, than those dream of who have not been slaves to the practice, and only the voice of God commanding, and the grace of God helping, can enable some to get the victory. But to return to the narrative.

The next day brother Witherow was powerfully converted, and at once took standing as a man of God. On one occasion after this I had an exhibition of his generous spirit. While at his house my horse was violently attacked with botts, and died. Brother Witherow put one of his own horses before my buggy, and told me to use it until I was better supplied; and then he passed about among his friends, and in a short time raised funds to purchase an excellent horse, which they presented to me. This kindness, both unsolicited and unexpected on my part, was gratefully received as an expression of their love. I knew that such things were not uncommon when the preacher was poor, but as it was known that I was independent in my temporal circumstances I had not expected it. Judging, however, from what experience I have had in such things, I am inclined to think that Churches are gainers even more than the preachers when there is such kindness shown. Every cord that binds the hearts of preacher and hearer together makes the preaching more effective, and all the labors of the pastor more hearty and successful.

We had on this circuit only two local preachers, and they were both venerable with years, and so infirm as not to be able to go forth as they had done in their younger days. But fathers Minshall and Gould still helped us with their influence and prayers. Among the excellent of the circuit was old brother Watson and his family, constituting quite a group, and presenting the delightful spectacle of a Christian family. James Foster was a valuable man, acquitting himself handsomely in the several offices thrust upon him, both in Church and State. He was blessed with ample means, and these he used ungrudgingly in aiding to promote every good word and work. John Fisher, who was his neighbor, was a man of kindred spirit and worth. Jesse Watson was another upon whom God was pouring wealth, and who was, with a liberal hand, devoting his means to worthy uses. Quinn Minshall, too, though not at that time in the Church, had generosity corresponding to his wealth, and afterward gave himself and all to God. May the blessing of Heaven be upon him and his! Isaac Fisher, leader and steward at Mt. Sterling, and Isaac Moore, of the same place, Stephen Moore and John Dungan, of London, were all men esteemed and honored by the Church, and who met the official responsibilities placed upon them in a manner profitable to all concerned. Brother Andrew Johnson, of Midway, was a first-class exhorter. His labors were attended with an unction and success that was seldom excelled. But how shall I arrest my pen while so many names of never-to-be-forgotten friends come crowding upon the memory, men of renown, such as the Bonds, and Pancakes, and Warners, and Lotspeiches, and Slagles, and a long list of such, whose names are in the book of life?

During this year the affliction of my wife culminated. The most eminent physicians agreed in pronouncing it an "ovarian tumor." It had reached such enormous proportions that it was estimated that it would weigh twenty-five pounds. It already pressed upon the vitals, and, in the opinion of the physicians, only a surgical operation gave any hope of her surviving any length of time. She laid the matter before God in prayer, and received the impression that it was not her duty to resort to such means, but that she should leave the matter in the hands of the Great Physician. She thus rested her case, and though a great sufferer, she was very happy. A choice circle of Christian friends made special supplications for her recovery. Brother Warner, a very earnest Christian, assured her that he had received direct answer that she would recover. My son and his family, who had taken a transfer to the Rock River Conference, visited us on their way thither, and they united very fervently in these prayers. To the unspeakable satisfaction of her friends she began to improve. A desire sprang up in her mind to accompany my son to the West, and visit our eldest son and family at Monroe, Wisconsin. She was carefully conveyed to the cars, and by the aid of pillows and wrappings made as comfortable as might be; and, strange to say, she improved constantly, though slowly, from that time. As the tumor had been about six years coming, so it was about the same time disappearing. I place the incident upon the record here especially in recognition of my gratitude to Almighty God, who heard and answered prayer, and to encourage any who may be similarly afflicted.

CHAPTER XXVIII.

PICKERINGTON CIRCUIT, AND LANCASTER DISTRICT, OHIO.

1854-56.

THE Conference held its forty-third session at Portsmouth, Ohio, commencing September 6, 1854, Bishop Scott presiding. The following persons were received on trial: Carmi A. Van Anda, Levi Hall, Fielding Harper, Earl D. Fink, Uriah L. Jones, James W. Alderman, Robert D. Stephenson, James Q. Lakin, Noah Speck, John Kemper, John Q. Gibson, Stephen Ryland, W. C. Filler, Asbury C. Kelley, J. T. Finch, D. Harlocker, Addison Nichols—17.

Our ranks, during the past year, had suffered no diminution by the death of any of our traveling preachers, nor had any withdrawn, or been expelled.

As I had spent four very pleasant years on the Portsmouth district, I had the privilege during this session of the Conference of seeing a large number of old and cherished friends. I was appointed to Pickerington circuit, with Rev. Stephen M. Merrill for my colleague.

After the adjournment of Conference I returned to London, moved my goods to the parsonage at Pickerington, put things in order, laid in supplies for living, and then went to Wisconsin, where my companion was visiting with our children, to accompany her home. I found her improved in health, and after a brief visit with the boys we returned to Ohio, and I entered upon my work.

Brother Merrill, my colleague, was one of the strong men of the Conference, but so impaired was his health at that time that the presiding elder released him from the charge, and employed brother Hannawalt, a good local preacher, to take his place.

It was by far the lightest work I had ever filled, there being only eight appointments on the circuit; namely, 1. Pickerington; 2. Powell's Chapel; 3. Reynoldsburg; 4. Taylor's Station; 5. White Chapel; 6. White Hall; 7. Winchester; 8. ——— School-house.

We had good meeting-houses, good congregations, and good times on the circuits, and a good parsonage to live in, and good neighbors full of good will. We felt that the lines had fallen to us in pleasant places. The Lord poured out of his Spirit on the charge, and we had some glorious revivals of religion. At Pickerington and Powell's Chapel, especially, we had a good ingathering. The year was one of prosperity and enjoyment, and wound up very satisfactorily.

A host of good people, the excellent of the earth, endeared themselves to us on this circuit. And even now the Taylors, and Powells, and Fowbles, and Pickerings, and Fords, and Pattersons, and Stephensons, and a long list of such crowd upon my memory, and I seem to see their smiling faces, and hear their words of sympathy and affection, as in former years. May the grace of our Lord Jesus Christ be with them and their posterity through all the generations to come!

The Conference held its forty-fourth session at Athens, Ohio, commencing September 5, 1855, Bishop Morris presiding. The following were admitted on trial: Daniel Lamont, Charles Bethauser, Ezekiel Sibley, George W. Nuzum, John J. Stillians, Samuel M. Donahoe, Jonathan W. Stump, William C. Holliday, Dugald Thompson, Alonzo Chapman—10.

PICKERINGTON CIRCUIT, OHIO.

Rev. Henry Forest Green, a lovely young man of great promise, had fallen by the hand of disease during the past year. He was born in Somerset, Ohio, February 18, 1830. During the great revival at Bainbridge, Ohio, referred to in the preceding pages, Henry consecrated his heart and life to God and his service. He commenced the study of medicine, but so strong were his own convictions and those of his brethren, that God had other work for him to do, that he left his medical studies and entered the Ohio Wesleyan University to prepare more fully for the work of the ministry. He was received on trial in the Ohio Conference in 1851, and preached with great acceptability for several years. His last Conference appointment was to Zanesville City Mission. In the Spring of that year, however, he was sent to supply a vacancy which occurred in Portsmouth. His health, however, soon began to decline, and he was persuaded to retire from labor for a time, with the hope of recruiting his health. But his pulpit work was now done. He suffered on until the 6th of May, when the Master said, "It is enough, come up higher." Shouting "Glory! glory! glory!" he closed his eyes upon earthly scenes to open them upon the brighter scenes of heaven. "He died as the Christian minister might well wish to die—mature in the grace of the Spirit."

This session of the Conference was unusually pleasant to me from the fact that I enjoyed the society of many relatives and friends living at Athens and thereabouts. We elected the following brethren to represent us at the General Conference, which was to meet the next May: Z. Connell, J. M. Trimble, S. Howard, J. M. Jameson, J. Young, and U. Heath.

I was appointed to Pickerington circuit, with Charles Bethauser for my colleague, and Rev. James L. Grover for my presiding elder.

Soon after my entrance upon my work, I received a commission from Bishop Morris to take charge of the Lancaster district in place of J. L. Grover, resigned. I appointed brother Hannawalt to succeed me on the circuit, and entered at once upon the work of the district.

At Lancaster I found Rev. J. M. Jameson in charge. He had been my presiding elder for several years past, and now welcomed me in our changed relations. He had this year a great revival, and gathered more than one hundred souls for Christ.

At West Rushville I found in charge my old friend Rev. C. C. Lybrand, of whom I have spoken in preceding pages.

At Baltimore, Samuel M. Bright, Henry Gortner, and J. T. Donahue, sup. Brother Bright had a clear logical mind, and discharged his duties with dignity and grace. Brother Gortner was a faithful worker, and gave evidence of a good mind, well improved.

At Newark, Eastern charge, Joseph H. Creighton; Western charge, A. B. See—both valuable men, but of different style of talent. Brother Creighton had a good memory and exuberant imagination, was always interesting, and oftentimes attained to lofty flights of eloquence, which carried all before him. Brother See, though not so brilliant, was a close student, well acquainted with Methodism, capable of defending her doctrines and Discipline against all objectors. His was not the rapid growth of the soft maple, but rather that of the rock maple. I anticipated that every year would add to his permanent value to the Church.

At Granville I found that strong thinker and clear-headed preacher, Rev. Stephen M. Merrill, now editor of the Western Christian Advocate.

At Alexandria, Banner Mark, a man tall in stature, and having in him more possibilities of usefulness than had ever been fully developed.

At Johnstown, Abraham Cartlich and A. M. Alexander, both good men and true—men who, if they ever took prominent position, you could be sure that it was without any wire-pulling or management upon their part. They were both modest and retiring men, best loved by those who knew them best, and possibly sometimes left in the humbler fields of labor because they were content, while others, less deserving, were promoted because they clamored for promotion.

At Etna, Samuel Tippett, a man whose soul was in his work. He had a fine imagination, and was an interesting and successful preacher.

At Pickerington, Rev. George Hannawalt, a local preacher held in high estimation, took my place as preacher in charge, and did good work. The junior preacher, brother Bethauser, was just commencing his itinerant life. He was recommended to the Conference from Newark, and gave promise of being a successful Methodist preacher.

At Groveport I found Rev. Francis A. Timmons and Jacob Martin. The preacher in charge, as I have had occasion to record in a former chapter, was of the old and excellent Methodist stock. Brother Martin was a well-posted theologian and a very valuable man, but his great modesty caused him to shrink from thrusting himself into any position of prominence.

At Royalton, George G. West was preacher in charge, and John Kemper the second preacher. Of Mr. West, a good and useful man, I have already spoken. His assistant was in feeble health, but was faithful in the expenditure of what strength he had for the advancement of the cause of God.

At Maxville, Levi Hall, Jonathan W. Stump. They were both growing men, faithful and popular among the people.

Brother D. Cadwallader had charge of the *Welsh Mission*,

but this year closed his missionary work and he went home to his reward. More of him hereafter.

The year passed rapidly, so full was it of important and responsible work; it also passed pleasantly, as the brethren in the ministry and the members of the Church gave me hearty welcome, and the labors of the year were crowned with gratifying success.

CHAPTER XXIX.

JACKSON DISTRICT, OHIO.

1856-60.

THE Conference held its forty-fifth session at Newark, Ohio, commencing September 3, 1856, Bishop Ames presiding. The following persons were admitted on trial: Elias W. Kirkham, Henry L. Whitehead, John W. Lewis, Elias N. Nichols, Frederick S. Thurston, William S. Taylor, John M. Shuly, Thomas M'Intyre—9.

During the past year the following had died: William Catlin, David Cadwallader, and Isaac D. Day.

Rev. William Catlin was born in the State of Maine in 1811; in 1852 joined the Ohio Conference on probation. His itinerant career was short, but he did his work faithfully, and left among the people that he served the fragrance of a holy life.

Rev. David Cadwallader was born in North Wales, Montgomery county, May 28, 1791, and died at his residence in Newark, Ohio, October 19, 1855. He became a Methodist in 1812, and commenced preaching the Gospel in 1814. He came to the United States and settled in Delaware county, Ohio, in 1821, and in 1828 joined the Ohio Conference and was sent forth as a missionary among the Welsh people. He continued his labors in that department, at intervals, during the rest of his life. He was a man of God, and a minister greatly respected and loved, and will doubtless have many stars in his crown in the great day.

Rev. Isaac D. Day was born in Petersburg, Penn., April 9, 1809, and died at Dumontville, Fairfield county, March 30, 1856. He served the Church faithfully as a local preacher for several years, and then joined the traveling connection in 1819, in which he continued to the end of his life. He was a good, plain, zealous preacher. He was more than ordinarily gifted in prayer, and as a sweet singer he had few equals. His singing often produced a most thrilling effect upon the congregation. He died peacefully, and doubtless rests with the redeemed on high.

Bishop Ames put forward the business of the Conference with his usual dispatch, and yet had time for some social intercourse with his brethren. I recall with much pleasure his kind attentions to me. He invited me to his room to talk over the reminiscences of our earlier life, as we were brought up in adjoining townships, in Athens county, Ohio.

I was appointed to the Jackson district. From the list of charges in it, and the preachers supplying those charges, I found that I would be at home. Almost all of the territory had belonged to Portsmouth district when I traveled it, and many of the preachers had been associated with me either on that work or in Virginia. In the following list I shall only speak of the characteristics of the preachers now for the first time under my charge, having spoken of the others in former pages.

Jackson—Charles H. Warren. *Jackson circuit*—Timothy Wones, F. S. Thurston. These brethren were both faithful, popular, and successful. Brother Wones, as I think, afterward made a great mistake in retiring from the work. No doubt there are circumstances, pecuniary and domestic, that sometimes justify a preacher while in good health and useful in the work to retire from it, but certainly it is a step that calls for searching self-examination and earnest prayer before it is decided upon.

Richmond—Edward P. Hall, J. W. Alderman. Brother Hall was a man of superior pulpit popularity, and did valuable work for the Church. Brother Alderman was a young man of attractive and commanding personal presence, and made so favorable an impression on his congregations at his first efforts, that some feared he could not sustain himself up to that standard during the year. In this, however, they were agreeably disappointed. They both grew upon the people, proved to be true yoke-fellows, and accomplished a good work for that charge.

M'Arthur—Joseph Morris. He had a glorious revival, from which I doubt not he will have stars in his crown.

Hamden—D. H. Cherington. With a manly, open countenance, dignified Christian bearing among the people, and earnest faithful labor, he seldom failed to have a revival. This year God poured out his Spirit abundantly upon his charge.

Mount Pleasant—James T. Holliday. During the year he went to Kansas, and I had to supply the work from the local ranks.

New Plymouth—John Dillon, W. C. Holliday. Brother Holliday possessed good natural ability, and only needed a measure of heavenly lightning poured into him to have made him a man of power.

Furnace—Uriah L. Jones. He was an efficient man, and usually had the honor of reporting the fruits of revival on his charge. It was so this year.

Kigerville—John R. Prose. Unlike the brother last named, brother Prose seldom reported results from his labor. He was uniformly pious, and was also faithful to his appointments, but for some reason his ministry seemed to be unfruitful. Had he felt it to be his duty to retire to the local ranks, I would not have dissuaded him from that course.

Gallipolis—Thomas J. N. Simmons. He was prompt, active, dignified and affable, and a workman that needed not to be ashamed.

Gallipolis circuit—Daniel Harlocker, William S. Taylor. These brethren were of kindred spirit. They possessed rare adaptation to the itinerant work. They won the hearts of the people to themselves without effort, and put forth all their efforts to lead them to Christ. They were knit to each other like David and Jonathan.

We had a pleasant home at Jackson, and the year was one of home enjoyment and district prosperity.

The Ohio Conference held its forty-sixth session at Chillicothe, commencing August 26, 1857, Bishop Morris presiding. The following preachers were admitted on trial: Jacob Hathaway, William P. Grantham, William Glenn, Peter V. Ferree, Joseph H. Adair, Isaac B. Brodrick, T. Welles Stanley, John W. Dillon, William R. Copeland, John W. Wakefield, Jeremiah Slocum—11. Some of these I had introduced to the Christian ministry, and felt much anxiety for their success. Thus far they are meeting my expectations, and give promise of continued usefulness in the Church.

The venerable Abner Goff had closed his pilgrimage, and his memoir was spread upon the journal of the Conference. He was born in Vermont, November 4, 1782. In 1819 he was admitted on trial in the Ohio Conference, and continued a laborious, useful, and effective preacher until 1841. His health having failed, he was placed on the supernumerary list, and continued either on that list or the superannuated list, until he closed his life in the city of Columbus, March 15, 1857. He was a good man, and maintained a high place in the confidence and affections of all that knew him.

I was re-appointed to Jackson district, with the following list of charges and helpers:

Jackson—Joseph Morris. He had a year of great prosperity, and gathered more than a hundred precious souls for the Master.

Jackson circuit—William S. Benner, F. S. Thurston. Brother Benner was one of my new men, and proved to be a good and useful man in the work.

Richmond—Peter V. Ferree. Had brother Ferree enjoyed health so that his physical vigor had been equal to his mental ability, he would have accomplished much more than he did.

M'Arthur—Stephen C. Frampton. Brother Frampton had an investigating, critical, and well-cultivated mind; was constantly gathering the materials of greater efficiency and usefulness.

Hamden—D. H. Cherington.

Mount Pleasant—C. H. Warren, William R. Copeland. The junior preacher was brought into the Conference under my administration. Small of stature, a slight impediment in his utterance was somewhat against him at first; but such was his talent, and unction, and industry, that he surmounted those embarrassments, and succeeded well in the work. This year he had the advantage of one of the very best colleagues.

New Plymouth—Uriah L. Jones, William C. Holliday.

Furnace—John Dillon.

Kygerville—John R. Prose.

Gallipolis—H. Z. Adams. Brother Adams was a diligent pastor; affable in his intercourse with the people, prepossessing in his personal appearance, he was blessed with elements of success.

Gallipolis circuit—J. W. Alderman, J. W. Wakefield. I had the pleasure of introducing brother Wakefield to the traveling connection. He was able-bodied and strong-minded, and willing to expend his strength in the vineyard of the Lord.

During a portion of this year my labors were much increased in consequence of the failing health of my venerable father. He was living at his old home on Hocking, where he had settled in 1802. He had reached the great age of ninety-five years, and it was evident that his end was near at hand. It was his desire as well as my own that I should be with him in his last moments. To secure this privilege, I made journey after journey on horseback over the hill country intervening Jackson and Athens. Though I was not allowed finally to be with him when he crossed the river of death, yet it was a great comfort to us both that we had enjoyed so much of each other's society during the year. He died calmly resting on the atonement, and went to join the loved ones in heaven.

The Ohio Conference held its forty-seventh session at Marietta, Ohio, August 25, 1858, Bishop Janes presiding.

The following were admitted on trial: William Chadwick, Isaac F. King, John E. Sowers, Bradford Crook, John N. Pilcher, John P. Calvert, Caleb W. Cherington, Edward I. Jones, Robert Callahan, Eli H. Taylor, Henry R. Miller, John A. Acton. Several of these had been licensed by quarterly conferences over which I presided, and I always felt special interest in the success of such.

I was returned to Jackson district, with the following list of assistants:

Jackson—Joseph Morris.

Jackson circuit—D. H. Cherington, J. R. Prose.

Richmond—C. H. Warren, J. W. Wakefield.

M'Arthur—S. C. Frampton.

Hamden—P. V. Ferree.

Mount Pleasant—Daniel Harlocker, Caleb W. Cherington. The junior preacher was of good Methodist stock, and was licensed under my administration.

New Plymouth—U. L. Jones, William R. Copeland.

Furnace—John Dillon.
Kygerville—W. S. Benner.
Gallipolis—H. Z. Adams.
Gallipolis circuit—J. W. Alderman, F. S. Thurston.
Gallia—William S. Taylor, E. S. Jones. Brother Jones was a Welshman of education, refinement, and good preaching ability. I had the pleasure of introducing him into our traveling connection, and in so doing thought I was doing a good work for the cause of God, and was confirmed in that opinion by his subsequent course.

The Ohio Conference held its forty-eighth session in the Town-Street Church, Columbus, O., commencing August 31, 1859. Bishop Ames presided, assisted by Bishop Morris. The following persons were admitted on trial: Isaac Crook, Henry Bolby, Wilder N. Middleton, William H. Mullenix, John P. Lacroix, George W. Isaminger, Robert W. Manley, Joseph Robinson, F. F. Lewis, William J. Griffith, Wellington Harvey, H. K. Foster—a good class, some of whose original licenses to preach I had the pleasure of signing.

It was my privilege to enjoy the hospitality of brother Bartlett's excellent home, and of having Bishop Morris for my companion at this Conference. The Bishop preached us one of his characteristic sermons on Sabbath, from this passage: "The common people heard him gladly." Mark xii, 37. It was laconic, suggestive, finished, and full of marrow and good things. I was returned to Jackson district, with the following work and workers: Jackson, Stephen C. Frampton; Richmond, C. H. Warren and U. L. Jones; Jackson circuit, D. H. Cherington and J. W. Wakefield; M'Arthur, Banner Mark; Hamden, P. V. Ferree; Mount Pleasant, Daniel Harlocker; New Plymouth, F. S. Thurston; Furnace, John R. Prose; Wilksville, Joseph Barringer and C. W. Cherington; Gallipolis, Edward P. Hall; Gallipolis circuit, J. W. Alderman and J. W. Copeland; Gallia, William S. Taylor and E. S. Jones. We elected the following brethren as delegates to General Conference; namely, J. M. Trimble, Z. Connell, F. Merrick, J. M. Jameson, and D. D. Mather.

The four years spent on this district were pleasant and profitable years. We lived in Jackson, where we formed many and endearing friendships. The society in this place contained some choice Christians, whose time, and intellect, and property were consecrated to God. They had projected and commenced the erection of a church edifice in Jackson, before I took charge of the district, which proved to be a heavy work, but they persevered, through years of toil and sacrifice, and at last had the privilege of seeing it completed and dedicated. They did me the honor of calling it Stewart's Chapel. My constant prayer to God is that it may prove to be the spiritual birthplace of many hundreds of precious souls.

CHAPTER XXX.

MINISTER AT LARGE—WESTERN TOUR.

1860-61.

THE Ohio Conference held its forty-ninth session in Gallipolis, Ohio, commencing September 19, 1860, Bishop Simpson presiding. The following persons were admitted on trial: Charles C. M'Cabe, William H. Wolf, Henry Berkstresser, David H. Moore, William H. Gibbons, W. B. Guthrie, Wilson Gardner, T. H. Manley, S. R. Porter, Timothy S. Stivers, John F. Dickson, J. M'Kendree Shultz, George Murray, and James D. Fry. In this class was choice and promising material.

Though the announcement had already been made, through the organs and pulpits of the Church, that Rev. Jacob Young and Samuel Harvey had gone to join the fathers on the other side of the river, yet there was deep and solemn stillness in the Conference-room when the memoirs of these good and honored men were about to be read.

Brother Young had been identified with the history of Methodism in the West from the very beginning of the century, and during the greater portion of that time he had been regarded as one of the strong, progressive, and most enterprising of our ecclesiastical leaders. Though for many years past he had struggled either with pecuniary embarrassment or bodily affliction, yet he had always kept abreast of the great moral and religious movements of the age, and was ambitious that the Church of his choice should meet its full responsibility in every department of religious and educational enterprise. We now felt indeed that a prince had fallen. Though the memoir spread upon the Conference journal was eloquent in its eulogies, yet we felt that it was none too strong. As I have spoken of brother Young at length in an earlier part of my narrative, I will not go into any further detail at this place than simply to record that on the 15th of September, 1859, after pronouncing his blessing upon those who surrounded his dying couch, he exclaimed, "Sweet heaven! sweet heaven!" and his happy spirit entered its rest.

Brother Samuel Harvey was born in Mifflin county, Penn., February 15, 1806, and died January 30, 1860. He entered the traveling connection in 1833, and thenceforth became one of our most reliable and influential laborers. He had intellectual strength, and vigor, and culture sufficient to attract attention and make an impression, but in the gift of holiness he especially excelled. Large portions of his time were spent in secret prayer—close communion with God. He died just as we would expect such a man to die. When told by his attendants that he was dying, he inquired, "May not you be mistaken?" "No, brother Harvey, you are dying." He replied, "Well, be it so. I would like to have seen my wife and children." He then closed his eyes as if in reflection and prayer; then opened them, smiling, and exclaimed, "To die is gain. O, what a gain!" and without a struggle or a groan he passed away.

As the next session of the Conference would be its fiftieth, it was proposed that we should celebrate that occasion in a becoming manner. A committee was appointed to consider the subject and report. They presented the following report, which was adopted:

"The committee to whom the consideration of the semi-centennial celebration of the Ohio Annual Conference was referred, beg leave to report that, in their opinion, it will be very appropriate and even advantageous to our cause to hold a semi-centennial celebration at the next session of our Conference. We have not had time nor opportunity to consider properly what would be appropriate exercises for such an occasion, but recommend the passage of the following resolutions:

"1. *Resolved*, That the Ohio Annual Conference celebrate its Semi-Centennial at its next session at Circleville.

"2. *Resolved*, That we invite all former members of the Ohio Conference to be present with us at the celebration.

"3. *Resolved*, That a committee of five be appointed as a Committee of Arrangements, who shall prepare a programme of exercises suitable to the occasion, and publish the same in the Western Christian Advocate before the next session of our Conference.

JOSEPH M. TRIMBLE,
BENJAMIN ST. JAMES FRY,
Z. CONNELL."

The following Committee of Arrangements was appointed: Joseph M. Trimble, Z. Connell, Benjamin St. James Fry, John W. White, James M. Jameson.

The Bishop appointed me to Midway circuit, with permission to spend any portion of the year that I might choose in traveling at large.

The shadows of age were falling upon my pathway, and my companion and self had for several years desired the privilege of making a good visit among relations and friends scattered over the North-west, and of preaching to them once more before we should go hence. In the kind providence of God that opportunity was now offered us.

Soon after Conference we started on our journey. Stopping a few days at Cincinnati, we enjoyed the hospitality of the kind families of brothers Langley, Ewan, Kilbreth, Mears, and our ministerial brethren. It was an exceedingly pleasant commencement of our trip, and prophesied a year of great enjoyment.

As the Rock River Conference was about to hold its session at the first Methodist Episcopal Church of Chicago, of which our son was pastor, we hurried there to enjoy that occasion. We were not disappointed in the anticipation we had indulged. Added to the glad welcome tendered us by our children, we formed many pleasant acquaintances among the preachers. Bishop Janes presided, assisted by Bishop Simpson. As I witnessed their manner of transacting business, I thought that I had not been introduced to any Conference in the connection composed of more competent and efficient traveling preachers.

My son had completed his constitutional term in charge of the first church, but as he had inaugurated in the city a temperance movement that appeared to be accomplishing much good, and had taken much interest in street preaching, and kindred missionary work, it was thought desirable that he should remain in the city and take charge of the city missionary work. As this appointment opened a wide field for the employment of the available unemployed ministerial force of the city and vicinity I entered into sympathy with it at once, and during the remainder of my visit there was no lack of opportunity to preach. Besides the mission points at which he organized Sabbath-schools, and maintained preaching in view of developing Churches, he had services at the city Bridewell, the city hospital, in the city cemetery, the North and West Side market-houses, the Lake Park, in front of the armory, and at various other outdoor places, where those who needed the Gospel were accustomed to congregate. Through the influence of these meetings many who were utter strangers to the interior of our church buildings were reached and saved. During my stay I had opportunity of preaching each Sabbath.

Dr. Eddy, editor of the North-Western, Dr. Tiffany, who took charge of the First Methodist Episcopal Church, Rev. brother Stone, pastor of the Des Plaine-Street Church, and Rev. brother Whipple, pastor of the Indiana-Street Church, showed me much courtesy and kindness, and brothers Milner, and Hitt, and Hamilton, and Lawrence, and many others paid me such attention as added much to the enjoyment of my visit in Chicago.

Having spent about two months, we journeyed on to Monroe, Wisconsin, to visit our other son. His family gave us a very hearty welcome. My son being a member of the State Senate, and that body then being in session, was at the State capital attending to his duties. After spending some two weeks, and twice filling the pulpit, and forming the acquaintance of the excellent pastor, Rev. brother Sweetland, and of brothers Ball, and Beers, and Newton, and Evans, and White, and others who received me as a father in the Gospel, I went up to Madison to visit my son.

To my surprise I found here at the capital of Wisconsin quite a company of cherished friends of other years: Yocum, and Farnandis, and Hood, and Spencer, and Chilcoat, and Reed. The first on the list was pastor of the church, and the last on the list was a Professor in State University, located in the suburbs of the capital.

I was introduced to the Legislature, and invited to open one of its sessions with prayer. After preaching several times to the people of Madison, and enjoying my visit well, I returned to Monroe by the way of Janesville, at which place I spent a Sabbath, and supplied the pulpit in the absence of brother Jenne, the highly esteemed pastor.

The war was making heavy drafts on both the ministry and membership of the Methodist Episcopal Church. Rev. Mr. Walters, presiding elder of the Madison district, and Rev. M. Tilton, presiding elder of the Janesville district, had both given up their districts at the call of patriotism. Though they were greatly loved, and could be ill spared from their ecclesiastical posts, yet such was the loyalty of the people that they would not complain.

After spending a few weeks more at Monroe we set out to visit our friends in Iowa. On the way we touched at Freeport, Illinois, where we enjoyed the hospitality of Mrs. Streeter, and of Hon. Thompson Wilcoxon, formerly of Scioto county, Ohio. He had settled with his family in Stephenson county, Illinois, in an early day, and by real estate investments and energetic business operations accumulated a large property, which he was liberally using for public and religious uses.

Passing through Burlington, Iowa, we reached Mt. Pleasant, and were warmly received by my sister, Mrs. Sarah Warren. In this beautiful town, the seat of the Iowa Wesleyan University, and per consequence the rallying point for ministers and laymen of the Methodist Episcopal Church, who wish to furnish their children with the best advantages for higher education, we spent several exceedingly pleasant weeks. I there found some of my former Conference associates, and some of my dearest ministerial friends. The venerable Charles Elliott, the world-renowned author, and editor, and educator, had his pleasant home here, though he was at this time editing the Church paper at St. Louis, Missouri. There the saintly Bishop Hamline was living, in the simplicity and purity of a primitive Christian Bishop. Feeble in health, but mighty in faith, he was waiting the Master's call to the better home above. There was M'Dowell, and Ingalls, and Shelton, and Bradrick, and White, and Miller, and Reynolds—almost a Conference of splendid men. Such was their kindness to us, and so did we fall in love with the place and people, that we felt strongly inclined to abide there. By the kind invitation of the pastors, I had the opportunity of delivering a message for my Master to both of the congregations.

At Marshall, fifteen miles north of Mt. Pleasant, we visited a number of old acquaintances and family connections, who showed such appreciation of our visit as made us very happy—the Warrens, and Flemings, and Gardners, and Moreheads, and many others, who had in former years been members of my pastoral charges. We took much comfort in the family of Wheeler Warren, an old Ohio Methodist of the primitive stock, and were gratified to see that God had blessed him with a numerous and very reputable family, and a goodly heritage in this world. Rev. brother White, the preacher in charge, gave me the free use of his pulpit during the two Sabbaths that I remained, and the people listened with much earnestness to the Gospel message that I brought them.

Returning by the way of Mt. Pleasant, we journeyed on to West Point, where we visited my oldest brother, Colonel William Stewart. He had emigrated with his family to Iowa in an early day, and having brought with him both capital and business ability, he had made for himself property and influence. His children had grown up, married, and settled about him, until he seemed almost a patriarch. Alexander Stewart, a younger brother, also the head of a large and interesting family, resided in the neighborhood. Besides this extensive family connection, we found here Simeon and Asahel Cooley, and other cherished friends of our earlier days in Ohio. At the invitation of the worthy pastor, Rev. brother Williams, I preached to the people of West Point on Sabbath, and felt that God was with us of a truth.

At Fort Madison, the county-seat of Lee county, a beautiful town on the banks of the Mississippi River, we visited other family connections and friends. The pastor of the church, Rev. J. G. Thompson, and the chaplain of the State prison, Rev. Mr. Thomas, endeared themselves to us by many very kind attentions. They were jointly engaged in a protracted meeting at that time, and their labors were highly appreciated and fruitful. I doubted somewhat the propriety of officiating as much in the meeting as they desired me to do, but felt indeed that my labors were not in vain. We visited the State prison, and were much pleased with the evidences of good management, and with the high estimation placed upon the labors of the chaplain by both officers and prisoners. Brother Thomas, if I mistake not, is destined to make his mark in the Church of his choice, as an able minister of the New Testament.

At Farmington, twenty-five miles west of Fort Madison, we had the melancholy pleasure of visiting the grave of a beloved cousin, recently deceased, Rev. William Arnold. He was a good man, and was faithfully serving his generation, but in the midst of business and usefulness was called to a better seat above. A widow and three lovely daughters mourned their loss, and by the propriety of their lives were reflecting honor upon him and increasing their influence in society.

After a pleasant visit with them and the Rainses and Kinneys, we passed over into Missouri and visited some friends in Clarke county, in the neighborhood of Chambersburg. Among these were Captain Jesse Long, and the Reynoldses, and Colberts, and Pilchers, and Spencers, and many others from Athens county, Ohio.

During this visit we attended a Baptist protracted meeting, and were not a little surprised to find the tone of the congregation in unmistakable sympathy with the rebels of the South. In their Sabbath-morning prayer-meeting they constantly reminded the Lord of the great misfortune he had allowed to befall the country in the recent election of

Mr. Lincoln to the Presidency. As all in the congregation were invited to take part, I ventured to offer up prayer, but in a spirit so different from those who had preceded me that they looked upon me with evident surprise and wonder. But no one offered to interrupt me in any way. The disloyal spirit, however, became so rampant afterward that my brother-in-law, Captain Long, and others who were uncompromisingly loyal, had to abandon their homes and property, and seek safety in other localities.

After making a short visit with my old friend Hubbel Reynolds, we retraced our steps to Fort Madison, calling by the way on Joel Bethel, an old Ohio friend, and touching at Farmington, and West Point, and Knapp's. After spending a few days in company with the last-named connection, Jonas Knapp, a prosperous farmer and large-hearted gentleman, we passed up the river to Burlington, and thence, bidding good-by to Iowa, crossed the Mississippi and set our faces toward Chicago.

The visit had been a very pleasant one, and I thought that if God would only bless my ministry to the salvation of my dear relatives who are out of Christ, I would rejoice through all eternity that I had made the visit.

We reached Chicago in safety, and found plenty of work in the department in which my son was engaged. He had secured a large corps of helpers, and was pushing the work in the destitute and depraved parts of the city with much vigor.

While here, I received a communication from the committee of the Ohio Conference requesting me to preach the memorial sermon at the coming semi-centennial anniversary of the Ohio Conference. Not without a good deal of hesitancy and misgiving, I accepted the honorable duty assigned me, and addressed myself to the work of preparation.

The latter part of January, 1861, leaving Mrs. Stewart,

with the children, in Chicago, I returned to Ohio. On the way I visited my old friends Rev. A. Eddy and Bishop Ames, at Indianapolis, Ind. With the former I had been associated in the work in Ohio, and was glad to see him once more in the flesh. I also called upon a very dear friend, Rev. Thomas H. Lynch, formerly a professor in Augusta College, Kentucky. He had ministered consolation to us when the shadows of death rested upon our habitation, and he will always have a very sacred place in our affections. I also found there and had the pleasure of seeing that elect lady, Miss Lydia Haws, who was with us during the same period of affliction, and rendered us sympathy and kindness never to be forgotten. She was a remarkable woman, and will doubtless shine in the kingdom of God forever.

Rev. William I. Fee, pastor of the Christie Chapel at Cincinnati, gave me the hospitality of his house and the freedom of his pulpit. I protracted my visit for some time, and by the invitation of the pastors preached in most of our churches. I visited, in Covington, Jesse Grant, father of General U. S. Grant. I found him full of anxiety and confidence in regard to the efforts of his son, who was at that time thundering at the gates of Vicksburg. Brother Grant extended to me the same cordial welcome that he had been accustomed to do in former years when I was his pastor. He offered to secure me an appointment as chaplain in the army. The war excitement was now all-pervading; not only the young men and strong men, but tender boys and infirm old men were offering themselves for such positions as they might be able to fill. My venerable friend, Rev. J. F. Wright, had just taken a chaplaincy, and I was much tempted to do the same, but after mature reflection, I decided to expend what of strength remained to me in labors at home, and let the younger and stronger go to the field.

Early in February I left Cincinnati and made my way to Athens, visiting in my route Chillicothe, Jackson, Portsmouth, and Pomeroy, at all of which places I met smiling faces and grasped warm and friendly hands, and at some of them had time to preach the Gospel to my old friends.

Again I turned my face toward the North-west, taking Springfield in route. About the middle of March I found myself again at the residence of my son in Chicago, and was grateful to God for the kind providence that had preserved us all during our separation. We spent the remainder of the month in Chicago, reading, writing, and helping in the city missionary work. The first of May I made a brief visit again to my son in Monroe, Wisconsin; thence to Freeport, Illinois, enjoying the hospitality of brother Wilcoxon; thence to Rockford, where I enjoyed the hospitality of that successful inventor and manufacturer, and faithful Methodist, J. B. Skinner. His plows and other farm machinery are widely known and appreciated in the West and South, and he is liberally spending his revenue to sustain the institutions of the Church of his choice. May the blessing of God be upon him and his family! Returning to Chicago, I now gave myself more earnestly to the task that was before me for the next session of my Conference.

The 10th of July we started south and passed through Springfield, the home of President Lincoln. I could but think of the rapid and wonderful changes that take place with men and things in this world. A poor young man, splitting rails for a living—the same man, self-made, presiding over the most powerful nation of the globe! A few small colonies struggling against the yoke of a tyrannical mother government—one-half of the States of a mighty republic, sacrificing millions of treasure and rivers of human blood, to perpetuate slavery in a land called the "land of the free!"

At Virden, Illinois, William Gamble, Esq., met us with his family carriage and conveyed us to his pleasant home, fourteen miles east of that place. He had been a citizen of Illinois some thirty years, and settled about him was a large family of children, mostly married and all prosperous and respectable. We spent among these friends several very pleasant weeks, and during the time made many acquaintances among their neighbors. Purposing to go from there to Carrolton, where another circle of their and our family connection were living, brother and sister Gamble took us in their family carriage. Here were several families who had come from Athens county; namely, Rev. M. Osborn, and the Halberts, and Pilchers, and Caricoes, and Simmonses, and Gambles. While we visited in this neighborhood we made our head-quarters at the residence of James H. Vanarsdale, son-in-law to the now sainted William Gamble.

The latter part of July we bade adieu to these kind friends, and turning westward made a brief visit at St. Louis, Mo. We found our venerable friend, Dr. Charles Elliott, at his post and earnestly at work. The spirit of rebellion was rife in St. Louis, and it required no small measure of courage for the Doctor to throw to the breeze the stars and stripes, and declare himself and the "Central Advocate" uncompromisingly on the side of the Union, but he never faltered. Firm as Gibraltar, he not only inspired his paper with the spirit of patriotism, but he filled the pulpit for the little band of Methodists who had not and would not bow the knee unto Baal. The Doctor gave me a warm invitation to spend the Sabbath with him and preach to the people,-but not feeling impressed with any special message for St. Louis, we determined to retrace our steps to Ohio.

On the way we spent the Sabbath at Moore's Hill, a

beautiful town, containing a population which indicated its excellence by the schools, churches, and college which they had gathered about them. Here resided some of our cherished friends, the Franklins, and Spencers, and Jenningses, and others. The visit was pleasant, and I had special enjoyment in ministering to them of the Word of Life.

We spent a week in Cincinnati and Covington, preaching in each place and enjoying the kindest attentions from many friends. The first Saturday and Sabbath in August we spent at Mount Washington, visiting my friend Leroy Swormstedt, who so long and efficiently served the Church as Agent of the Western Book Concern.

August 11th we arrived at Jackson, Ohio, having now been upon the wing for eleven months. These kind friends, among whom we had made a happy home while serving the Jackson district, welcomed us back, and, as we reviewed the labor and danger through which we had passed, and how God had protected and blessed us, we felt unutterable emotions of gratitude filling our hearts. We had not been conscious of any miraculous deliverances, as from the wreck of blown-up steamers or collided cars, but we felt that God had so wonderfully directed our steps that we had not even taken passage upon steamer or cars that were destined to explosion or wreck. We erected here our "Ebenezer," and gave ourselves anew to God.

After resting for a few days at Jackson, we visited M'Arthur, Hamden, and Athens, where we visited until time to start toward Conference. *En route* I visited Chillicothe, Dryrun, New Holland, and Columbus, at the last of which places I called on brothers Trimble, Jameson, and Brush, and enjoyed the hospitality of brother Bartlett. From Columbus I went to London, where I visited many of our old friends. From there I went to Springfield, and attended the session of the Cincinnati Conference, and at its close returned to London, and spent Sabbath, the 8th of September, preaching for the people. Monday I visited James Foster and Rev. J. Martin, and dined at brother Moore's, of Mount Sterling, on my way to Circleville, where the Ohio Conference was to commence its fiftieth session on the 11th.

The session was one of interest and profit. I was able to report, in regard to my year's travels and labors that I had delivered about one hundred sermons to nearly as many different congregations, scattered over a very large circuit, and that the year had been one of blessings to myself, and I had reason to think that God had made me, to some extent, a blessing to others.

This being the fiftieth session of the Ohio Conference, as before stated, arrangements had been made to celebrate it with suitable services. Rev. Zachariah Connell was to deliver a historical sketch of the Western Conference, Rev. Dr. Trimble a historical sketch of the Ohio Conference, and I was to preach the commemoration sermon.

CHAPTER XXXI.

FRANKFORT CIRCUIT, OHIO.

1861-62.

THE Ohio Conference held its fiftieth session in Circleville, Ohio, commencing September 11, 1861, Bishop Janes presiding. The great and absorbing interest at this Conference was the semi-centennial memorial services. In accordance with the invitation sent out by the Ohio Conference, many of its former members were present to enjoy those services. Monday was set apart for this celebration, and with it came a great crowd of people. As the memorial sermon, which was assigned to me, was set for eleven o'clock, A. M., I entered the crowded audience with a good deal of tremulousness. The congregation, however, gave me very close attention, and at times such demonstrative evidences of their appreciation of the discourse as I had not expected. At three, P. M., the vast audience gathered again to listen to the essay of Rev. Z. Connell on the "History of the Western Conference." It was an able and appropriate sketch, and gave much satisfaction to the hearers. At night they gathered again to hear "A Historical Sketch of the Ohio Conference," by Rev. J. M. Trimble, D. D. The task was accomplished in the style and with the ability of that popular minister. The day was one of great interest and profit. The memorial sermon will be found in the appendix to this volume.

The appointment assigned me was Frankfort circuit, and

my colleague W. W. Cherington. Being well acquainted with both, I felt grateful to the Bishop for dealing so kindly with me. The circuit was a fragment of the territory embraced in Deer Creek circuit as it was in 1826-27. I hardly anticipated finding many who were active members in that early day, but I expected to find their children and grandchildren. In this I was not disappointed. The circuit received us with great cordiality, and we settled down in Frankfort, near the dust of our little Asbury, who had been buried here some thirty-four years ago. The plan of appointments embraced 1. Frankfort; 2. Estell Chapel; 3. Cline's School-house; 4. Morris Chapel; 5. Teeter's Chapel; 6. Lattaville; 7. Roxabell School-house; 8. Mount Pleasant; 9. Pleasant Hill. It was a year of considerable mortality, and it fell to my lot to preach a larger number of funeral sermons than I had ever preached before in a single year. Among them were some of the early settlers, who had been in my congregations when I first preached there. Of those whom we buried, perhaps no one was more universally respected than Rev. Dennis Blacker, a local preacher. In earlier years he had at times been under the dominion of strong drink, and on more than one occasion it had been necessary to dismiss him from the Church on that account. But he would still return with so much penitence and humility to ask another trial, that the Church always received him back with open arms. At length he gained complete victory over this besetment, was licensed as a local preacher, commanded the confidence of all classes of people, and labored very acceptably, diligently, and usefully as a local preacher for many years before his death.

My colleague was a good man and true. We held protracted meetings at all of the appointments, and had encouraging results.

We were now in the midst of the excitement of war times

The great rebellion had commenced, and the loyal people of the land were rallying to the standards of the country. As our Church, with few exceptions, was intensely loyal, the volunteering made sad breaches in our classes. We furnished from our Church not only material for chaplains and officers, but companies of privates, many of whom were members that we would have been loth to spare for any other cause. Those of us who remained at home addressed ourselves to the work of raising supplies, and sending comforts to our brethren and loyal fellow-citizens who had gone to the field. So constantly did our prayers and discourses indicate the deep anxiety we felt for the overthrow of the rebellion, that the few who were in sympathy with the South turned with loathing from Methodist Churches and pulpits.

Bating whatever was unpleasant in these regards, we had a comfortable year, and take great pleasure in placing upon the record a few names of the excellent of that circuit as a sample of the membership. They were such as the M'Neils, and Hainses, and Smitherses, and Blackers, and Pancakes, and Blacks, and Hopkinses, and Snyders, and Lattas, and Lucases.

CHAPTER XXXII.

DEER CREEK CIRCUIT, AND CHILLICOTHE DISTRICT, OHIO.

1862-64.

THE Ohio Conference held its fifty-first session at Zanesville, Ohio, commencing September 3, 1862, Bishop Morris presiding. The following persons were admitted on trial: William F. King, Thomas R. Taylor, E. C. Wayman, and James L. Grover was re-admitted. Brother Grover, after trying the pasture in that ecclesiastical organization which claims to be *the Church*, came back to the old pasture, and we gave him a cordial welcome.

During the year three of our brethren had died; namely, John W. Clarke, Uriah Heath, and John P. Calvert.

Brother Clarke was born September 21, 1803, in Maryland, and emigrated to Ohio, and settled near Cincinnati, in an early day. In 1825 he entered the Ohio Conference, and died August 26, 1862, at Mt. Pleasant, Ohio. During his ministry he was twelve years in the office of presiding elder, and in every relation that he sustained he exhibited such qualities of mind and heart as caused him to be valued and honored as a minister of Jesus Christ. Near his last moments, he said to his colleague, "Tell the brethren of the Ohio Conference that we shall meet in heaven."

Brother Heath was born near Xenia, Ohio, April 11, 1809, converted in his youth, and in 1835 was admitted to the Ohio Conference, of which he remained a laborious member until his death. He served the Church in various departments, and whether on a circuit, station, or district; whether gathering funds for school, churches, or tract distribution, his time and strength were given, and his labor was crowned with success. He died at his post in Zanesville, Ohio, March 28, 1852, and devout men carried him to his burial, and made great lamentation over him.

Brother Calvert was born in Belmont county, Ohio, October 23, 1833. He joined the Conference on trial at Marietta, in 1858. When the rebellion broke out six of his brothers enlisted to defend the old flag. In 1861 he felt that he could stay back no longer, and enlisted in company K of the Seventy-seventh Ohio. He fell in the memorable battle of Shiloh. He was a faithful Christian worker in the army, as at home, and died a Christian patriot.

We moved back to Deer Creek circuit, on which we had already spent two constitutional terms with much satisfaction. Our friends rallied about us, and congratulated us on the greatly improved health of my wife. We were soon settled in the parsonage, and at our work. Colleague, Rev. T. J. N. Simmons; Z. Connell, presiding elder. In a former chapter promise was made to furnish some statistics of the history of this circuit, which promise it will be proper now to fulfill.

Deer Creek circuit was formed from a portion of the Scioto circuit in 1808, so that it is several years older than the Ohio Conference. Perhaps, however, it will be gratifying to my readers to have the genealogy of the circuit traced back to its origin:

SCIOTO CIRCUIT—
  1800. Alex. M'Caine, P. E., Henry Smith, P. C.
SCIOTO AND MIAMI CIRCUIT—
  1801. Wm. M'Kendree, P. E., Henry Smith.
  1802. "   "   " Benj. Young, E. Bowman.

Scioto Circuit—
1803. Wm. M'Kendree, P. E., John Sale, Stephen Timmons.
1804. Wm. Burke, P. E., Wm. Patterson, Nathan Barnes.
1805.   "   "   "   Luther Taylor, C. W. Cloud.
1806. John Sale, P. E., James Quinn, Peter Cartwright.
1807.   "   "   "   Anthony Houston, Milton Ladd.

Deer Creek Circuit—
1808. John Sale, P. E., Benjamin Lakin, John Crain.
1809.   "   "   "   John Collins, Wood Lloyd.
1810.   "   "   "   John Collins, Francis Travis.
1811. Sol. Langdon, P E., Ralph Lotspeich, J. Haines.
1812.   "   "   "   R. Cloud, C. Waddle.
1813. James Quinn, P. E., Samuel Parker, Alexander Cummins.
1814.   "   "   "   Alexander Cummins, H. B. Bascom.
1815.   "   "   "   Isaac Quinn, Sedosa Baker.
1816.   "   "   "   Walter Griffith, Isaac Pavey.
1817. David Young, P. E., Charles Waddle, Samuel Glaze.
1818. John Collins, P. E., Shadrach Ruark, R. W. Finley.
1819.   "   "   "   William Swayze, R. W. Finley.
1820.   "   "   "   John Brown.

This year Chillicothe was taken from the circuit, and erected into a station. Brother Swayze reported a membership of one thousand five hundred and eighty-eight, and brother Brown reported one thousand three hundred and seven, and brother J. Quinn, the first pastor of Chillicothe station, reported a membership of three hundred.

1821. Samuel West, P. E., William Stephens, A. Kinnear.
1822. G. R. Jones, P. E., Andrew M'Clain, I. C. Hunter.
1823.   "   "   "   Isaac Quinn, William Simmons.
1824.   "   "   "   Zachariah Connell, J. T. Wells.
1825.   "   "   "   James Collord, Nathan Walker.
1826. Rus'l Bigelow, P. E., Jacob Delay, G. W. Young.
1827.   "   "   "   John Stewart, John Ferree.
1828. John Collins, P. E., John Stewart, A. Sellers.

Brother Delay reported to me nine hundred and ninety, and I reported to my successor one thousand and five. For the plan of appointments, indicating the geographical area of the circuit, the reader can refer to the appropriate chapter in this narrative.

1829. John Collins, P. E., Francis Wilson, J. T. Donahoe.
1830.   "   "   "   Francis Wilson, John Ferree.
1831.   "   "   "   Adam Poe, Solomon Minear.
1832. Aug. Eddy, P. E., J. H. Power, J. Gurley.
1833.   "   "   "   David Lewis, Joseph A. Reeder.

DEER CREEK CIRCUIT—

1834. John Ferree, P. E.,	David Lewis, C. C. Lybrand.
1835. J. B. Finley, P. E.,	C. C. Lybrand, Edward Estell.
1836. " " "	James Armstrong, Henry Wharton.
1837. James Quinn, P. E.,	Wm. S. Morrow, F. H. Jennings.
1838. " " "	Wm. S. Morrow, Wesley Rowe.
1839. Mich'l Marlay, P. E.,	Rob. Cheney, W. Rowe, J. F. Conrey.
1840. " " "	E. H. Field, W. M. D. Ryan.
1841. " " "	E. H. Field, B. A. Cassat.
1842. " " "	David Reed, Philip Nation.
1843. J. M. Trimble, P. E.,	Z. Wharton, J. D. Webb.
1844. " " "	Z. Wharton, Alexander Meharry.
1845. J. F. Wright, P. E.,	Henry Wharton, B. L. Jefferson.
1846. " " "	H. Wharton, J. W. Locke.
1847. D. Kemper, P. E.,	J. G. Dimmitt, C. C. Lybrand.
1848. " " "	J. G. Dimmitt, Wm. Sutton.
1849. J. M. Jameson, P. E.,	A. Nelson, J. Laws.
1850. " " "	John Stewart, D H. Sargent.
1851. " " "	John Stewart, Samuel Middleton.
1852. J. W. Clarke, P. E,	D. Smith, H. F. Green, W. A. Prettyman.
1853. " " "	D. Smith, J. Williams, Lem. F. Drake.
1854 " " "	Samuel Bateman, J. Kemper.
1855. " " "	Samuel Middleton, Samuel Bateman.
1856. J. M. Trimble, P. E.,	N. Westerman.
1857. " " "	N. Westerman, William Morris.
1858. " " "	Edward Estell, Wm. Morris.
1859. " " "	Edward Estell, E. H. Dixon.
1860. D. D. Mather, P. E.,	R. Pitzer, A. Cartlich.
1861. Z. Connell, P. E.,	R. Pitzer, F. A. Timmons.
1862. " " "	John Stewart, T. J. N. Simmons.
1863. " " "	" " " "

Early in this year brother Connell died, and I was appointed to supply the district. An examination of this long list will show that Deer Creek circuit has had the services of many of the most distinguished ministers of the denomination.

The Ohio Conference held its fifty-second session at Lancaster, Ohio, commencing September 3, 1863. Bishop Baker having failed to reach the place, Rev. Zachariah Connell, by appointment, opened the session and presided with dignity and efficiency during the first day of the session. Bishop Baker arrived the next day and took the chair.

What was remarkable at this session was, that we neither admitted a probationer nor recorded a death. The fact that no probationers were admitted had its explanation in the return of the ministers who had been in the army.

I was appointed to Deer Creek circuit, with Rev. Z. Connell for presiding elder, and Rev. T. J. N. Simmons for colleague. Early in the Winter, however, our beloved presiding elder was called from labor to rest, and the Bishop appointed me to take his place on the district. I had supposed that my age would excuse me from any further service on district work, but as it seemed to be the desire of my brethren that I should fill the gap until Conference, I gave brother Simmons charge of the circuit, employed Rev. Z. Wharton to assist him, and entered at once on the duties of my new relation. The following is a brief outline of the field and the workmen:

Chillicothe—J. H. Creighton and I. F. King. Brother Creighton, of whom I have spoken in previous pages, had charge of the Walnut-Street Church, and brother King of the Main-Street Church. They were prosecuting their work with diligence and perseverance.

Washington—E. H. Dixon. He was a minister possessed of a clear perception of truth, and of a ready and forcible utterance. Self-possessed and logical, he was appreciated by the people and did good service.

Bloomingsburg—A. Cartlich, Joseph Morris. Brother Morris went as chaplain to the army, and C. Phillips, a young man of promise, supplied on the circuit.

Staunton—T. G. Ross, J. Q. Lakin. Brother Ross was an able preacher. His sermons were well prepared and well delivered, and furnished timely and nourishing food for his congregations. Brother Lakin was a strong and well-developed man physically, and though forty-five years of age, was putting forth commendable effort to develop his intellectual powers. He had good native ability, and was doing good service.

New Holland—N. Westerman, J. B. Bradrick. Brother Westerman was a man of extensive reading, possessed a large fund of knowledge, both general and critical. A stranger would wonder why he did not occupy a more prominent position. The junior preacher possessed the elements that gave promise he would take rank among his brethren. He had a pleasant manner, his sermons contained good matter, and in his work he had that something which the Western people call "snap," an element indispensable to the successful circuit or station preacher.

Deer Creek circuit—T. J. N. Simmons, Z. Wharton. Brother Simmons succeeded me in charge of the circuit, and administered the Gospel and Discipline according to his usual ability. Brother Wharton was an experienced and able minister, popular in his address, and capable of filling any pulpit.

Frankfort circuit—Edward Estell, C. H. Warren. These men were pure coin, and the circuit was fortunate that secured the service of either of them. Brother Estell finished his work this year, and died at his post with the harness on. His memoir will appear in the next chapter.

Bainbridge—William H. M'Clintock, F. A. Timmons. Brother M'Clintock was an energetic and successful man. He seldom failed to have a revival. Of my friend of many years, brother Timmons, I have already spoken in previous chapters.

Massieville—William Morris. In 1849, while in charge of the Portsmouth district, I had the pleasure of signing the license of brother Morris, and of carrying his recommendation up to the Ohio Conference. He had proved to be a good man for the work, but this year he felt it his duty to go to the field of battle to defend his loved country. I employed brother Moore to supply his place, and he did well.

Waverly and Sharonville—D. Tracy, a good preacher and able-bodied man; he gave good satisfaction.

Kingston—Richard Pitzer, W. W. Cherington. Of the worth of these good men I have spoken heretofore.

I had on my list of preachers the name of Rev. Wesley Prettyman, missionary to Bulgaria. He was a man of mercurial temperament, enterprising, efficient, and eloquent; of the best Methodist stock, and devoted to the Church of his fathers.

The year was one of military excitement and intense anxiety, but of a good share of devotion to the cause of God, and was not without a measure of prosperity.

CHAPTER XXXIII.

WEST RUSHVILLE CIRCUIT, OHIO.

1864-65.

THE Ohio Conference held its fifty-third session in Chillicothe, commencing October 8, 1864, Bishop Ames presiding. We admitted on trial the following persons: William H. Scott, Francis A. Spencer, Francis S. Davis, Benjamin F. Thomas, James M. Weir, Charles A. Phillips, John W. Baker, Henry Berkstresser.

We placed on the list of our sainted dead the names of our dear brethren Edward Estell and Zachariah Connell.

Brother Estell was born May 5, 1801, in Lucerne county, Pennsylvania, and died at the parsonage in Frankfort, Ohio, April 2, 1864. He embraced religion in early youth, and joined the Ohio Conference in 1834. During the thirty years of his ministerial life, the Ohio Conference had no more conscientious, faithful, and devoted minister than Edward Estell. The work of God was the work of his mind, and heart, and hands. He was subject to seasons of despondency, doubtless, in a great measure, the result of diseased condition; but he gave unmistakable evidence to the Church and the world that he was a man of God. Now, when he lay upon the borders of the spirit world, all gloom was dissipated, and he sent this message to his brethren of the Ohio Conference: "I feel that the hull is sinking, but the cargo is insured."

Brother Connell was born in Connellsville, Penn., September 11, 1794, and died December 13, 1863, in the forty-sixth year of his ministry. Early in his ministry his pulpit and administrative abilities secured for him a permanent position in the Ohio Conference. He was many years in charge of the most important districts and charges in the Conference, and was frequently elected to represent the Conference in the General Conference. He was truly a Christian gentleman, and though at the time he was attacked by his death-sickness, he was almost three-score and ten years old, yet he possessed a mental and physical vigor that gave promise of continued valuable services for the Church of his choice. He died in the midst of friends and usefulness, and ascended to heaven.

During this session of the Conference we enjoyed a rare treat in a reunion with the members of the Cincinnati Conference. That Conference was holding its session at Greenfield, only twenty miles distant, and arrangements having been perfected through appropriate committees, on Tuesday, headed by Bishop Simpson, the Cincinnati Conference came to Chillicothe, and was welcomed by the Ohio Conference, headed by Bishop Ames and the venerable Bishop Morris. It was arranged that Bishop Simpson should deliver his address on the state of the country. The circumstances were such as to call out fully his great ability: two Conferences of Methodist preachers, strongly bound to each other in affection, and overflowing with patriotism; a vast concourse of lay members, running over with the same enthusiasm; a vast army of citizens, looking on with wonder and admiration. It was undoubtedly one of the greatest of Bishop Simpson's masterly efforts.

Brother Moody addressed the vast audience at night, but it was as the shining of moonbeams after the setting of the sun. He is usually a master, but the excitement of the day and the overwhelming effect of the Bishop's discourse had been too intense. Human nature can not endure such excitement long until it begins to flag. On other occasions I have heard the stately, and learned, and eloquent Moody when he seemed almost peerless, but this was not one of those occasions.

I was appointed to West Rushville circuit, the smallest charge, geographically, that I had ever served. It was a two-weeks' circuit, having the following appointments: 1. West Rushville; 2. Asbury Chapel; 3. Bremen Chapel; 4. Collins Chapel. This territory was embraced in the Fairfield circuit in 1817, when I traveled that circuit; but nearly a half century had intervened, and the stream of time had borne nearly all of my then hearers beyond the sea.

I now had my first experience of a two-weeks' circuit, and found it well adapted to my age and growing desire to be as much at home as duty would allow. I transcribed all the names of my members into my visiting book, as had been my custom for years, and visited all the members methodically and Methodistically. It required unusual effort to keep the minds and hearts of the people stayed on God during the excitement and passions incident to the terrible war that had now been agitating the republic for so many months.

Though the Methodist Church in both its ministry and membership was in harmony with the loyal spirit of the administration, yet there was occasionally a discordant string in both. When J. F. Given was allowed to step out at the back door of the Church, the ministry was relieved, and the most of the members who had possessed the spirit of Given and such, had either withdrawn or had come to see that they had been misled, and deceived, and injured. There were noble men and women who appeared to sympathize with the rebellion during the early years of the war, who were loyal at heart, and when the old prejudice or party discipline that blinded them was taken away, they stood shoulder to shoulder with the best friends of the country. Now that the war is over, we can well afford to throw the mantle of forgetfulness over the extravagant sayings and the bitter feelings that were then uttered and engendered.

We had excellent neighbors at West Rushville, and cherish the memory of many dear friends there and at the other appointments of the circuit. Among them I now recall the names of Dr. Evans, and brothers Jackson, and Miller, and Drivers, and Anderson, and Webb, and Deans, and Hamocks, and Collins, and Gardner, and Melix, and Vanzant, and Hutchens, and Neely, and Kelsey, and many others of the same spirit, whose families showed us multitudinous kindnesses. May the richest blessings of God be upon them!

CHAPTER XXXIV.

ROYALTON CIRCUIT, OHIO.

1865-66.

THE Conference held its fifty-fourth session in Bigelow Chapel, Portsmouth, Ohio, commencing September 21, 1865, Bishop D. W. Clark presiding. Our veteran and model Secretary, Rev. Joseph M. Trimble, having, by the General Conference of 1864, been appointed Assistant Secretary of the Missionary Society, we consented, at his request, to excuse him from the responsibilities he had so long and faithfully met at our table, and we elected as our Secretary Rev. S. M. Merrill. The following persons were received on trial: Charles B. Lewis, S. N. Marsh, D. H. Moore, A. H. Windsor, Thomas H. Braderick, John E. Moore, James H. Gardner, George L. Sites. Three more names were placed on the roll of those who had been discharged from the Church militant and gone to join the army of the skies. They were John C. Havens, Henry Wharton, and Leonidas L. Hamline.

Bishop Hamline was born in Burlington, Conn., May 10, 1797. In 1828, through sanctified affliction, he was led to Christ and joined the Methodist Episcopal Church in Zanesville, Ohio. In 1832 he was received on trial in the Ohio Conference. His extraordinary ability placed him soon in the very first rank of his brethren, and in 1844 he was elected to the Episcopacy. His humility grew as rapidly as he was promoted, and his zeal for the cause of God and the Church of which he had been made a chief pastor was intense and almost consuming. In 1852, his health having failed, he resigned his office as Bishop and was granted a superannuated relation in the Ohio Conference. He removed to Mount Pleasant, Iowa, where he spent the rest of his days. On the 22d of February, 1865, he entered the rest that remains for the people of God. He was a man who would have stood among the first in any department he might have selected. Possessed of genius, learning, and large pecuniary means, he counted all loss for Christ, and preferred to preach the Gospel on a Methodist circuit to sitting among the chieftains of the State. He now doubtless realizes fully that his choice was a wise one.

Brother Havens was born in Newark, New Jersey, in the year 1802. He was received on trial in the Ohio Conference in 1825. Either as effective, supernumerary, or superannuated he continued to labor for the Church from that time to his death. He was not a man of popular talent, after the standard of the world, but he was faithful in the work intrusted to him, and will doubtless have stars in his crown of rejoicing in the day of the Lord Jesus.

Brother Wharton joined the Conference in 1835. He was a man of a meek and gentle spirit. The people were instinctively drawn to him, and his constant and greatest endeavor was to lead them to Christ. His mild and amiable features, his musical voice, and all his bearing in the pulpit tended to give effect to his ministry. He aimed to reach the hearts of the people, and so spoke from the depths of his own heart. He was an eloquent preacher and a careful, diligent shepherd. Few of our brethren who have departed are more affectionately remembered by their charges than is brother Henry Wharton.

At this Conference the brethren almost embarrassed me by their kind attentions. I had always regarded myself as the least among my brethren, and only regarded myself as their equal in the ability to love them and pray for their success in the work of saving souls. They passed the following resolution:

"*Resolved*, That, as our venerable brother, Rev. John Stewart, will have completed his fiftieth year in the effective ranks, should Providence preserve his life till our next annual meeting, he is hereby requested to deliver a semi-centennial sermon at some suitable hour during the session, to be designated by the Conference.   B. N. SPAHR."

I was appointed to Royalton circuit, with Rev. J. W. White for my colleague. His first year in the Conference had been associated with me as my assistant, and now, after a lapse of thirty years, I was to spend my last and fiftieth year in the effective work as his assistant. As I had been accustomed to have charge of work for so many years, the change seemed somewhat awkward for a time; but brother White was an able and efficient minister, and honored me as an affectionate son in the Gospel. The kindness of himself and his excellent family to me and mine has endeared them to me beyond the ability of my pen to write. May the great Head of the Church deal kindly with them and theirs through all of their generations!

We found a pleasant home in Royalton. The following was the list of appointments: 1. Royalton; 2. Union; 3. Mount Zion; 4. Wesley Chapel; 5. Fairview; 6. Pleasant Grove; 7. Amanda; 8. Hedges Chapel; 9. Bloomfield.

I prepared my visiting list, and went to work with the earnest prayer that God would crown my last year in the effective work with much success. My colleague was earnest and able in the pulpit, and we pushed the battle, but after all did not see the outpouring of the Spirit on the Churches as we hoped. We comforted ourselves with the assurance that we had sowed good seed, and had sowed it with a liberal hand. God had promised that the Word should not return void, and we trusted him for the results.

We had one local preacher on this charge, Rev. Lewis Peters, a man of sterling worth, and a host of laymen of intelligence, and generosity, and piety. I can only mention a few as a sample of the many. They were such as brothers Williamson, Strodes, Bolembaugh, Peters, Ebright, Allan, Raber, Hedges, and a long list of kindred spirits at all of the appointments.

As I had been requested by the Conference to deliver a semi-centennial discourse at its next session, my mind was much employed in reviewing my ministerial life. It was difficult for me to realize that a half a century had passed since I threw my saddle-bags over my arm and went forth from my father's house to join the band of itinerants; but, as I traveled over the circuits in memory, year by year, they truly had been years of real travel, and real toil, and real sacrifice; but, thank God! years, too, of real enjoyment, and some of them years of real triumph.

CHAPTER XXXV.

SUPERANNUATED LIFE.

THE Ohio Conference held its fifty-fifth session at Columbus, Ohio, commencing September 26, 1866, Bishop Janes presiding, assisted by Bishop Morris. The following persons were admitted on trial: John Y. Rusk, W. W. Martin, Henry Culp, Samuel Loomis, Joseph L. Durant, Levi T. Hannawalt, William F. Hughey.

The following brethren were not with us to occupy their accustomed places in the Conference-room, they having been called during the past year to loftier seats among kings and priests: Henry T. Magill, William C. Filler, D. H. Cherington, and C. A. Phillips.

The emotions of my heart in attending this session of the Conference were peculiar. With it would close the first century of American Methodism, and with it would close my itinerant effective life, which had embraced the last half of the closing century. My brethren had appointed me to deliver before them a semi-centennial discourse; that duty performed, I would ask to be placed upon the superannuated list. The same indescribable feeling of dread which came over my spirit fifty years ago, when I stood upon the threshold of an itinerant life, now stole over my spirit again as I was about to retire from the active field.

The Conference set apart $10\frac{1}{2}$, A. M., on Monday, October first, as the time for the delivery of my discourse. With trembling, at the appointed time I entered the crowded sanctuary and ascended the pulpit. Casting myself upon God for help, he sustained me, and the great audience gave me very respectful attention as I tried to set forth the might of the Methodist Episcopal Church as one of the great evangelizing agencies of the past century, and to show the source of her power. The Conference received the effort very kindly, and placed the following resolution upon their journal:

"*Resolved*, That having heard with much pleasure, and, we trust, with profit, the very interesting and instructive semi-centennial sermon, delivered this day before the Conference by our venerable and beloved brother, John Stewart, we do hereby very respectfully request him to have it published in such form as he may think best, for our benefit as well as for the interest of those who were not present at its delivery. B. N. SPAHR."

This action of the Conference, followed up by the personal solicitation of many of my brethren of the ministry and membership, had much to do in deciding me to prepare the present work for publication. I did not flatter myself that my autobiography would have an extensive and permanent circulation, but after hearing the desires of personal friends, and revolving the question in my own mind, it occurred to me that if it could accomplish any good in strengthening the bonds of attachment to our Zion and to the Great Head of the Church, it would be a source of gratitude and thanksgiving to me.

None but those who have had the experience can imagine my feelings when, in the examination of character, the Bishop called the name, "John Stewart." The presiding elder replied, "Nothing against father Stewart. He has completed fifty years as an active minister among us, and now asks a change of his relation. I move that he be granted a superannuated relation." The motion was carried unanimously, and then, in their great kindness, they spread upon their journals the following resolution:

"*Resolved*, That as the venerable John Stewart, who, at our present session, has, at his own request, been placed upon the superannuated list, is about to leave our bounds to spend the remnant of his days with his sons in the West, we consider it to be but a just tribute to his worth to say, that for the last fifty years he has sustained an effective relation to this Conference, and that during all that time he has maintained the highest character, not only for his honesty, veracity, and integrity as a man, but for his piety as a Christian, and his prompt, faithful, and laborious services as a Christian minister. He leaves with our most heart-felt good wishes and earnest prayers for his welfare and happiness.

B. N. SPAHR,
J. W. WHITE."

I served on several committees during the session of Conference, and had the satisfaction of contributing five hundred dollars as my Centenary offering toward the endowment of the "Morris Professorship" in the Ohio Wesleyan University.

Having made all my arrangements for the purpose, as soon as Conference closed, myself and companion started for the North-west. We left Columbus, Ohio, October 3d, at 3 o'clock, P. M., and arrived at the pleasant residence of my son, J. W. Stewart, in Monroe, Wisconsin, at 6 o'clock, P. M., the next day. We received a warm welcome, and our dear children did all that lay in their power to make us feel at home. Though we had been endeavoring for some ten or twelve years to prepare ourselves for an entrance upon superannuated life, we could not avoid a feeling of loneliness in entering upon a year without a pastoral relation and responsibility.

I had been there only a few days, however, when I

received an affectionate letter from Rev. Alfred Brunson, D. D., an old friend of mine, and a prominent minister in the North west. He gave me a very cordial welcome to my new home. Though forty-five years had passed since we had seen each other, yet his words of welcome were grateful, and abated somewhat the feeling of loneliness that had crept over me.

The first Sabbath that I attended church I experienced a feeling of awkwardness in my new relation. The pastor, Rev. J. C. Aspinwall, was already in the pulpit with glasses on and book in hand when I entered. I however advanced and introduced myself to him as a superannuated member of the Ohio Conference. He received me with kindness, and at once invited me to preach. I declined the invitation, but promised that at any time when sickness or necessary absence from the station should prevent his occupying his pulpit, I would be glad to assist him. Our acquaintance rapidly ripened into brotherly love, and we had many pleasant seasons together in the house of God.

At the next quarterly-meeting I met my old friend, Rev. E. Yocum, the presiding elder of the district. He preached at $10\frac{1}{2}$ o'clock, A. M., on Sabbath, and, by his request, I preached at night, and realized much enlargement of soul. The preachers and people of adjoining charges began to urge me to visit and preach for them, and soon I found myself itinerating and preaching on quite an extended scale. At the camp-meeting the brethren gave me such prominence as almost embarrassed me, but the Lord revealed himself in power, and we had a glorious time. At the end of my first year on the superannuated list I found, on looking back, that I had preached about one hundred sermons, besides holding frequent love-feasts and administering the sacraments of the Church.

The time of the session of my Conference approached, and

it was not without a feeling of sadness that I relinquished the purpose of attending. I however spent some weeks with my son, Rev. W. F. Stewart, at that time presiding elder of the Joliet district of the Rock River Conference, and assisted him in holding the quarterly-meetings on his district. As he had about two quarterly-meetings for each Sabbath, the people received me gladly as his substitute when he could not attend. When I finally abandoned the purpose of going to Conference, I addressed the following letter to my brethren:

"JOLIET, ILLINOIS, *September* 18, 1867.
" To the Bishop and Members of the Ohio Conference:

"DEAR BRETHREN,—For fifty years past I have enjoyed annually the greeting of my comrades in arms at the Conference. I am now upon the retired list, and am admonished by my great distance from you, and by the infirmities of age, that it will be prudent for me to sacrifice this enjoyment this year.

"I find here an abundance of work to do, and I thank God for strength wherewith I am still able to do something for Christ and the Church I love so well! To both myself and my companion the year has been one of usual bodily health and personal enjoyment, and I trust our labor has not been in vain. Since December last I have preached some eighty sermons.

"At the solicitation of my brethren, I have entered upon the work of putting upon paper the reminiscences of fifty years in the regular work. I have seen a host of giants fall out of the ranks, covered with victory, and I have seen a host of valiant young men step into their places and carry forward the work. Lewis, and Carper, and Ellis, and Brockunier have gone during the past year. There is with me a feeling of loneliness, in that they have left me behind, but there is also a feeling of gladness in the thought that they will be there to welcome me when I pass over the river.

"By the blessing of God my companion and myself are enjoying a contented and cheerful old age, and expect, before long, to finish our course with joy.

"Remember us, dear brethren, in your prayers, and may the grace of our Lord Jesus Christ be with you always! Amen. JOHN STEWART."

I have now been nearly four years in superannuated life, and what was the history and experience of the year just detailed has been substantially that of the subsequent years. I have found a more open field, and have been blessed with more strength to labor than I had anticipated. After comparing Methodism in the latitude of Lake Michigan with Methodism in the Valley of the Ohio, I find that, while they differ slightly in form and somewhat in the fervency of outward manifestation, they are, after all, substantially the same. I have sometimes thought I saw a cloud in the ecclesiastical horizon that boded no good, in a growing indifference to the class-meeting and the quarterly-meeting. I have earnestly prayed to God to save me from being a croaker, and I have prayed, too, that he would help me with all fidelity to stand firm to the faith If I should venture a suggestion at all to my excellent brethren of the ministry and membership in the North-west, it would be to work earnestly and conscientiously all of the established machinery of Methodism. It is adapted to meet the wants of the people, and with faithful administration it will fill the land with righteousness and the habitations of the people with joy.

May the blessing of the Father, and of the Son, and of the Holy Ghost abide with all who love our Lord Jesus Christ in sincerity, every-where, always! Amen.

APPENDIX.

APPENDIX.

I.

COMMEMORATION SERMON.*

I will remember the works of the Lord: surely I will remember thy wonders of old. I will meditate also of all thy work, and talk of thy doings. Thy way, O God, is in the sanctuary: who is so great a God as our God? PSALM LXXVII, 11–13.

FROM this portion of Scripture we learn that man may know something of God and of his doings; that he may treasure up that knowledge in his memory; that he may meditate upon it to his own advantage, and talk of it to the profit of others.

He who asks your attention during the present hour claims to know something of God and of his doings; that he has treasured up in his memory some of his doings; that he has found it profitable to meditate on that knowledge; and he is anxious to edify and comfort others while talking about his doings; and now may we all feel as the Psalmist felt when he said, "Thy way, O God, is in the sanctuary; who is so great a God as our God?"

When, in the month of May last, in the city of Chicago, on the shore of Lake Michigan, I received a communication from your Committee of Arrangements, through Dr. Trim-

---

* Delivered by request of the Ohio Conference, on the occasion of its fiftieth anniversary, at Circleville, Ohio, September 16, 1861.

ble, requesting me to prepare a discourse suitable for this semi-centennial occasion, I realized, as I had never done before, the fact that I have outlived my generation, and am now an aged minister. I ran back in memory to the laying of the foundations of the Church and commonwealth in this goodly land. As the events of more than half a century came crowding upon each other, they almost overwhelmed me; my sensations were peculiar—sadness mingled with joy. A feeling of loneliness and sadness would come over me as I inquired, Where are those fathers and brethren who welcomed me nearly half a century ago, when I, a youth, stood knocking at the door of the Ohio Conference? Your committee admonished me that I am now the oldest effective minister upon your Conference roll. But again these feelings of loneliness gave way to those of joy and hope, when I remembered that as God had discharged my fathers and co-laborers, he has called others into the field to occupy their places. I see gathered around me to-day a band of ministers possessing as much learning, and piety, and devotion to the cause of God and Methodism as were possessed by those who have gone before. This record of the past gives me hope for the future. I trust that when another half century shall have passed, and some one of these young brethren who may commence his itinerant life with this Conference shall stand up to preach the centenary discourse of this Conference, he will still look around him upon a body of Methodist preachers as able and true as any of their predecessors; and thus the line will be perpetuated through centuries, and till the Church militant shall have fully accomplished its mission upon earth.

The nineteenth century opened amid thrilling excitement in the New World. The foundations of a great republic had just been laid, and savage tribes were receding before the march of this giant young republic. The most interesting scenes were transpiring in the Mississippi Valley—a valley which the early pioneers had already predicted must become the garden of the republic. There was the excitement of pioneer life, of fortune-hunting, and of Indian warfare, over the mountains, through the vast forests, and along the rich savannas, the eager multitude carrying their effects or merchandise upon pack-horses, pressing their way, or floating down the majestic Western rivers on rafts and flat-boats.

The hardy pioneers who had made their claims were erecting or occupying rude log-cabins or block-houses, designed for strength rather than beauty—to be a defense from the storms of heaven and the more pitiless attacks of the Indians rather than to court admiration. A pioneer thus describes the house in which he was living at that period: It was built of round logs from the forest trees, the first story made of the largest that the men could put up, the second story of smaller ones, and made to jut over two or three feet, so that no one could climb up to the top of the house. The chimneys were built on the inside of the house. The doors were made of puncheon slabs, six inches thick, and were barred on the inside by strong iron staples driven into the logs on both sides of the door, into which were placed strong bars. In the upper part of the house were port-holes, out of which an enemy could be shot; and as there were no windows allowed, these port-holes answered both for light and ventilation.* The house being thus strongly constructed, the pioneer, with his fire arms and ammunition, was always prepared for war. The Mississippi Valley was also full of religious excitement among the hardy pioneers. The history of the Church in modern times will not record a grander and more wonderful uprising of the people, at the call of the trumpet of the Gospel, than was witnessed at the beginning of the nineteenth cen-

* Finley's Autobiography, page 35.

tury. Temples made by hands were few and far between, but the people resorted to the primeval forests, the grand old woods, and there worshiped the God of nature and of grace in his own temple. I am loth to leave this period without dwelling upon the history and results of the camp-meetings of that period. In view, however, of the many important events crowding the period that I am expected to review, I can only glance hastily at facts and scenes which will furnish to the historian matter for the most thrilling volumes. Two brothers in Kentucky by the name of M'Gee, representing two denominations, widely different in doctrines and usages, began to labor together as evangelists. Forgetful of all those peculiarities of faith in which their denominations could not agree, they dwelt upon the great fundamental doctrines of depravity, atonement by Christ, and salvation by faith. The Word preached by them was attended with such power that multitudes flocked to hear them. Coming from a distance, the people would find it necessary to camp out for the night, and then, under the powerful attractions of the Gospel, they would remain for several days. The meetings soon became known by the name of camp-meetings. In the Spring of 1801 William M'Kendree was appointed presiding elder of the Kentucky district; and after satisfying himself that, notwithstanding some extravagances incident to the excitement, the great work itself was of God, he encouraged the people to attend them. Rev. Henry Smith thus describes them: "At the first camp-meetings but little preparations were made. A piece of ground was selected in some grove and cleared of underbrush; a rude stand was erected, and a few seats provided near the stand. At some of the meetings two or three stands were erected, at which there was preaching at the same time, while singing and praying would be going on in circles at a distance from these stands. At first there was strong opposition, and not a little disorder, as might be expected. So many, however, of these violent opposers were 'knocked down,' as it was commonly called, that dread soon fell upon the multitude, and they were greatly restrained. Many fell under the preaching and exhortations; some who were not willing to yield when seized with conviction, ran to the woods to shake it off, but were pursued by the Spirit of God, and compelled to cry for mercy. It sometimes so happened that numbers fell about those first smitten, and the work extended over acres of ground. On such occasions little was heard but the loud cry for mercy, or the singing and shouting of heaven-born souls, and of their friends, rejoicing with and over them."*

Infidels and skeptical persons, not being able to comprehend this phenomenon, were often in great perplexity. Finley gives an account of one Dr. P., of Lexington, Kentucky, who was thus confounded. He had accompanied a lady to the Cane-Ridge camp-meeting. Having heard of the involuntary falling, and other exercises, they agreed upon the way that, should either of them be thus strangely attacked or fall, the other should stand by to the last. It was not long till the lady was brought down with all her pride before God, a poor sinner in the dust. The Doctor, agitated, came up and felt her pulse; but, alas! her pulse was gone. At this he turned pale, and staggering a few paces fell beneath the power of the same invisible Hand. After remaining some time in this state they both revived rejoicing, went home happy in God, and lived and died consistent Christians.† The most remarkable of these demonstrations of power was upon the part of wicked men and scoffers, who were stricken down in the very act of disturbing the worship of the people of God. The following instance oc-

---

* Recollections of Rev. Henry Smith, page 56.
† Finley's Autobiography, page 365.

curred at the same meeting referred to above, and is given upon the same authority. A leader and champion of a party of disturbers and opposers, mounted a large white horse, and rode into the midst of the praying circle, uttering the most horrid imprecations. Suddenly, as if smitten by lightning, he fell from his horse. At this a shout went up from the multitude as if Lucifer himself had fallen. His limbs were rigid, his wrists pulseless, and his breath gone. Several of his comrades came to look at him, and they too fell like men slain in battle. For thirty hours he lay, to all human appearance, dead. During this time the people kept up singing and praying. At last he exhibited signs of life, but they were fearful spasms, which seemed as if he were in a convulsion, attended by frightful groans, as if he were passing through the intensest agony. It was not long, however, till his convulsions ceased, and springing to his feet, his groans were converted into loud and joyous shouts of praise. The dark, fiend-like scowl which had passed over his features gave way to a happy smile which lighted up his countenance.* Such was the religious excitement amid which the nineteenth century had its birth, which, with the excitement of pioneer emigration, and frequent collisions with the Indians, made the period emphatically one of stirring events.

In 1799 Rev. Henry Smith was appointed to the Miami circuit. He crossed the Ohio River at the mouth of the Little Miami, on the 11th of September. Finding that brother Hunt was still supplying the circuit, and looking over a vast field yet to be occupied, he determined not to build upon another man's foundation, but to break up new ground. On the 23d of the same month, therefore, he started up the Ohio River to form a new circuit. Commencing on Eagle Creek, he thence directed his course to

---

* Finley's Autobiography, pages 364, 365.

the mouth of the Scioto, and thence up the river to Chillicothe. In three weeks the Scioto circuit was formed. In the Spring of 1801 he was returned to the circuit, and continued here till the Fall of 1801. Speaking of his adaptation to pioneer life, he says that he accustomed himself to eat any thing that was set before him, to sleep anywhere, and to accommodate himself to any inconvenience. His system, however, was not proof against the bilious and intermittent fevers which then prevailed to a great extent in this country, especially in the rich river valleys. Occasionally, when the body was debilitated by disease, the hardships of this circuit life would become formidable, and for a moment the courage of the hero would fail. Thus, when recovering from a severe attack of the fever he was feebly making his way from Paint Creek to New Market, a tremendous snow-storm mixed with hail overtook him; its pitiless peltings were so severe that for a little while he became despondent, and gave way to tears. Soon, however, he met a poor fellow not so well clad as himself, and exposed to the same storm. Then said the itinerant to himself, "He is not as well clad as I am, and he is out upon his own business; I am out upon the Lord's business." So he dried up his tears, and went on cheerfully to his work.*

The presiding elder who had charge of the Scioto circuit, traveled as far as the Holston circuit, in Tennessee, and embraced all of Kentucky and all of the North-Western Territory west of this valley. By reference to the General Minutes, it will appear that in 1801 the districts took names, and that in 1802 the names of Conferences appear for the first time. The Scioto circuit, which embraced this valley and all west of this circuit, was connected with the Western Conference. The Little Kanawha and Muskingum circuits, which embraced the territory of the present Ohio

* Recollections of Rev. Henry Smith, page 65.

Conference east of this valley, belonged to the Baltimore Conference.

Having so briefly glanced at the foot-prints of the pioneers who laid the foundation of the Church on the soil which we now cultivate, I come next to the organization of the *Ohio Conference*, whose semi-centennial anniversary we commemorate to-day. It was organized at the first delegated General Conference, in the city of New York, in the month of May, 1812. Its boundaries embraced all the State of Ohio, and parts of the States of New York, Pennsylvania, Virginia, Kentucky, and all the North-Western Territory not included in the Tennessee Conference. The year of its organization was also memorable in the history of the country, on account of the breaking out of the war with Great Britain. It was feared that the drain of the membership in supplying the army would materially injure the work, but the ministers kept at their work, so that amid the excitement of martial music, military demonstrations, and the conflict of arms, the cause of God still went forward. In reviewing the history of our Conference during the half century of its existence, I shall, for convenience, divide it into five periods. We shall be gratified to see that each decade has made large accessions to our membership. It will also appear to the credit of our Conference that each period of its history has witnessed the calling into existence, through its instrumentality, some new agency, or some grand movement for the conversion of the world.

The Conference was organized, as above stated, in 1812, and held its first session in Chillicothe; and from the Minutes of that Conference we learn there were sixty-one traveling preachers and twenty-three thousand two hundred and thirty-four members. These sixty-one traveling preachers were generally regulars, well drilled in the exercise, ready and willing to do the work assigned them. They fully and cheerfully submitted to the appointing power which was lodged with Bishops Asbury and M'Kendree, the general superintendents of the whole body of American Methodists. These holy men of God were anxiously looked for annually, to preside in the Conferences. Seldom, if ever, did they fail to meet expectations. By them the business appertaining to an Annual Conference was presented and disposed of in due form; the reports of the doings and success of each preacher were heard by them in Conference, and their eyes were open to see for themselves, and their ears open to hear from others, both what should be done for the preachers and the charges. They were accessible both to preachers and people. It was understood by all concerned, that to go forward as a Church successfully and harmoniously, there must be upon the part of the preachers a full relinquishment of the right to choose their own charges, and upon the part of the membership a full relinquishment of the right to select their own preacher. Without such surrender to the appointing power, disorder and dissatisfaction would be inevitable. Out of sixty-one preachers twenty might be specially sought after by the charges, and out of forty-five charges ten might be specially sought after by the preachers. The twenty preachers could not supply all the charges, nor the ten charges accommodate all the preachers; but on the plan to which all should submit the sixty-one preachers have work assigned them, and no charge is left without a preacher; every preacher is employed and every charge supplied. It may so happen every year that some preachers and some charges are not so well accommodated as they could desire. They may feel that their lot is a hard one; it may be so, and yet it may be for the best; some one must have this charge, why not I? All the preachers want work, and they all have it; all the charges want a preacher, and all have them. Thus the work goes on from year to year. Fifty years have passed since the Ohio Conference commenced acting on that principle, and the cases of demur, either on the part of the preacher or on the part of the charge, have been few and far between; and in no case, as far as I have been capable of judging, has the rebel preacher or the rebel charge made that rebellion profitable, either to the Church or the rebel. It is to be hoped that the good reasons for introducing such a policy will always be appreciated. It is not becoming in any preacher to insist on having a particular charge, or in any charge to insist on any particular preacher. There may be and often are good reasons known to the Bishop why such an appointment should not be made, and at the same time be improper for him to divulge those reasons. A conformity to the Golden Rule will always have a salutary effect; that rule is valuable above all price, and all may profit by it. I assume the fact that the appointments, under God, come from one who loves the Church, and intends, with the means in his hands, to advance, as best he can, the general good.

The Conference had five districts and forty-five circuits, each of which included territory from four to eight times as large as that of districts and circuits of this day. Stations had not then commenced among us. Our first set of presiding elders were all men of mark; namely, David Young, Jacob Young, James Quinn, John Sale, and Solomon Langdon. David Young was then in the seventh year of his ministry, a man of undoubted piety and great zeal. His oratorical and reasoning powers were not surpassed by any. Jacob Young, then in the ninth year of his ministry, was a man of deep, uniform piety, sound judgment, and a great advocate and defender of Methodism. James Quinn, of precious memory, was in the thirteenth year of his ministry, an able divine, efficient in the work; his name is embalmed in the hearts of all who knew him. John Sale was in the sixteenth year of his ministry, and had given strong evidence of his ability, and of his devotion to the itinerant work. Solomon Langdon, in the twelfth year of his ministry, was an excellent preacher—commanded great respect wherever he labored. Long since the powerful voices of most of the giants in our Israel have been hushed in death. The two Youngs lingered with us the longest, but they, too, have now gone to join their co-laborers on the other shore. At that day, though there was great honor attached to the office of presiding elder, those men, though they gained character by it, did not suffer the office to depreciate in their hands. We are thankful that the office remains, and that worthy men in the main, from first to last, have filled it. The succession has been, and we humbly trust will be kept up, and that those only who are well qualified will be appointed to it. There were others, many others of the sixty-one who received appointments at the first Conference, as worthy of honorable mention as those already named. Such were Samuel Parker, Alexander Cummins, James B. Finley, John Brown, William Lamden, John Strange, Moses Crume, Benjamin Lakin, Isaac Quinn, Marcus Lindsey, John Collins, Charles Holliday, William Burke, and others.

The circuits during that decade continued large, the preachers having appointments for almost every day of the month, and in some instances more appointments than there are days in the month. With the preachers it was literally a protracted meeting from Conference to Conference.

To give a definite idea of this, look at the boundaries of Letart Falls circuit, the first I traveled, in the year 1817, and much smaller than some I traveled afterward: Starting from Letart Falls, I went up the Ohio River five miles, and crossed into Virginia, and preached at the mouth of Mill Creek; from there to Statt's, eight miles up Mill

Creek; from there took the back track, passed over into Ohio, and down to Letart, there preached Sabbath and Sabbath night; from there I crossed the Ohio River into Virginia, and took my course down across the flats and over the mountains, crossing the Big Kanawha, filling appointments on the way, till I got opposite the mouth of Big Raccoon; then crossed the river into the State of Ohio, preached at Lanford's, at the mouth of Raccoon; from there up the creek to where Patriot now stands; from there on to Syms Creek, and down it to its mouth, filling three appointments on the way; from there down the Ohio River four miles below, where Burlington now stands; from there I passed on in a north-west course through the forest, to Oak Hill, near where Jackson now is; from thence eastward, to Buck's, where Centerville now is; from thence to Kirkpatrick's, near Ridgeway; from thence to A. Donley's; from thence to William Cherington's, both not far from Gallipolis; from thence to Long's, near where Porter now is; from thence to Edmonson's, near where Ewington now is; from thence to Abraham Hawk's, near where Wilksville now is; from thence to Edward Williams's; from thence to Daniel Rathburn's, on Leeding Creek, seven miles from its mouth; from thence to Vining's, up the creek; from thence across the hills to Cowderey's, on Shade River, a small distance above where Chester now stands; from thence eastward to Graham station, on the Ohio River; then up the Ohio to Letart Falls, the place of beginning, two hundred and fifty miles travel; poor roads at best, much of the route no roads at all, many streams not bridged, oft high water; still the journey was performed every four weeks, and twenty-five stated appointments filled, and frequently appointments at night that enter not into this account. The Methodist Episcopal Church has thirteen charges within what was then Letart Falls circuit.

During this decade, at the General Conference of 1820, a branch of the Book Concern was established within the bounds of the Ohio Conference, at Cincinnati, and Martin Ruter was appointed to its agency. The wisdom of this movement has been demonstrated by the wonderful prosperity and power of this agency among us for good. From a diminutive depository, with a single agent, it has grown to a mammoth publishing house, rivaled by none in the Mississippi Valley. It issues one monthly periodical, with a circulation of 39,500, and four weeklies, in two languages, with an aggregate circulation of 78,000; periodical sales amounting to $195,297.47, and book sales to $133,482.34, and upward of 4,000,000 pages of tracts. It employs a capital of $359,860.21, embracing its real estate, and a working force of ninety men and thirty women.

At the same General Conference the Kentucky Conference was formed, and took from the Ohio Conference its territory lying in that State, and fifty-five preachers and 13,526 members.

The great event of that decade, however, and that which will immortalize both the period and the Conference, was the rise of the Foreign Missionary Society, as connected with the Methodist Episcopal Church.

The Ohio Conference had the honor of leading our Zion in this department of labor. In 1819, in the city of New York, at a meeting of preachers, a committee was appointed to prepare a Constitution, in view of the organization of a Missionary Society. The following preachers were present: Freeborn Garrettson, Joshua Soule, Samuel Merwin, Seth Crowell, Nathan Bangs, Laban Clark, Thomas Mason, Samuel Howe, and Thomas Thorp. A resolution in favor of forming a Bible and Missionary Society was passed, and the 5th of April and Forsyth-Street Church selected as the time and place when the Constitution should be submitted to a public meeting for discussion. The historian gives us no intimation of the numbers present at that meeting, or the zeal with which they entered into the work. A Constitution was adopted, the names of subscribers taken, and the following officers elected: President, William M'Kendree; Corresponding Secretary, Thomas Mason; Treasurer, Joshua Soule. At the first meeting of the Board of Managers, an address and circular, prepared by a committee appointed for that purpose, were adopted and ordered to be printed in the Methodist Magazine, and in pamphlet form. As the Constitution of the Society contemplated action upon the part of the oncoming General Conference, the subject came before that body at the session of 1820. An able report, prepared by the late Bishop Emory, was presented and adopted. That report opens with this language: "Your committee regard the Christian ministry as peculiarly a missionary ministry. 'Go ye into all the world and preach the Gospel to every creature,' is the very foundation of its authority, and develops its character simultaneously with its origin. After referring to the missionary spirit as the life of the Church, and to the zeal and success of the Wesleyan Church in Great Britain in this department, it goes on to spread out the special field which this society should attempt at once to enter and cultivate. In that connection we find this language: "In a particular manner the committee solicit the attention of the Conference to the condition of the aboriginals of our country, the Indian tribes. American Christians are certainly under peculiar obligations to impart to them the blessings of civilization and Christian light. That there is no just cause to despair of success through grace in this charitable and pious undertaking, is demonstrated by the fact that there are already gathered into Church-fellowship about sixty members of the Wyandot tribe in the State of Ohio, and that a successful mission, under our direction, is now in operation among them. Why might not similar success attend other missions among other tribes?"*

From this historical record these two things appear: 1. A foreign mission had been successfully planted before the organization of the Missionary Society; and, 2. That mission was in the bounds of and under the care of the Ohio Conference. As this department of Christian effort has since grown to such colossal proportions, and produced such grand results, it is with honest pride that we trace the origin of Methodist Episcopal missions to our own Conference. Let us then pause for a little while to contemplate the circumstances under which our first mission among a pagan people was planted.

In the year 1816 a free colored man by the name of John Steward, residing in Marietta, Ohio, felt strangely impressed by the Spirit of God to travel toward the North-west, that he might preach the Gospel to the lost sheep of the house of Israel. He saw in his vision an aged Indian man and woman, with imploring countenance, looking to him for the Word of life. He communicated his impressions to his religious friends, but the scheme to them looked so unpromising that they gave him no encouragement. He could, however, find no rest to his mind except when he was yielding to those impressions. Finally, God having given him some special sign which he had asked, he determined to obey the call. By this time his class-leader had come to sympathize with him in his strange impressions, and they spent a great part of the night preceding his departure together in prayer, that God's blessing might attend him. And what a scene was that! I have read of great gatherings in splendid temples on taking leave of missionaries, but I confess that the gathered multitude, the splendid temple, the eloquence and feeling of those occasions have

* Bangs's History of the Methodist Episcopal Church, Vol. III, pages 143-145.

never, to my mind, reached the sublimity of that occasion, when this humble colored exhorter and his class-leader were wrestling with God together, that he would direct the willing feet of his servant to the place where he might shed light upon the minds of those sitting in the region and shadow of death. The handful of corn was about to be planted upon the top of the mountain, which, in the providence of God, in after years should shake like Lebanon. Steward, with his little bundle in his hand, started on foot and alone in a north-westerly direction, sometimes pursuing his way through the trackless forest, veering to the right or left, according to the impressions made by his inward monitor. After some days he came to a settlement of Indians at Pipetown; he now supposed that he had reached his destination. He spent the night with them, and opened to them the Gospel. In the morning, however, he felt impelled to continue his journey. After some days he reached the Wyandot nation of Indians, in Upper Sandusky. He called upon Mr. Walker, a sub-agent of the Government among these Indians. He had no Episcopal credentials to present, nor educational endowments or personal presence to recommend him. He related to Mr. and Mrs. Walker his Christian experience, and how God had sent him to preach the Gospel to the Indians. They listened to his story, and being convinced of the purity of his motives, threw no obstructions in his way. His first sermon was preached to an old Indian woman. The next day two aged Indians, a man and a woman, came to hear him. He took courage, for though his congregation was small at his first sermon, it had increased a hundred-fold in a day. But what gave him the greatest encouragement was, that he recognized the two persons who constituted his second congregation as the same persons he had seen in his vision while passing through the singular mental exercise at Marietta. At the close of his sermon they came forward and gave him the hand of welcome. He was now fully assured that this was to be his field of labor, and so diligently and efficiently did he bring the Gospel home to the understanding of these two aged Indians, that they were soon converted to God. Around them soon gathered a congregation, first curious, then serious, then in deep distress, calling upon God for mercy, and finally joyful in the hope of the Gospel. Among these converts were several influential chiefs of the nation—Between-the-Logs, Mononcue, Hicks, and Scutash; also, two of the interpreters, Pointer and Armstrong. Nothing pleased the missionary more than the conversion of Pointer, the colored interpreter. At first this boy had performed the office of interpreter of the Gospel with a good deal of indifference and reluctance. Sometimes after interpreting a sentence he would add, "So Steward says, but I do n't know whether it is so or not, and do n't care." Now that he was converted, he would be more efficient and earnest as a helper in the good work. In 1819 the mission was taken under the care of the Ohio Conference, and attached to the Lebanon district, of which Rev. J. B. Finley was presiding elder. At the Conference of 1820, held at Chillicothe, deeply interesting interviews were had with a delegation from the Wyandot nation, who brought a petition for the appointment of a missionary to their people from the Ohio Conference. The petition was granted, and Rev. M. Henkle was appointed.

My time will not permit me to follow this history further. This was the first of our missions among pagan populations. In less than forty years, behold what God hath wrought! Missions have been established among other Indian tribes upon this continent, and our missionaries have crossed oceans, planting the standard of the Cross on the shores of Africa, and among the vast pagan population of China and

India. The Methodist Episcopal Church has among the aboriginals of this country 21 missionaries and 1,557 members; in India, 20 missionaries and 82 members; in China, 5 missionaries and 56 members; in Africa, 25 missionaries and 1,498 members. The missionary contributions for the first year—1820—were $823.04, and $85.76 expended. The last year—1860—the missionary collections were, as the Minutes show, $258,849, and all expended; $10,334 of that amount from the Ohio Conference, to say nothing of amounts raised by other branches and offshoots of American Methodism. As though God would set his seal of approbation to this missionary movement, the same year was signalized by special revivals of religion within the bounds of the Ohio Conference. At Chillicothe 320 were converted and added to the Church, among whom was the man who was erecting the Methodist church in that place, together with all his family, and all the workmen employed upon the house. During this first decade of our Conference history, the ministry in the Church at large had increased from 688 to 891; and the membership from 195,357 to 281,146. The Ohio Conference had increased in the ministry from 61 to 88, and the membership from 23,281 to 34,178.

I now pass to the second decade of our Conference history. The year 1822 witnessed gracious outpourings of the Spirit of God within its bounds. Bangs's History makes special mention of that which attended the Scioto campmeeting. This meeting was held at White Brown's campground, within the bounds of what is now Deer Creek circuit, and was under the charge of Samuel Parker and Alexander Cummins. About sixty of the converted Wyandots were present, and their thrilling and powerful experiences melted all hearts. Those who had been accustomed in other days to meet the Indians in their savage state on the bloody field of strife, were deeply moved by what they now witnessed. The Word of God powerfully prevailed, and the revival spread in all directions.

During this decade, as of interest in the general history of American Methodism, should be mentioned the establishment of the Christian Advocate and Journal, the parent of a now large and influential family of Advocates. The paper was issued in New York city, in the month of September, 1826. The next year, namely, 1827, the *Sunday School Union* was organized. These appliances have exerted an incalculable amount of good since their establishment. Our denomination had indeed given some attention to Sabbath-schools on this continent at an earlier day, but not till this period had the subject taken organic shape, or demanded so large attention. During this decade, too, the polity of the Methodist Episcopal Church underwent the most thorough and searching investigation. The cry was raised that her government was not in harmony with the republican principles of the land. Giant minds came in conflict, and in some places the collision threatened to prove disastrous to the interests of the Church. The principles of our government were irrefutably defined by the able pens of Bond, Emory, and others, and firmly administered by the majority of our presiding elders and pastors. The incurably disaffected seceded and organized the Protestant Methodist Church. The heat of that controversy has long since passed away, and the historian will make up his verdict from the comparative success of the so-called Reformers, and the Church against whose government they so earnestly battled. If the Reformers improved upon the polity of Methodism, it is but fair to demand the proofs of this improvement in the history of the growth and success of the Church which they formed. They were led on by men of giant intellect, and whose names had been a tower of strength in the denomination for years. A careful examination of history will sufficiently demonstrate the wisdom of our fathers in their course.

During this period, namely, at the General Conference of 1824, the Pittsburg Conference was organized, taking from the Ohio Conference all the territory east of the Muskingum River, except Marietta and Zanesville, together with what then lay in Virginia, Pennsylvania, and New York. About 40 preachers and 12,000 members went with the territory.

The important event of this period, which reflects honor upon the Ohio Conference, was an effort to found an institution of learning of a high grade. Before this time, several colleges and academies had been projected in other parts of the Church, but to this time no persevering and successful effort had been made to plant and endow an institution of learning so as to give promise of permanence and extended usefulness. At the Conference of 1820, held in Chillicothe, a plan was agreed upon, and commissioners appointed to select a location. In consequence of the offer upon the part of the trustees of Bracken Academy, to loan the Church the use of $10,000, on condition of its location at Augusta, the institution was fixed at that point, in the State of Kentucky, and on the banks of the Ohio River. This location was also esteemed advisable in view of having the Kentucky Conference to unite in the founding and support of the college. In 1823 John P. Finley was appointed by the Kentucky Conference in charge of the infant institution. In 1825 a commodious college edifice was erected, and with the organization of an able faculty, the institution rapidly increased in popularity. Its students gathered from all parts of the land, and soon filled up its halls. For about a quarter of a century Augusta College accomplished a large amount of good. It enjoyed the labors, in its boards of instruction, in the prime of their days, of such men as Finley, Tomlinson, Fielding, Bascom, Durbin, Ruter, Trimble, M'Cown, and others, men who had few superiors, either in the recitation-room or in the pulpit. It survived to see its graduates in high places, both in Church and State, all over the land. When at last a proslavery fanaticism struck the fatal blow at the old institution which had done so much for the development of the mind of the Mississippi Valley, it had the pleasure of looking over the land and witnessing how large a band of institutions had sprung up all around it to supply its place. Had this first successful Methodist college which the world ever saw been planted upon free instead of slave soil, it would doubtless have strengthened with years, and flourished for centuries. When the Kentucky Legislature repealed the charter of the College, commissioners were appointed by the Ohio Conference to close up its affairs, and so much of its endowments as could be saved by our Conference was loaned to the Ohio Wesleyan University, where they now constitute part of the endowment fund. When Augusta College was founded, the State universities and colleges were generally controlled by other denominations, and it was not uncommon to hear remarks made touching educational enterprise which were by no means complimentary to our Church. Thirty-five years, however, have made a vast change in this respect. The Methodist Episcopal Church now has in the United States a larger number of universities, colleges, and seminaries, and in their halls a larger number of students than any other denomination. Besides which, she now takes a leading part in the management of State and other non-denominational institutions of learning. She purposes honestly and faithfully to do her full share in the education of the youth of the land. She now has 24 universities and colleges and 126 seminaries.

At the close of this decade, namely, 1831, there were in the Church 2,010 traveling preachers and 513,114 members;

and in the Ohio Conference there were 132 traveling preachers and 34,178 members. The increase of traveling preachers was 1,119, and of members 231,968; in the mean time the increase in the Ohio Conference was 44 traveling preachers and 6,458 members; a fine increase, considering the number set off to Pittsburg.

We now take up the third decade of our history. The general spirit of the Church for the evangelization of the world was advancing. The Ohio Conference having set an example by sending missionaries to the pagan tribes on our own shores, the Church now followed that example by sending them abroad. In the year 1833 Melville B. Cox, a man of great firmness of purpose, meekness of spirit, and burning zeal for the cause of God, offered himself as a missionary for Africa. It was feared by many that he would fall a martyr to the climate of that country. Being asked by some one what should be written on his tombstone, should he die in Africa, he replied, "Let thousands fall before Africa be given up." Though the brave missionary lived but a few months, he accomplished a work, under God, of incalculable value to the Church at home, and to the heathen abroad. The mission planted by him has grown and prospered till a Conference has been established, embracing 25 traveling and 33 local preachers and 1,566 members. The next year after Cox offered himself for Africa, Jason and Daniel Lee offered themselves for a missionary expedition to the Flat-Head Indians, beyond the Rocky Mountains. The call to which they responded was one that thrilled the heart of the Church. The Flat-Heads, having a tradition that away toward the rising sun there lived a people who could instruct them in the true religion, after discussing the matter in their council, determined to dispatch a messenger to find that people and get that instruction. The messenger made his tedious and toilsome way to the valley of the Mississippi, and in response to the Macedonian cry for help, the evangelical Lees turned their backs upon home and civilization, and scaled the Rocky Mountains, and proclaimed to the inquiring savages the Gospel of the Son of God.

During this decade, namely, in 1836, the boundaries of the Ohio Conference were still further contracted by the organization of the Michigan Conference. It took from us Michigan Territory, and four presiding elder's districts in the State of Ohio, and of our preachers 129, and of our members 23,867.

The great event of this period, however, as connected with the Ohio Conference, and which we regard as one of the most important historical events of modern Christianity, was the founding of missions among the Germans. We would do unpardonable injustice to this Conference and this occasion did we not direct special attention to this sublime work. In the year 1835, after a somewhat protracted discussion in the Ohio Conference, William Nast was appointed missionary to the German population of Cincinnati. The soil to be cultivated seemed to be barren and unpromising enough. The German mind had become deeply and widely poisoned with the infidelity of rationalism. The pantheistic philosophy had taken possession of leading German minds at home both in and out of the Church. And the masses of people who flocked to this country to make money gave poor encouragement for an evangelist. There was encouragement, however, to that class of persons who felt that while the Gospel was a stumbling-block to some and foolishness to others, it still remained the power of God and the wisdom of God to every one who would receive it. William Nast had the demonstration of this in his own experience, and he had hope for his countrymen. His fitness for the mission will appear from a consideration of his personal history, and from the results of his plans and efforts. He was born at Stuttgart, the capital of Wurtemberg, in Germany. During his university course, he was in the labyrinth of pantheism. He declined, therefore, entering the three years' theological course, which follows the philosophical course, preferring to sacrifice all his property in paying back to the State what it had spent upon his education, rather than to enter the ministry, solemnly promising to preach doctrines which he did not believe. It was urged that many of those highest in the Church held and taught the same doctrine which he held; but this would not satisfy his conscience. He positively declined to enter the pulpit. In 1828 he came to America, and some time after became tutor in a Methodist family. He there formed the acquaintance of several ministers of the Baltimore Conference. He became deeply convicted for sin, but for a time he labored under the error of supposing that it was inconsistent with the Divine justice that the sinner should be absolved from the guilt and penalty of sin without suffering in part himself for his sins. He passed through mental struggles dark and terrible as those which marked the experience of the other great German Reformer. His case attracted attention, and many persons became deeply interested for him. Some already seemed to have a premonition that he was designed by God for a special work. A pious old lady by the name of Patrick, while encouraging him on one occasion, said, "William, do n't doubt, you will yet get the blessing. The Lord has a great work for you to do. You will yet take the Gospel trumpet and publish the Savior's name to your countrymen." While occupying a place in the Board of Instruction at Kenyon College, he made several journeys to Zanesville, to converse with Rev. Henry S. Farnandis, from whom he received much encouragement. After this he attended quarterly-meeting in the town of

Danville, Knox county, Ohio, at which Rev. Adam Poe was the presiding elder. A powerful revival was in progress. He went forward for prayers, but after praying long and earnestly, he arose discouraged, and started to leave the house. As he approached the door, he looked back upon the happy converts, and as he listened to them shouting the praise of God, suddenly these words, "There is bread enough in my Father's house," were impressed with divine power upon his mind. His spiritual eyes were opened to see the fullness of the merits of Christ. In a moment, thinking no more of his want of qualification, he resolved to approach the mercy-seat again. He hastened back to a corner of the house—fell on his knees to plead once more with God for mercy. But as he this time offered nothing but Jesus, the moment he opened his mouth to ask his prayer was answered. Happy in God, he returned to Kenyon College, called the professors and students together, and after telling them what God had done for him, kneeled down and prayed with them, and gave thanks to God. Soon after this he was licensed to preach, and at the Conference held in Springfield, as above stated, he was received into the traveling connection, and appointed as German missionary to Cincinnati. Such, then, were the qualifications of the missionary—thoroughly educated, not only in general literature, but in those phases of infidelity which had swept the great mass of his countrymen from the true foundations of Christian faith; a man of deep and genuine experience, and willing to give his time, talents, and life to the cause of God among his countrymen. If the man appeared to be the appropriate person for the work, the results of his labors have completed the demonstration. The limits of my discourse prevent me from going into details of this stupendous work. The revival commenced in Cincinnati spread to other points within the bounds of the Ohio Conference, extending to other Conferences, crossed the Atlantic Ocean, and made a profound impression upon the great German heart in the Father-land. Rev. Dr. Nast does not now stand alone; but around him gather as his spiritual children, and the results of his labors and faith, 241 traveling and 205 local preachers, and 21,000 members in this country; and 18 preachers and 1,354 members in Germany. To assist them in their work, two papers, with an aggregate circulation of 26,000, are issued by the Cincinnati Book Concern. A tract publishing house has been established in Germany, and Dr. Nast is now preparing and publishing an original commentary on the Bible in the German language. While we thank God for what has already been done, we can see that it is only the commencement of a revival destined to regenerate Germany.

I come now to the fourth division of the history, reaching from 1841 to 1851. During this period the Methodist Episcopal Church was visited by the most extraordinary revivals, and rent by internal dissensions. The net increase of the membership of the Methodist Episcopal Church for 1842–43, as reported by the General Minutes, reached the astonishing aggregate of 257,465. The year 1844 precipitated a collision between that portion of the membership of the Methodist Episcopal Church which clung to the primitive doctrine of American Methodism on the subject of slavery, and that portion of the membership which had become, to some extent, leavened with the spirit of slavery. The slavery question had agitated the Church to a greater or less extent during its whole history. Stringent laws had sometimes been enacted, and then followed by compromises and attempts to conciliate those who professed to be aggrieved. Whatever of compromise or laxity of administration had marked any portion of our history, there was one place in the economy of the Church where slave-holding has never been allowed. Our general superintendents had kept pure from this contamination. At the General Conference of 1844 it began to be whispered that Bishop Andrew had become the owner of slaves. No bishop was more dearly beloved, none had been more abundantly honored throughout the borders of our Zion. The question was started in many hearts as between duty and affection: Shall we arraign Bishop Andrew, or shall we wink at this thing? It was not, however, of difficult solution. Two men, both of Southern antecedents, both well known as strongly conservative men—men, too, who were strong personal friends of Bishop Andrew—Rev. J. B. Finley and Rev. J. M. Trimble, offered a resolution requesting the Committee on the Episcopacy to examine and report the facts in regard to the rumor of Bishop Andrew's connection with slavery. The report fully sustained the rumor, and the Bishop himself fully explained the circumstances of the case. It is thought that he would have promptly resigned, but the Southern leaders supposing that they never would have the opportunity of discussing the general subject under more favorable circumstances, insisted that he should maintain his position. After full and prolonged discussion, the Conference passed a resolution, setting it forth as the "sense of that General Conference, that Bishop Andrew desist from the exercise of his office till this impediment should be removed." What immediately followed, the protest of the minority, the answer of the majority, the plan of separation, and the means by which the great mass of the members of most of the Southern Conferences were induced to secede from the Methodist Episcopal Church, are matters of familiar history upon which I can not now dwell. As might have been anticipated, the Southern secession has continued to tend toward slavery, till all of the old landmarks have been broken down, and her strong men have become principal champions of the divine right of slavery. On the other hand, the Methodist Episcopal Church has continued to speak out with a clear and more emphatic voice at every General Conference, till to-day her influence in the behalf of freedom is more powerful than ever before. Whatever of honor may attach in history to the General Conference of 1844, for taking so firm a stand, and arresting, so far as the Church was concerned, lax views and lax legislation on this vital question, a great part of that honor must belong to the Ohio Conference, leading members of whose delegation, as before stated, introduced the resolution which brought the matter to an issue.

Upon the period extending from 1851 to the present I do not propose to dwell. Its scenes are fresh in the memory of us all. At its beginning we suffered a large bereavement of ministers and members, as well as territory, in the organization of the Cincinnati Conference. It took from us 188 preachers and 34,239 members. The period has been marked with missionary zeal and liberality, educational and Church extension enterprise, and an encouraging degree of religious prosperity. The Conference to-day enrolls 178 traveling and 248 local preachers; 34,136 members; 489 churches, valued at $533,129, and 89 parsonages, valued at $74,340; 551 Sabbath-schools, 6,327 teachers, 32,708 scholars, 104,994 books in library. The Methodist Episcopal Church now enrolls 6,987 traveling and 8,188 local preachers and 994,447 members; 9,754 churches, valued at $19,552,054; 2,674 parsonages, valued at $2,663,318; 13,243 Sabbath-schools, 146,120 teachers, 793,131 scholars, 2,672,482 books in library. The rates of increase or decrease during each decade have been as follows: In the Methodist Episcopal Church, in the first, increase, 31 per cent.; in the second, 82 per cent.; in the third, 66 per cent.; in the fourth, the decrease was 15 per cent., owing to the

Southern secession of nearly 400,000; and in the fifth, increase 37 per cent. In the five decades, the per cent. of increase was 364. In the same periods the Ohio Conference, first decade, increased 46 per cent.; the second, 19 per cent.; the third, 33 per cent.; the fourth, 25 per cent.; the fifth, 49 per cent. decrease, by the heavy draw on its membership to form the Cincinnati Conference.

Leaving this period to younger and abler pens, I turn now to review very hastily the past, and gather up some of the lessons with which this day and this occasion should impress us. The record of the Ohio Conference during the half century of its existence is one of which we need not be ashamed. We have seen that she has had honorable connection with many of the important moral and religious movements of the age. During her first decade she planted the first foreign mission of the Methodist Episcopal Church. During her second, she projected and founded, in connection with the Kentucky Conference, the first successful Methodist college in the world. During the third, she started the great domestic missionary movement among the German population, which in its growth and success has equally surprised and delighted the Christian world; and during the fourth period, through her delegation in the General Conference, she was instrumental in arresting the Church in her pro-slavery tendency, and to elevate her in the eyes of the world as ready to sacrifice every thing else for the preservation of her purity. In 1836 the General Conference selected one from among us for the work and office of a Bishop; and in 1844 selected another. The former is now the senior, and is an ornament to the bench; the latter served the Church in that office efficiently for eight years, and, in consequence of affliction, retired. They live, and will live, in the confidence and esteem of the Church. During the first fifty years past 872 persons have been admitted on trial into the Ohio Conference; 800 of them, after two years probation, were received into full connection. They came in classes varying in numbers from three, the smallest class, to thirty-three, the largest class. These have all stood before the Conference, been publicly examined by the Bishops, according to the forms of our excellent Discipline. As only 72 out of the 872 were discontinued at the expiration of their probation, it would seem that the Conference has exercised commendable caution. I would earnestly call the attention of the Conference to this point, in order that all who are added to the body be such as will add to its strength and efficiency. The door of admission both on trial and into full connection should be guarded with a watchful eye. During the half century 168 preachers of the Ohio Conference have located. The causes of these locations are not matters of record; some of them had sufficient reason, and were prompted by pure motives, in retiring from the regular work; others, possibly, were prompted by trivial or selfish considerations. Some of them, in after years, were re-admitted to the traveling connection. Others applied, but failed of being re-admitted. I have been a careful observer of these things for many years, but have seldom known a preacher who retired from the field from other causes than a failure of health, to be either contented in his mind or prosperous in his business. I would ask my young brethren in the ministry when tempted to leave the Word to serve tables, to weigh the matter well. The Conference may easily supply your place, but if your location is not in the order of God, all your fond anticipations will fail.

Scattered along through the General Minutes are the memoirs of fifty-six of our fathers and brethren, who have died at the post of duty. Having taught the lessons of holy living, they taught also the lessons of happy dying.

Preachers die, and all must die. We may preach the funerals of others; let us still bear in mind that others will soon officiate at our funerals, and let us be ready when the Master comes to call us. The youngest of those fifty-six was twenty-five years old at the time of his death, and the oldest was ninety-one. The average age was fifty years. The contemplation of the death of our fathers and brethren is in one sense sad. There is, however, one other item that we glean from our Minutes, unspeakably more sad than the death of the preachers. I refer to their expulsion on account of immorality. Would to God that such an instance had never pained our hearts or tainted our records! But, alas! in a few instances, Christ and his cause have been scandalized in the eyes of the world by wickedness among the ministers of the Gospel. During the history of our Conference nine have thus disgraced themselves, wounded the cause, and compelled us to expel them from the ministry and the Church. I am unspeakably happy, however, to announce that all but one of the nine afterward gave evidence of deep repentance, and again found a home and consolation in the Church they had so greatly wounded. Some of them were eventually restored to the ministry, but they have never regained the position and influence from which they fell.

My beloved brethren and sons in the Gospel, I know you will receive a word of exhortation from me on this interesting occasion. Let brotherly love continue; be not envious of each other's talents, or positions, or influence, but strive together in love, as also ye do, each esteeming others better than himself, and he that is ambitious to be the greatest, let him be willing to be servant of all. Deal kindly with those who have worn themselves out in the work. And the widows and orphans of those who have died in the work; see to it that they are cared for. You yourselves will be aged by and by, or if called from your sphere of labor here, you will leave families to be cared for by your brethren; let your kindness to the aged and sympathies with the bereaved be such as you desire may be meted out to you and yours. Give your best energies and thoughts to the work in which you are engaged. Never let your work as Methodist traveling preachers be subordinate to any thing else. Literature, politics, and money-making are all proper in their place; but all of them sadly out of place when they become the primary matters of solicitude or attention upon the part of a Methodist itinerant. Finally, brethren, be true to the Gospel of our Lord Jesus Christ, and to the Church through whose instrumentality you have been saved and made what you are. Men of splendid parts have deserted and gone off from our communion, thinking to better their condition; few of them but would have gladly come back again could they have hoped to wipe out the past and regain what they had forfeited. Cling to the Bible and book of Discipline, and keep your hearts richly baptized with the Holy Ghost, and then a glorious future awaits you as individuals and as a Conference. Brethren, the task you assigned me upon this occasion is about done, and yet my heart is full. It is possible, as I intimated in the beginning, that some of you may live to participate in another meeting like this, when another half century shall have passed. I shall not. If, however, disembodied spirits are permitted to return to earth to mingle with those they have loved, and in whose success they feel interested, then may I come back fifty years hence to see the labors you shall have done, and the victories you shall have gained through the grace of Jesus Christ.

May the peace of God, which passeth all understanding, abide with you forever! Amen.

II.

SEMI-CENTENNIAL SERMON.*

I will tell of the glory of thy kingdom, and talk of thy power. PSALM CXLV, 11.
Awake, awake, put on thy strength, O Zion, put on thy beautiful garments, O Jerusalem. ISAIAH LII, 1.

IT was the good fortune of the speaker to commence his itinerant career at an eventful period of the history of the Methodist Episcopal Church. It was in the year of our Lord 1816, the middle year of the just closing first century of American Methodism. That year some of her grandest historical characters were just passing away, and some of her grandest institutions for the accomplishment of her mission were about coming into existence. During that year her Asbury, and Jesse Lee, and George Shadford closed their pilgrimage and labors; and within three years from that date her Bible and Missionary Society and her Tract Society were organized—societies that were destined to become mighty agencies in carrying forward the work of the Church. As that year (1816) was the closing year of the first half-century of American Methodism, it may be well to pause and spend a few moments in contemplating the departure of those moral heroes whose personal narrative makes up so much of the history of the times in which they lived.

Bishop Asbury's eventful history, which had extended

---

* Delivered by request of the Ohio Conference, on the completion of half a century in the regular work, at Columbus, Ohio, October 1, 1866.

through fifty-five years of ministerial labor, forty-five of which he had spent in this country, was now about to close. In the Spring of that year he reached Richmond, Virginia, having traveled in his private carriage from Tennessee, through South and North Carolina. Worn by fatigue and reduced by disease, his friends saw that his end was near. They entreated him to spare himself from further labor. The heroic man said he desired once more to deliver his testimony in Richmond. Unable either to walk or to stand, he was assisted from his carriage to the pulpit, and seated on a table that had been prepared for that purpose. His text was Romans ix, 28: "He will finish his work and cut it short in righteousness, because a short work will the Lord make upon the earth." His debility was such that he was compelled to make frequent pauses in the course of his sermon, yet the audience was much affected by the manner in which he delivered his solemn message, but much more with his appearance, venerable with age, standing on the borders of eternity, pale and tremulous with debility, while the deep intonations of his commanding voice, rising with the grandeur of his subject, gave a solemnity to the whole scene of the most impressive character. Having so faithfully delivered his last message, he lingered only a few days. On the 31st of March his friends saw that he was dying, and asked him if he had any communications to make. He replied that "he had fully expressed his mind in relation to the interests of the Church to Bishop M'Kendree, and had nothing to add." How sublime that answer! Those whose lives have been of religious leisure are apt to be in a hurry when they come to die—much to do, and little time in which to do it. But those who, like Wesley and Asbury, have made life wonderful with its religious enterprises and activities, when they come to die, have calmness, and leisure, and rest, on the borders of eternity. Sitting in his chair, without a struggle or a groan, he passed from earth to rejoin his companions who had preceded him to the Church triumphant. He had seen the Methodist Church on the continent grow from a membership of 1,160 to that of 224,853.

In the Autumn of that year the Ohio Conference met at Louisville, Kentucky. A goodly band of young men stood ready to fill up the ranks which had been thinned by death and locations. The following preachers were received on trial: Thomas A. Morris, John C. Brooke, Stephen Spurlock, Ezra Booth, Samuel Glaze, William Holdman, William Westlake, Samuel Baker, John Linville, Daniel D. Davisson, William Williams, Samuel Demint, Thomas Carr, and Simon Peter—fourteen. There not being enough, however, to supply the work, Rev. Jacob Young, presiding elder of the Muskingum district, called me out, and sent me to assist Rev. John Summerville, on the Letart Falls circuit. Young, inexperienced, and trembling, I responded to the summons, and started forth in the name of the Lord to do the best I could. The race which I then commenced I have been enabled, by the blessing of God, to continue for fifty years, and now, a monument of God's mercy, am here to witness the closing up of the first and the commencement of the second century of American Methodism. At that time the Ohio Conference had about sixty-seven preachers, and the territory embraced Ohio, Kentucky, Indiana, and parts of Virginia and Pennsylvania. Within the same bounds there are now some ten or twelve Conferences and more than one thousand traveling preachers. There were then in the bounds of what now constitutes the Ohio Conference two districts, arranged and supplied as follows:

Muskingum District—Jacob Young, presiding elder. Letart Falls, John Summerville, John Stewart as supply; Fairfield, James Quinn, John M'Mahon; Zanesville, John

Waterman, Thomas Carr; Marietta, Cornelius Springer, Thomas A. Morris; Knox, Shadrach Ruark.

Scioto District—David Young, presiding elder. Pickaway, Michael Ellis, Samuel Brown; Paint Creek, Jacob Hooper, William Westlake; Scioto, Thomas Sewell, Robert W. Finley; Columbus, William Swayze, Simon Peter; Brush Creek, Elijah Truitt; Salt Creek, John Tevis; Deer Creek, Charles Waddle, Samuel Glaze.

I have omitted from the list the charges that lay outside of our present Conference bounds, and have inserted the names of the supplies as far as they are known to me. When you called your roll at the opening of this Conference, I listened attentively, but though you called over one hundred and fifty names, yet except my own I heard not one of the names that I have just read in your hearing. One other is still living, who is now the senior Bishop of the Methodist Episcopal Church; but with that exception my old comrades in arms have all gone home—elders, deacons, licentiates—they have all gone. The same year, and only about a month after the decease of Bishop Asbury, the General Conference met in Baltimore, and now for the first time in its history did the superintendency of American Methodism devolve solely on native American hands. Asbury had come forty-five years before, a missionary sent by Wesley, and had given his noble life, with all its energies, to the work of founding and building up the Church on this continent. He had outlived most of his co-laborers, and now he, the last and greatest, had left the battle to be fought by others.

The delegates from the Ohio Conference to the General Conference were James Quinn, Charles Holliday, Marcus Lindsey, Jacob Young, Samuel Parker, Isaac Quinn, David Young, John Sale, and Benjamin Lakin, all of them giants in their day. They assisted in electing Enoch George and

Robert R. Roberts to strengthen the Episcopacy, which then had but one member, the saintly M'Kendree, and he in very feeble health.

The Bishops elected, and our delegates who assisted in electing them, are all gone, and now, doubtless, mingle together in the sublimer enjoyments of the better world; possibly to-day as ministering spirits interested in this Centenary jubilee, they may mingle with us, rejoicing in the results of one common toil. For so it is, the workmen who in their day seem to be essential to the continuance of the work are called home, but the work goes forward, steadily, surely, grandly it goes forward. As I stand here to-day, calling up the memories of the half century that has passed since I entered the itinerant field, and glance down through the vista of the on-coming century, I can hardly tell which interests me most. I think of what God has wrought for Methodism throughout the world during the past century, and I feel to "tell of the glory of his kingdom, and talk of his power." My heart grows warm as I antedate the possibilities of the future, and I cry out, "Awake, awake, put on thy strength, O Zion, put on thy beautiful garments." If we and our successors sufficiently appreciate the available strength and responsibility of the Methodist Episcopal Church, and will be true to our mission, our future will eclipse in grand results even the magnificent achievements of the past. The study of her history demonstrates that she has wielded wonderful strength; an examination of her genius, polity, and ecclesiastical enterprises, shows that she has large resources of strength upon which to draw at pleasure; these resources indicate her responsibility, and call for a girding of herself with all her possible strength for another campaign of a hundred years. Had Methodism not possessed strength she could not have extended her lines against active and constant opposition, till her standards are planted on all the populous portions of this continent; she could not have planted and sustained missionary stations on all the continents of the globe; she could not have erected on this continent 9,922 church buildings, building them during a portion of the time at the rate of one every day. She could not have founded 77 seminaries and 25 colleges and universities; she could not have gathered into her fold 928,320 members, and into the various branches of the Methodist family on this continent and the neighboring islands 1,986,420 communicants, and into her congregations nearly 8,000,000 of people. Wherein has she this great strength? and where are the sources of her strength? Are they not found, first, in her discipline, or Methodism; second, in the activity of her laborers, and that peculiar feature of her economy—the great itinerant wheel—which puts and keeps the entire host in operation; third, in the intelligence of her membership, and her multitudinous appliances for the dissemination of knowledge among the members and the people; fourth, in the pure Gospel she always has, and always proposes to carry on all her banners, and publish to all her people; fifth, in the vital piety or holiness which she teaches as attainable, and which she urges upon all her people as indispensable to the fulfillment of her mission as a Church and people?

Allow me to spend a few minutes in illustrating these positions.

1. We have intimated that one of the secrets of the strength of our Zion, and one of the resources of her strength, is found in her *discipline*, that drill and discipline of her membership and ministry which enables her to marshal and direct and use her energies to the best advantage. *Methodists*, so called at first, by their enemies, sarcastically, because of their methodical way of doing their work, drilled themselves and disciplined their successors in the doctrine

and practice of each, doing work in the station and in the manner that the proper Church authorities should direct. Her muster-roll was called each week at the class-meeting. The absentees were marked, and then the leader himself or other members of the class detailed by the leader, hunted up the absentees, that they might be comforted if sick, brought back if stragglers, court-martialed if deserters. In a well-disciplined army, the officer in command needs only to give the order, "Take that battery," and the division receiving the command marches forward with fixed bayonets, and if the work is practicable the battery is taken; so has the Methodist Episcopal Church pulled down strongholds, and secured brilliant successes in consequence of this discipline of her army. Loyal to authority, her members have responded to her class-leaders, her leaders to her pastors, her pastors to her presiding elders, her presiding elders to her bishops, her bishops to the General Conference, and all to the Captain of our salvation—the great Head of the Church.

This discipline has never been irksome or galling to the speaker, but he has found the yoke of Methodism to be easy, and its burden to be light. In 1814 his name was placed upon her muster-roll by that efficient recruiting officer, Rev. Marcus Lindsey. Never by any selection or electioneering of his own, but in response to the recognized voice of Church authority, he served the Church successively as class-steward, class-leader, exhorter, local preacher, junior preacher, preacher in charge, and presiding elder. Though I feel that I have unworthily filled the different stations assigned, yet by the blessing of God I have so filled them that no official censure is on record against me, and think I may say with sincerity, that with singleness of aim I have endeavored during that long period to endure hardness as a good soldier. It is doubtless to this spirit of loyalty to Church authority, occupying carefully and faithfully the positions assigned to the members and ministers, severally, that we have heretofore, and shall hereafter, attribute much of our success.

2. We have intimated that the secret of success is found in great part in the activity of her workers, and that one of the resources of her strength is found in that feature of her economy, the great itinerant wheel, which puts the whole host in motion. We have had illustrations in the history of our own country, that an army may be thorough in its discipline, and yet maintain a masterly inactivity, spending its time and energies in the exercise and parade of its drill-manual, but carefully avoiding any forward movement. The hosts of Methodism were never organized for garrison duty. Wesley, in the Old World, and Asbury in this, proposed the occupancy of the world-wide parish in the shortest possible time. Hence they ordered constant movement, and that constant movement a movement of the whole army, a forward movement; nothing less than the conquest of the world for Christ was the aim, and each individual soldier was expected to be at the post of duty, and to do his full part in the campaign. It is said that during the late rebellion one of the commanding officers telegraphed to the Lieutenant-General, saying, "If we push the enemy I think we can take him; what shall we do?" Back over the telegraphic wire flashed the prompt and laconic reply, "Push." But no standard-bearer in the hosts of Methodism, under such circumstances, ever needs to telegraph to a superior officer for instructions; when he received his commission he received a special charge and standing orders to "push the enemy and take him." Wherever there is a stronghold of Satan, push and take it; wherever there is a rebel against the government of God, push and capture him; wherever there is a benighted heathen, push and rescue him. This

she regards indeed as marching order No. 1, issued more than one thousand eight hundred years ago, by the Chief Captain, when he said, "Go ye into all the world and preach the Gospel to every creature. He that believeth and is baptized shall be saved; he that believeth not shall be damned." In response to this order the general superintendents strike their tents and start upon the grand campaign. They sound the marching orders down the lines through the presiding elders to the pastors, and they to the leaders and members, and the vast army, cavalry and infantry, throughout the mighty host, are moving to the charge. How rapid and resistless has been this movement let records of the past and the position of to-day declare. You will pardon the weakness, if weakness it be, of an aged itinerant, in glancing over the march of half a century in this army. In 1816 Jacob Young, then in the strength of early manhood, and a fearless and successful champion, ordered me to push the battle, a junior preacher on Letart Falls circuit; a circuit, however, of twenty-five appointments, and spreading over what now constitutes eleven pastoral charges. Beardless boy as I was, I packed my clothing and library into my saddle-bags, mounted my horse, and started. I have had the honor of traveling thirty circuits—six of them only six months each—and five districts—two of them only one year each; these I found in seven of the States.

The circuits have usually been large ones, the largest having thirty-five appointments, and the whole list averaging twenty appointments to a circuit. If I had indulged in an estimate of my journeyings and labors during the half century, it is not to glorify myself, but in honor of that ecclesiastical system which so successfully keeps the wheels of its pastoral machinery in motion. I find, upon calculating the geographical boundaries of my several fields of labor and the number of preaching-places, and making an estimate of the ingathering of souls on those charges, the following results: I have traveled not less than 161,000 miles, mostly on horseback; a journey which, if continuously pursued around the world, would have taken me six times around the planet, and I should now be 11,300 miles, or nearly half-way round again. I have preached in the regular course of my appointments not less than 9,476 times. Were I to add sermons preached at protracted meetings and funerals, and occasional sermons, the number would be much larger; and, best of all, I have had the honor of welcoming into the Church of my choice not less than 5,000 souls. After half a century I stand bleached, and stiffened, and scarred in the service, but I love it still. If the Chief Captain would so appoint, gladly would I enter with you, my younger brethren, upon another fifty years' campaign. But this may not be. I am content to step down into the ranks or be placed on the retired list, and perform any service that any one of my years and infirmities may be equal to. If I may not longer pass into the fight I may lift up my hands to God, praying that the great itinerant wheel so efficient in the past, may be increasingly so till the commission is fulfilled and the world is saved.

3. The secret of the strength of Methodism is found in part in the intelligence of her membership, and one of the resources of her strength is her multitudinous appliances for the dissemination of knowledge among the people. It is true that when I entered the itinerant field we had not on this continent a single college, or seminary, or Advocate, or Sabbath-school library, or large catalogue of books of our own publishing. But even then we had in every place where we planted our standards organized societies or classes, the work of whose members was to assist each other in obtaining the clearest and most thorough theoretical and experimental knowledge of the plan of salvation.

What books we had were sound and solid—each preacher regarded it as a part of his regular work to supply the people with such books as would make them intelligent Bible Christians. I need not say that the Methodists in those days, though without colleges for the laity and Biblical schools for the ministry, were able to give a reason for the hope that was in them with a clearness and power that astonished and convinced their hearers. But they were not indifferent to these agencies with which God has so greatly blessed us in these later times. While I was on Fairfield circuit, in 1818, the Methodist Magazine, which still continues under the name of Quarterly Review, was issued. In 1823 a youth's paper was started; in 1826 the Advocate and Journal, the parent of the Advocate family, which now count their subscribers by hundreds of thousands and their readers by millions. The Book Concern, which had commenced in the early history of the Church upon a few hundred dollars borrowed from one of her members, had been gradually and noiselessly growing up among the publishing houses of the country, sending out her childhood literature and solid theological works for laymen and ministers, till to-day it stands the largest religious publishing-house belonging to any denomination on this or any other continent. It has an aggregate capital of $837,000, and the Agents in the last quadrennial report made an exhibit of sales for the last four years of $1,200,000. Who can tell how much of power is available to the Church through the more than thirty presses which are throwing off her millions of pages and papers? While her book and periodical interests have been developing, she has also given attention to secular education.

All our efforts to establish institutions of learning during the first half century of our history proved to be failures. Not, indeed, till 1823 did we make a successful effort in that direction. But the successful founding of Augusta College, in Augusta, Kentucky, was followed by an enterprise and success that has known no parallel in any age or country. In forty-three years she has founded one hundred and two seminaries, colleges, and universities, possessing endowments and other property to the amount of $3,055,000. Thus, since she really entered upon this work, has she founded institutions of learning at the rate of more than one for every six months. Now she proposes, as a grand Centenary offering, to accumulate a connectional educational fund which may greatly add to the magnitude of the source of strength.

There is still to be added to these appliances for the spread of denominational and general Christian intelligence her great Sunday-school system. Her Sunday-School Union was organized in 1827, eleven years after I entered the work. Its growth has been amazing, and its accomplishments wonderful. It now reports 13,400 schools, 150,000 teachers and officers, and 918,000 scholars, 19,000 of whom were reported as converted during the year preceding the last printed report. There are in her libraries 2,529,000 volumes of books, and these schools are supplied every two weeks with 260,000 Sunday-School Advocates. And what must thrill every Christian heart with joy and thanksgiving in this report, is the item that within eighteen years last past 285,000 have been converted in connection with the Sabbath-schools of our Church. These statistics need no comment. Here in great part is the secret of our success and the resource of our strength. Her class-meetings for instruction in matters of experience; her Sabbath-schools, seminaries, and colleges, for her children and youth; and her great Advocate family and publishing house for all, present a stupendous system—a system of appliances for sending light and influence every-where.

4. The secret of her success has been, in great part, found in the fact that she has adhered with tenacity to the pure teaching of the Gospel, and has given its vitalizing truths constant prominence.

At the time that Methodism arose the creed of the Established Church of Great Britain, as preached, differed widely from her faith as found in her books. Wesley found the pure doctrines of the Bible in the standard authors of the Church and preached them; but they were new doctrines to many of the Established clergy. How remarkably this is true may appear from the following extract from an English Review, edited by a clergyman of the Church of England at the time that Wesley and helpers were having such grand success in leading the people to the Savior. The article from which I quote was on the causes of the "increase of Methodism." It presents the following grave charges against the Methodists:

"1. The Methodists believe in a special Providence. 2. They believe in internal emotions wrought by the Spirit of God; that is, that the Spirit of God does produce spiritual emotions in the heart. 3. They are opposed to theaters, calling them hot-beds of vice, and to cards, dancing, and parties of pleasure. 4. They preach salvation by faith alone, and not by the works of righteousness. 5. They are desirous of making men more religious than the constitution of human nature warrants. 6. The doctrine of the Methodists is calculated to give power and influence among the poor."

The reviewer goes on to say, that "if this fanaticism continues, happiness will be destroyed, reason deserted, religion banished, and a long period of grossest immorality, atheism, and debauchery will succeed." The writer was much at a loss to find a satisfactory plan for the cure of this fanaticism. He recommends, however, "to ply it with ridicule." Either the writer was so ignorant of the faith of the Established Church as not to know that the doctrines which he charged upon Methodists were all found in the liturgy as well as in the Bible, or else he was so corrupt as to try to mislead the people and excite unwarranted hostility against the earnest men who were accomplishing a wonderful reformation among the people. The accusation furnishes from the pen of an enemy a striking proof of the purity of the doctrines and the consistency of the morals of the early Methodists.

In these respects, both in the Old and New World, has the Church of Wesley borne the same testimony. She has published from her pulpits, and in her standard writings and current periodicals, the depravity of man's nature, redemption by the Lord Jesus Christ, justification by faith, regeneration by the operation of the Spirit, the direct witness of the Spirit to the soul's relation to God, the completion of the work of sanctification in the full salvation of the soul. She has sounded the invitations of the Gospel to all as redeemed sinners; she has warned all of the danger to which they are exposed while neglecting the invitations of the Gospel; and while she has taught all Christians that it is their privilege and duty to be made perfect in love in the present life, she has faithfully warned them of the danger of making shipwreck of faith and of failing of the grace of God. She has uniformly set forth Christ Jesus, the God-man, the Savior of sinners, as the Alpha and Omega—the beginning and the end—the foundation and top-stone of faith, and hope, and joy. Her trumpets have given no feeble or uncertain sound.

In the year 1833 Melville B. Cox carried these doctrines to Africa, and after planting the banner of the Gospel truth firmly, he laid his bones beneath the sods of that distant continent, connecting forever the heart of the Church with the salvation of the millions of Africa. In 1833 Jason

Lee and others carried these doctrines to the Flathead Indians, beyond the Rocky Mountains. Her sons and daughters have carried these doctrines to China and India, and to the decaying Churches of the land of Luther and the Reformers. Her great army of itinerants at home have sounded them from mountain to mountain, from valley to valley, from prairie to prairie, over all this wide continent—all preaching Christ Jesus; in him a present, free, and full salvation; without him, no salvation at all. For a time the opposition of those who advocated predestination and limited atonement was active and positive. But long since that conflict has virtually ended, and nearly all the preachers of the Gospel in these States join in sounding the "whosoever" invitation in every pulpit and every place. It is a fact that has challenged attention and admiration, that while no other branch of the Church has been as lenient in doctrinal requisitions for Church membership, no other branch of the Church has had such unity of faith among her members, and such freedom from doctrinal wranglings and schisms. As she has not been ashamed of the Gospel, "which is the power of God unto salvation," so the Author of the Gospel has not been ashamed of her, and has given her wonderful success in the propagation of a pure faith.

5. The secret of her strength has been found in part in her adherence to the doctrine of holiness, and the distinct and earnest manner in which she has urged its experience upon all her members as being attainable in the present life, and as being the duty of all ministers and members, as a preparation for the successful accomplishment of their mission.

In the primitive Church, the disciples, by the command of the Master, tarried at Jerusalem to be endued with power from on high. So did Mr. Wesley and his early co-laborers tarry for the same baptism. In the Conference of

1765, a little more than one hundred years ago, Mr. Wesley asks the question, What was the rise of Methodism? and answers the question thus: "In 1729 my brother and I read the Bible; saw inward and outward *holiness* therein; followed after it, and incited others to do so. In 1737 we saw that holiness comes by *faith*. In 1738 we saw that we must be justified before we are sanctified; but still *holiness* was our point—inward and outward *holiness*. God then thrust us out to raise up a holy people." The writings of Mr. Wesley and other early Methodists furnish frequent illustrations of the earnestness with which the people sought this experience and the zeal with which the preachers urged it, and of the pentecostal baptism which they from time to time received. January 1, 1739, Messrs. Ingham, Whitefield, Charles Wesley, and about sixty others, at a conference with Mr. Wesley at Fetter-Lane, about three o'clock in the morning, while they continued instant in prayer, the power of God came mightily upon them, insomuch that many cried out for exceeding joy, and many fell to the ground. As soon as they recovered a little from the awe and amazement which the presence of the Divine Majesty had inspired, they thus broke out with one voice, saying, "We praise thee, O God; we acknowledge thee to be the Lord." Whitefield records a conference of some seven of these "despised Methodist" preachers not long after. They continued in prayer till three o'clock, and then departed with the full conviction that "God was about to do great things among us." How gloriously that "full conviction" has been realized, is shown in the remarkable biographies of such private members as William Carvosso and Hester Ann Rogers, and such ministers as Fletcher and a host of others.

The Church has never retired this doctrine from its prominent position, or lowered the standard set up at the beginning. Doubtless her continuous revivals for a century and a half are largely attributable to this. There is something in holiness that profoundly impresses the world. When the hearer is penetrated with the conviction that the one who prays, or preaches, or exhorts is really holy, or is groaning after holiness, the prayer, the sermon, the exhortation is clothed with power.

The world may be entertained by the sweet-toned instrument, delighted by the golden-tongued preacher, and influenced in some respects by wealth and social position; but if there is no soil of holiness underlying it all; no spirit of holiness permeating it all; no inspiration of holiness inspiring it all, it will fail to assault successfully the citadel of the soul. But where these really are, God will be recognized, and the presence and power of his Church confessed.

Thank God! the fire of holiness still flames upon the altars of Methodism. Her hosts still sing the holiness-inspiring lyrics of Charles Wesley; they still utter prayers panting after holiness as did the sainted Fletcher. Her ministers still recognize it as the mission of Methodism to spread Scripture holiness over all lands. The class-leader presses it upon the members in the social meetings. And as each candidate for holy orders stands before the Conference the Bishop asks him whether he is groaning after full redemption, and whether he expects to be made perfect in this life?

In this position of the Church touching the doctrine and experience of holiness is doubtless found, in great part, the secret of her success, and here will continue to be the hidings of her power.

I must now hasten to close. We have glanced briefly at some of the facts of the past of Methodism. We are not ashamed of her history. Distinguished divines of other communions have been lavish in their praises of our enterprises and success, and illustrious statesmen have pronounced glowing eulogies upon our denomination. Dr. Chalmers pronounced Methodism to be "Christianity in earnest;" and the lamented Lincoln publicly recognized the Methodist Episcopal Church as leading the Churches of the nation in patriotism and prayers. But let us be careful that we be not exalted above measure. Do all who carry the name of Methodist bring credit to that name? Are there not some who ignore the class-meeting, and are strangers to the prayer-meeting? Are there not some who give themselves irregularly and reluctantly, if at all, to the labor of the Sabbath-school? Are there not some who devote but little if any of their money to the support of the Methodist press or pulpit, or the educational or missionary enterprises of the Church? Would that each member of the Church, while reading her wonderful history, would inquire, "What have I done to bring about these grand results?" And if there is any one who has been a clog upon the wheel instead of a spoke in it, who has been a hinderance instead of a help, let such a one lay it to heart. Methodists will not be commended in the great day for what Methodism has done, but each individual will be commended or condemned in proportion as the individual has been faithful or false to responsibility. Had all our ministers and members fully met their covenant obligations, our showing would have been far beyond what it is to-day. We will leave this train of thought for those to whom it may be appropriate.

We are about to step upon the threshold of the second century of American Methodism. Not one of you, my brethren, will live to see its close. The majority of you will close your labors before it has run one-fourth of its course. I can hardly hope more than to see its commencement; and yet each of us in fancy casts the horoscope of the century, and we see the teeming millions that shall people this continent in 1966. In less than forty years, according to the calculations of one Church historian, more than one hundred millions of souls will people this land—a population equal to the present aggregate population of England, France, Switzerland, Spain, Portugal, Sweden, and Denmark. In about sixty-six years, says the same writer—Stevens's Cent. Vol., p. 227—this mighty mass of people will have swollen to the stupendous aggregate of 246,000,000, equaling the present population of all Europe. We shall not follow these calculations further, but raise the question, Shall we as a Church keep pace with this coming population? If such fond anticipations are realized, it will be because you and your successors are faithful to your trust. The heir to fortune having received it without sacrifice or effort upon his part, frequently settles down to its enjoyment, and not only fails to add to his inheritance, but scatters it. It may be so with our successors. Our earnest and powerful ministrations may die down into pompous dull formalities, such as the Church Establishment of England was in the days of Wesley, as compared with the ministry of Latimer, and Cranmer, and Ridley; such may be the Methodist ministry of 1966 as compared with its gushing, joyous, and powerful laborers of to-day. If we would write "success" upon the history of the oncoming century, let us adhere steadfastly to our doctrines, and our Discipline. We should cling to our doctrines because they are the vitalizing truths of the Gospel; we should cling to our Discipline, because a hundred years of trial has demonstrated its wonderful adaptation and efficiency.

It is with hesitancy and trembling, my brethren, that I detain you with a single word of exhortation; and yet, if I do not do it now, it is not probable that I shall ever hereafter. My life-work is nearly done—would that it had been done better! yet such is my reliance upon the atonement of my Savior, and such my anticipations of the continued successes that shall crown your labors, that I am ready to say with Simeon, "Now lettest thou thy servant depart in peace, for mine eyes have seen thy salvation." My soul pants and prays that the successes of the next century shall be much more abundant than those of the past; and surely this centenary year gives rich promise of it. What sweeping revivals, what extraordinary ingatherings, what extensive liberality has marked this year of jubilee! Since I put my pen to paper in the preparation of this discourse, thousands have joined the Church, and millions of dollars have been laid on her altars as a thank-offering, by her grateful people. One of our eloquent Bishops, catching the inspiration of those facts, exclaims, "I wish I had the power to bring before this congregation the grandeur of the position. Why, sir, we have a million of soldiers in the field; we have another million of cadets in our Sunday-schools; we have thirteen thousand recruiting stations and eight thousand recruiting officers. There is not a district or circuit between the two oceans that is not organized and moving in the work. Why, sir, in this organization there is a power to move the world; and when this marshaled host shall make their stately steppings on the earth, depend upon it they will shake the very gates of hell." (Bishop Janes.)

And now, my brethren, if our responsibility is to be measured by our ability, the summit on which we stand to-day, while the eyes of earth, and heaven, and hell are upon us, is awful as well as glorious. Let us not forget that it was upon that high and holy place, the "pinnacle of the temple," that Satan thrust sorely at our Master.

May the blessing of the God of Wesley and of Asbury abide in your habitations and your sanctuaries through all the generations to come! Amen!

www.ingramcontent.com/pod-product-compliance
Lightning Source LLC
Chambersburg PA
CBHW032009220426
43664CB00006B/193